AM

Six Spoons of Sugar

Six Spoons of Sugar

Richard Holdsworth

A catalogue record of this book is available from the British Library.

ISBN: 978-0-9558383-1-6 (hbk)
ISBN: 978-0-9558383-0-9 (pbk)

To order additional copies of this book please visit:
www.holdsworthwrites.co.uk

Published by: Holdsworth Writes (Publishing)
Greenways, Mustard Lane, Sonning, Berks RG4 6GH, UK

Tel/Fax: +44 (0)118 9696271

Email: holdsworthwrites@aol.com

Web: www.holdsworthwrites.co.uk

Cover design by Lucy Holdsworth and Ron Nicola and created by Image Corporate Ltd www.image-corporate.com

Printed and bound in Great Britain by Cpod, Trowbridge, Wiltshire, BA14 0XB

To my wife Heather,
my daughter Lucy and to my sister Helen.

Also to the memory of my Mum and Dad.

Acknowledgements

The author is indebted to the following individuals and organisations for help in researching material and allowing its use within *Six Spoons of Sugar:*

The BBC for the use of extracts from news broadcasts up to and including WWII.

The Imperial War Museum and the National Archives, London, for providing illustrations and other material.

The British Library Newspapers, Colindale, London, for help in accessing newspapers over the period of WWII.

Express Newspapers for the extensive use of news reports covering the war.

Express Newspapers for the references to Rupert Bear column and Rupert Bear books.

A P Watt Ltd on behalf of W E Johns (Publications) Ltd, for the references to Biggles and the use of extracts from the Biggles books.

The Daily Telegraph for use of the illustration depicting a Spitfire fighter plane.

Acknowledgements

The 101st Airborne Screaming Eagles for the front cover illustration © Terrance Collins e-mail photofolio@ntlworld.com. Actual picture depicts The Screaming Eagles, Living History Group, UK. www. screamingeagleslhg.co.uk

Reading Library for help in researching the bombing of Reading in February 1943.

The author is also indebted for the recollections of Harold Heffner, 1st Battalion, A Company 2nd Platoon, 101st Airborne, 501st Parachute Infantry, who was billeted in Berkshire before parachuting into Normandy on D-Day, June 6, 1944.

And, most especially, the author is indebted to the family of Robert Bowen for permission to use extracts from *FIGHTING WITH THE SCREAMING EAGLES* – With the 101st Airborne from Normandy to Bastogne.

Contents

Acknowledgements | vii

Prologue   **Up the Steps and Through the Door**   1

Chapter 1   **Indian Summer**   3

Chapter 2   **And the Man on the Wireless Said**   17

Chapter 3   **Far and Away**   27

Chapter 4   **The Back of Beyond**   37

Chapter 5   **So, It's War**   47

Chapter 6   **Enter the Artist's House**   65

Chapter 7   **Into the Lion's Den**   75

Chapter 8   **The Ghostly Apparition**   93

Chapter 9   **It Never Rains but...**   107

Chapter 10   **Time for Action**   125

Chapter 11   **Your Dad's an Enermie Spy**   147

Chapter 12   **In the Wrong Place at the Wrong Time**   179

Chapter 13   **The Americans Cometh**   193

Chapter 14   **We're All on the Same Side**   203

Chapter 15   **Day of Reckoning**   219

Chapter 16   **Will the Real Winner Please Stand Up...**   233

List of Illustrations | 239

About the Author | 241

Diary of WW11 | 243

Bumblethorpe village

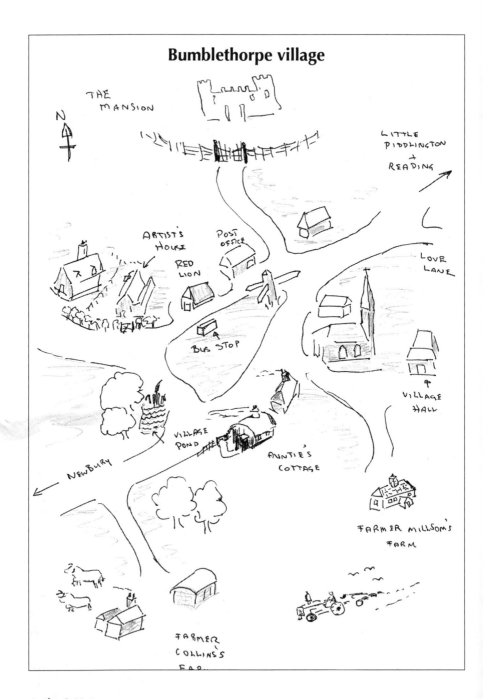

Author's Note

Some place names, geography and people's names have been changed in this account of my boyhood experiences as an evacuee.

Prologue

Up the Steps and Through the Door

February 10, 1943.

Today's special is corned beef. Soup of the day is vegetable; the girl in a white apron and starched cap ladles it out as though there is no tomorrow. "Get it while you can. There's no second 'elpings in this war."

All this for under a shilling. And a cream cake (no cream) for tuppence extra. The People's Pantry is heaving even though it is Wednesday and Reading's early closing day.

Nice Miss Ballantine pops in for tea and a biscuit, as she does every day. She'll be back behind her desk at Pringle & Pringle (Solicitors, established 1901) in just ten minutes, Mr Pringle (Senior) allowing no lassitude from his staff, even in these difficult times.

Mrs Meadows and her daughter, Emily, 12, are heading for the People's Pantry, down Minster Street and past the town hall. It is the place to eat, she's been told on the bus coming in. "A square meal at a fair price." They'll both have the soup, she declares. It's a cold day and Emily needs warming.

1

Up the steps and through the door. Yes, it looks cosy in here. "Perhaps we'll have a cream cake as a treat." Emily's mother is smiling. It has been a good shopping day despite the shortages.

Suddenly, there's a shadow. Gone in the blink of an eye, a roar and an ear-splitting crash… and the People's Pantry on the corner of Friar Street and opposite the town hall is no more.

I am ten and mad keen on aeroplanes. Only Smith Junior says he can recognise a German bomber quicker than I can. I know this is a Dornier as it skims the roof tops and I run helter-skelter with my mum as two long cylinders come tumbling from its belly…

I'm picking myself up; there is a ringing in my ears so I can barely hear. There is dust in my eyes so I can hardly see. And there is dryness in my throat so I can scarcely cry out… *Mum, where's my mum?*

Chapter 1

Indian Summer

The summer of 1938 is one of the best for ages. Mum says so. And she writes it down in her diary along with the other things. Essentials my mum calls them. Like our birthdays, the recipe for the Christmas cake and my shoe sizes.

"Goodness, son, how you're growing. Into size sevens already and still not out of short pants."

Our Doctor, Dr McGilligan, has said I'm going to be a beanpole of a lad when I grow up. "Sure, you don't have to look twice, Mrs Holdsworth," he told Mum, and put a cold thing with rubber tubes next to my chest, and listened to the other end while I coughed and said "nointy-noin." He's from Ireland and doesn't talk like us.

"Well my, it's only a chill he's got. But you can never be too careful," said Dr McGilligan, giving Mum some embrocation to rub into my chest. "Such a nice young boy too. And him the height of someone much taller…"

That was then. Now it's now, the best summer for years, and I watch Mum write it down in her diary along with all those other essentials. "I can't remember when we last had a summer like this," she writes, smiling with her bright blue eyes and blotting it carefully with the blotter. Then tugging my sun hat down against the glare: "Don't want to get your precious face burnt now, do we?"

August is the hottest. The days stretch out before us and me and Big Sister are in the middle of our school holidays, enjoying every minute of it. Dad's taking time off for his garden; pottering is what he calls it, and how it beats burying your head in a stuffy old bank. "It's no contest," my Dad tells anyone who stops to ask.

Dad hates the mowing but has it done for another week. "Behind him" he calls it, and the edges trimmed too. Dad says Mum's flowers are the prettiest for miles. Quite the best he's seen. The sun beats down and we're having tea on the lawn. There isn't a care in the world.

Big Sister says if it keeps up like this we'll soon be enjoying an Indian summer.

I ask "What's an Indian summer?" but don't expect an answer. And don't get one. Things like Indian summers are for grown ups and older sisters.

Like *my* sister. She's 13, eight years older than me, and really grown up. Her name is Helen but I call her Ingie because I couldn't say things properly when I was little and just came out with it… *Ingie*. I don't know why and I can't remember how.

"It's the way of little ones," Gran says, stroking my head, like I was the cat. "Getting words mixed up." Being nice. Being Gran with her wrinkles and whiskers and a spare set of teeth grinning at you from the shelf beside her bed.

What a pity she doesn't come over more often, Mum says sadly. "But what with the buses and those funny old feet of hers." They're the worst possible things to take on a Number 47 from Clapham.

I still call my Big Sister Ingie, even now. Her friends at school have picked it up (worst luck for her), and she would rather stay Helen. She thinks a nickname is something you should avoid, although there are far worse. Like Esmeralda, her school friend, with her head stuck in a book… "You won't see Swat today," they all sing, "she won't be out to play."

4

Now Mum is calling out from the verandah, "Come and get the tea, children!" and the grass prickles our feet as we run across Dad's new-mown lawn, Ingie with her flowing hair and see-through green eyes, a gift from Heaven Gran says. I think I'm a gift too, although I'm not so sure the day I stepped on those funny old feet.

Ingie is laying the tablecloth now, on the slope running down beside Mum's most colourful flowerbed, and I have the forks and spoons and the napkins. We set it up, like we always do, in the shade beneath the honeysuckle bush and next to the lupins Mum has lavished with equal quantities of love and affection and Mr McBean's Patented Flower Feed. That's what Dad says, anyway.

Very prim and proper. That's what Mum calls tea on the lawn. And says we're not to be surprised if we're all feeding peacocks and playing croquet by this time next week. It's what Posh people do, Mum reckons, and says in a funny voice, "Would you like another cucumber sandwich, my dear? Oh rather..."

"You're taking them off again," Ingie insists and thinks she shouldn't.

Mum's talking about these Posh people, I think, although I don't know about Posh people, even where they come from. Some foreign land, I suppose. I expect I'll find out about it in lessons one day – Indian summers in the morning and Posh people in the afternoon. Ingie promises I'll learn lots when I get to the Seniors.

Now Mum's bringing the tray with four cups and a big pot of tea.

Dad stops pottering and comes over and plonks himself down on the lawn with a groan. He says the hard ground isn't doing his bones any favours. "It's about time us gardeners had a spot of rain." And Dad says a man to help with the mowing wouldn't go amiss either. Every now and again, at least.

Mum tells Dad he looks out of place on the lawn despite his sun hat and sandals. His trousers pull up and show little bits of white leg which stand out against the black socks he wears when he goes off to the bank. "Take those stuffy old socks off, Father, and let your feet breathe."

Dad says his feet are breathing just fine, thanks very much.

Ingie reckons he's more at home in the bank than pushing the mower. "But you're happiest when you're listening to your gramophone, aren't you Dad." His favourite is a man called Richard Wagner and his hero, Siegfried, who Ingie says stomps about our living room to an orchestra full of timpani and tales of derring-do and Timmy, our cat, taking cover.

Mum says that's where I got my name from. This favourite composer of Dad's.

"Well, there's not much derring-do in the bank these days," Dad has to say. "Can't wait for retirement... and a bit more Wagner." And the Now-and-Again man on the end of the mower, of course.

Dad's going to tune into his wireless tonight, the BBC at six o'clock. He says he needs to catch up with the news about a man called Hitler and a place called the Sudetenland. "That's all they talked about in the bank this week." He'll tune in even if it's not what he wants to hear. "Someone needs to find a solution, and find it fast."

Ingie and me have to stay hushed while Dad listens to the news he doesn't want to hear.

"Hitler's a dreadful man if you believe Miss Fosdyke," Ingie says, and tells us how she spent the whole history lesson telling them just how dreadful. "Yes, the *whole* history lesson. Can you believe it?"

"We'll just have to go to war with him," Miss Fosdyke told them, with her tight little mouth and accusing eyes. The sooner the better. And then she wrote on the blackboard: HISTORY SAYS NOT TO APPEASE BULLIES and got them all to copy it in their history books.

Mum can't see why we should risk a war over somewhere so far away and nothing to do with us. "It's ludicrous," she says. "After the last one." It was the war to end all wars, apparently.

Dad tunes in, then seems pleased. "Mr Chamberlain, our Prime Minister, is going to Germany to sort it out, face to face with Mr Hitler. First thing in the morning, in an aeroplane."

"Well, I hope he does," says Mum. "We've had enough of wars... all that killing. No-one wins."

Dad tells us that you have got to have some sympathy for the German people and talks about a thing called a treaty that brought more problems with it than it solved. "A treaty imposed after the First World War," Dad tells us, and says how Mr Chamberlain will find a solution if anyone can. Bending over backwards, that's what he'll be doing. "I'll tune in again tomorrow to see how he gets on." We're to keep our fingers crossed.

I just hope it doesn't get in the way of some Rupert Bear. Dad's the best storybook reader in the whole street and I'd like a few pages if I can. Or Biggles if there's the time. They've given him a new aeroplane, the fastest ever, and I can't wait to hear what happens next. I bet Dad can't either. After he comes home from his bank, of course.

And after Mr Chamberlain's done some bending over backwards.

"Here is the 6 o'clock News from the BBC for September 30, 1938

The British Prime Minister has been hailed as bringing Peace to Europe after signing a non-aggression pact with Germany.

PM Neville Chamberlain arrived back in the UK today, holding an agreement signed by Adolf Hitler which stated the German leader's desire never to go to war with Britain again.

The two men met at the Munich conference between Britain, Germany, Italy and France yesterday, convened to decide the future of Czechoslovakia's Sudetenland.

Mr Chamberlain declared the accord with the Germans signalled "peace for our time", after he had read it to a jubilant crowd gathered at Heston airport in west London.

The German leader stated in the agreement: 'We are determined to continue our efforts to remove possible sources of difference and thus to contribute to assure the peace of Europe.'

But many MPs are bound to criticise it as part of the Prime Minister's appeasement of German aggression in Europe.

And Mr Chamberlain's personal pact will be little comfort to the Czechoslovakian Government, which has been forced to hand over the region of Sudetenland to Germany, despite not being present at the conference."

A face is pressed against our fence and it wants to know why we had tea on the lawn. It's Podgy, a right little tyke, according to my mum, and his dog is at his side yapping. Podgy's mum and dad haven't got time for tea on the lawn. "We 'ave ours indoors on a table like everyone do." And they don't like peacocks either and his mum says croqueting is all 'oles.

And out comes his tongue when I tell him that's silly.

"Mum's right," says Ingie, "tyke means troublemaker and that Podgy is a right little troublemaker if ever there was."

"He's not that bad," I say. But I don't sound very convincing.

Podgy only moved next door a month ago from a place called West Am and we play together with the football we found in the park. But only if I don't talk like he talks – cor blimey and gotcha, for a start. Mum's got a list of things I mustn't do or say, and cor blimey and gotcha come right at the top.

"And another thing," Mum's saying, straightening the collar of my fresh white shirt. "Don't let me catch you near that dreadful dog of his." And I'm not to forget to tie my shoelaces either. Tripping over your shoelaces isn't as bad as getting attacked by Podgy's dog, but it's on Mum's list all the same.

Even Mr Trimble, our postman, runs down Podgy's footpath and runs back again. He says a postman's worst enemy is a dog with sharp teeth and Podgy's is as bad as they get. "He'll 'ave yer privates, that dog," I hear him shout as he gallops past.

"What are your privates, Mr Trimble?" I call out after him. But he doesn't hear. Or perhaps he does and won't tell. Perhaps they're like Posh people and Indian summers and I'll only learn about them when I get to the Seniors.

Mum says dogs have diseases like distemper and if I got distemper in my bloodstream I'd be a goner, dying an agonising death even before Dr McGilligan could get to me, clutching my throat, crying out and keeping the whole street awake.

"Even Mr and Mrs Jenkins from over the back fence, Mum?"

"Especially them," Mum says. Everyone knows God-fearing Mr and Mrs Jenkins deserve a good night's sleep if anyone does. "No-one in their right mind would want to keep them awake, now would they?"

I think it's best to say no and try a question of my own. "Where's my privates, Mum?"

Mum looks as though someone's going to have to go to their room. But it's not me this time. "You've been talking to that postman again, haven't you?" I think Mum's going to have a word in Mr Trimble's ear next time she sees him.

Ingie says I shouldn't take too much notice of Mum's nagging, keeping the Jenkinses awake or Podgy's dog, or anything. She says all mums do a bit of nagging before they can be called proper mums. Ingie says she got it in the neck when she was little. "Now it's your turn, Little Brother."

Podgy's face is still at the fence and now he's not happy about Ingie's name. "What sort of name do you call that?" Podgy thinks it's daft. "In't it?" he says, pressing against the railings and saying how I'm going to get a beating the next time we play football together. "Ten nil, probably more." I'm not going to get a look in, he says.

I gulp, look down, drawing circles in the dust with the tip of my shoe. I know Ingie would have an answer and Mum and Dad definitely would.

I could try the one about a little boy who couldn't pronounce Helen when he was very little, but I don't think I will. Not with Podgy from West Am, anyway. Then I remember Isobel from next door, on the other side, with pigtails and freckles, who has a crush on me (so Ingie says), and who calls things by funny names – flutterbyes for butterflies and cowbobs for cobwebs.

"A crush," Ingie said, "means she wants to marry you when you grow up."

"Over my dead body," Mum declared. "No girl who does handstands and shows her knickers is going to marry my son."

Podgy's still there, dog yapping, and he's still on the attack. And now it's my dad's turn. "Your dad's a silly old dad with a silly old bank... Mine's a greengrocer and much more important." Podgy's got two lines running down his face from the railings and I think I'd better tell him before he gets stuck like that. "You want a punch or somefin'?" Anyway, he's decided to keep the football and there's nothing I can do about it. "Don't bovver" he tells me. "Finders keepers" he says, even though I saw it first.

Mum's halfway through her daily routine with the Hoover as it Beats as it Sweeps as it Cleans, just as the salesman promised when Mum plumped for the deluxe model with its extension piece for all our out-of-the-way places.

"Never mind all that," Ingie says. "Our mum wouldn't put up with any nonsense from that troublemaker Podgy. She'll know what to say. Go on, ask her."

Quite how Mum had met Dad was never said, apart from it being very romantic. "It was at the Saturday dance," Ingie's sure. "Dad wasn't very good so Mum showed him. The twirly bits, especially." And Dad kept standing on Mum's toes; that didn't help. Ingie's sure of that too. But he asked if he could walk her home afterwards and all was forgiven. "And then they went out on a date, boating on the Serpentine, or something." Ingie giggles and her eyes sparkle. "Fancy, on a boat. How romantic!" Dad was from a "well-to-do" part of London while Mum came from working-class Clapham, a family of eight and their dad out of work. Ingie says they were hard up and had to scrimp and save; fight for everything they got.

The Hoover roars to life again but not before Mum has done just as Ingie said and told me what to say. "Tell that Podgy of yours that your dad has an important job in the bank and secondly, if vegetables come into it, your father grows his own at the bottom of the garden." Mum reckons you can't get better than that.

"Even if his carrots shrivel up a bit and make people laugh?"

I'd heard Dad tell how Mr Higgins laughed at his best ones, right in Dad's face. "You don't call them proper carrots," he said, with something called a smirk and an allotment that grew carrots the size of tree trunks.

"So what?" Mum says. "It's the thought that counts... growing your own... and that's what your father does. When he's not in the pub, anyway."

Of course my dad's the best dad in the world, I know that. But a few pointers won't go amiss and here's Mum coming up with two smashers – the one about Dad's bank and, secondly, Mum knows why Dad's carrots make Mr Higgins laugh and it's all down to horses' doings.

And this is how my Mum knows. The treat of the year for Mum and her family was to dress up in their Sunday Best and go out and watch the Lord Mayor's Show with its horses and carriages and then keeping cavy while Mum's dad sneaked out into the road to gather the horses' doings for his vegetable patch. "That'll grow 'tatoes on concrete," he told them. He was admiring the pile in the bottom of his bucket when he said it, apparently.

Now I know what Dad's carrots need and all I have to do is ask for some in my prayers tonight. Not another minute wasted, I'm on my knees the moment Mum has the lights turned out and I've got my goodnight kiss.

Reverend Runcon always says that God works in mysterious ways and I'm sure God does because the horses' doings turn up, out of nowhere, in a sack just a few days later.

"That'll put paid to Mr Higgins laughing," Mum says.

And what with Dad's important job in the bank, I reckon it'll be a knockout blow for Podgy the trouble maker.

Mr Chamberlain seemed very happy with Mr Hitler when he got back from this place called Munich. And he had his piece of paper to prove it. The man on Dad's wireless said Mr Chamberlain smiled and people patted him on the back.

Even Reverend Runcorn's happy. Mum's off to the shops and has me in tow while Reverend Runcorn raises his hat and says, "Wonderful news, isn't it?" and calls out to the back of Mum's head, "See you in church, perhaps?" But Mum's already on her way. "I'm not spoiling a perfect day for anyone," she says.

But Dad's not so sure. I watch him in his big, fat, lazy leather chair, puffing on his pipe, listening to what the man on the wireless is saying, a glass of whisky at the ready. The man is measuring his words carefully. "Now that Hitler has the Sudetenland… he has no other territorial claims… Mr Chamberlain is confident…"

Or is he?

Dad's turning it over in his mind, arguing it this way and that, trying to convince himself.

But we are safe for the moment and there's still time for the tale of Rupert Bear and the Enormous Balloon. Dad's his usual brilliant best as Rupert, and his Professor is no less amazing. "The balloon is the biggest I've ever seen," says a kindly Professor as he unties the rope and the Enormous Balloon drifts away on the breeze. Rupert waves and Algy waves and the kindly Professor waves. The chums are off on the most wondrous adventure.

But Dad still isn't happy with Mr Hitler. He doesn't trust him further than he can throw him, which isn't far on two whiskies. So Mum says.

Rupert and Algy float over the countryside. The Professor is just a little dot on the horizon now. They can hardly make him out, he's so far away. Everything in the world is peace and tranquillity.

I just hope the chums get down before there's another Sudetenland.

"Here is the 9 o'clock News from the BBC for March 31, 1939

The British Prime Minister, Sir Neville Chamberlain, told the House of Commons today of the assurances his Government have given the Polish people if their independence is threatened by a Third Party.

He told a packed House that any action threatening Polish independence and which the Polish Government considered vital to their national interest, His Majesty's Government would feel bound to lend the Polish Government every support.

Mr Chamberlain also said that he had spoken to the French Prime Minister, Edouard Daladier, and the French Government had issued similar assurances to the Polish Government.

This follows last week's statement by the German Foreign Secretary, Herr Ribbentrop, that German interests lay in the return of the Free State of Danzig to the German Reich and the construction of road and rail across the Polish Corridor to link East Prussia with the rest of Germany."

Dad's listening to his wireless again.

"That'll give you indigestion," Mum says. Dad has a glass of whisky. He tells Mum it'll make the news easier to digest. "It's getting very gloomy again," he says.

* * * * *

Mr Trimble, our postman, swings his bike into our drive, leaving track marks in the gravel, and digs deep into the brown satchel hung across his shoulder. "Got a few letters in 'ere for your mum and dad," he says, and hands them over – one, two, three. Dad has his summer seed catalogue and Mum the knitting patterns she ordered last week; but there is also a brown envelope lurking in there and it has all the makings of bad news about it.

Mum puts it on the mantelpiece for Dad to read when he comes home from the bank. Mr Trimble has delivered one to every house in our street, and the next one and the next, and is whacked. "It's a hard life for a postman," he tells Mum. "And getting harder."

Mum says, "I expect you'll be in the Dog and Duck tonight."

Mr Trimble's letter has the word OHMS on the bottom left-hand corner and Mum says she has never known anything from OHMS that did anyone any good, and leaves it on the mantelpiece next to the clock so Dad won't miss it. "Looks like trouble to me," she says.

I stand there and look up at Dad's letter before I go off to school and again when I come home in the afternoon. Ingie does the same only from a bit higher up. "Mum's right," Ingie says and calls it "ominous".

Dad is home now and we rush to greet him. I'd like to tell him how well I have done at times tables; but the brown envelope is much more important. Even Ingie coming second in French (Esmeralda coming first) can't compete.

"It's from a man called Ohms, Dad."

Dad says OHMS stands for On His Majesty's Service and it could be from those sneaky people in the tax department who have one hand in his pocket.

But it isn't. It's from Civil Defence and it's telling Dad what the Government is going to do if there's a war.

"This calls for a sit-down," Dad tells us, taking to his big, fat, lazy leather chair and his pipe. Then he gives his glasses a huff and a polish with his hanky and lets out a "Hmmm" when he gets to the start bits. "It says here that in the event of war some people will be moved to places of safety. People from vulnerable areas. They'll be moved to the country... be evacuated."

This is not what Mum wants to hear at all and calls it a silly letter. And there's worse to come. "These people will be the old, infirm and the children... the children," Dad repeats.

"My children sent away? How on earth can that be?"

"Well, if you're looking for someone to blame, I'd blame the men who drew up the Versailles Treaty... a flawed treaty," Dad calls it. "I've said before how its shortcomings would return to haunt us one day, and now it seems they have."

Mum doesn't understand. Nor Ingie. And me especially. Dad's thing with a funny name that's come back to haunt us.

Now he's explaining how Hitler wanted the Sudetenland and how he wants Danzig in Poland too. "There are lots of German people there and Hitler says they deserve to be part of Germany." Dad tells us that Hitler isn't the sort of person to back down. "And worse," Dad says, "now that our government has given a commitment to Poland we could find ourselves drawn into a conflict."

There's more to come from Dad's OHMS letter. The bit he's reading now. "Any such conflict could result in an attack on Great Britain and this will put the people living in the most vulnerable areas at risk... you live in one of these areas... you might be at risk."

"The Red Brick House?" Mum sounds startled, not quite believing what Dad's reading from his letter.

"Yes, the whole of south London, Coulsdon included. And with Croydon Airport just down the road we could be a target."

Mum doesn't like this bit especially. Us being a target.

"It's not a foregone conclusion, though," Dad says, making it sound not so bad, and tells Mum how we've got to wait for a further communication.

I don't understand what Dad's saying, these funny-sounding places, Danzig and Poland. "And what's evacuation, Ingie? And why does Dad have to wait for a communication?"

Ingie says we might have to be sent away, that's what evacuation means. "Children like you and me. Dad will only know when he gets another communication... another letter..."

15

"Like the one that Mr Trimble brought today? Another silly one?" Ingie thinks so.

Dad's still reading. Ingie says his face is as black as thunder now.

That night I lie in bed and hope Dad's silly letter doesn't mean we'll be evacuated. I am happy here in the Red Brick House with Mum and Ingie, and Dad coming home in the evening, playing his tricks and reading my storybooks. Rupert Bear and Biggles.

Even Podgy's not that bad. I beat him at football this morning even though he said he'd let me win. But I didn't mind. A win is a win against my friend Podgy.

Chapter 2

And the Man on the Wireless Said

Dad's home late and Mum's worried. It's gone eight and there's still no sign.

"He'll be all right, I'm sure. It's just his work." Mum sounds tired and on edge. Ingie says its not easy running a house with the threat of war hanging over your head.

Mum perks up a bit. "I'll read some of your book if you like. A nice Rupert Bear story to get you off to sleep..."

Dad and me started Biggles last night and Biggles is fighting for his life, behind enemy lines – miles from anywhere and running out of fuel fast. And isn't that Red Baron at 12.o'clock high? "It's got to be Biggles, Mum," I say. "I must find out what happens to him, he's my hero..."

Rupert Bear is being put back on the shelf, reluctantly, and Mum's reaching for Biggles with a sigh. "Well, at least the little bear doesn't get shot down," Mum says, sitting uncomfortably on the edge of my bed and readying herself for the doom to come, straining an ear for the sound of Dad's footsteps.

"You vill not escape Englisher dog. I 'ave you in my sights. I vill snuff out your leetle lights vunce and for all..." Mum's voice trails off, her face soft and her silky hair held neatly back with a clip, wondering what to say next. How we both want it to sound right, sound convincing...

I screw my eyes tightly shut, trying to imagine what it's like to be up there with Biggles and his seat about to be shot from under him. But all I get is the inside of my eyelids. "Mum," I say, "are you sure Red Barons talk like that?"

Now if only Dad was reading Biggles. He's the best. Mum would be the first to agree, I'm sure. Puffing up the characters, making them live. Putting you there...

"Buckle up, old son, we're going in low." That's just the sort of thing Dad says and we'd be ducking and weaving and turning the tables on that evil Red Baron. Real wind blowing in my hair and proper engines roaring in my ears. And Biggles coming thundering in through the open window. You don't get shot down with things like that.

There's the sound of feet on our gravel pathway and then the latch on the front door. "I'm home – at last."

Mum's closing Biggles swiftly, slipping him back on the shelf. "Goodnight Biggles." A kiss lands on my cheek. "And goodnight, Son. Don't have bad dreams..."

Dad's hanging his hat and coat wearily in our hallway. I hear him say it's been another hard day at the bank. The threat of war makes for lots of work... I catch his words as they float up the stairs. There's money to be transferred for the Kleinwarts, very important customers, and it's his responsibility, the Kleinwarts' account, and he's getting looks from his boss while he waits for it to be done. A man with a shiny head and less humour than the pencil he taps on his desk, hour after hour, day after day.

Dad's told the tale many times, making us laugh at the thought of this silly man. It's not just the Kleinwarts, his boss with the gleaming head, or his blessed pencil tap, tap, tapping on his desk. It's all the Money Men in the City, he says. None of them likes the way things are going. "The bank isn't the place to be if you want an easy life."

He's going off to his wireless now. "I'll catch the end of the nine o'clock news with any luck," I hear him say. "There might be developments."

But there aren't. Ingie finishes her homework and pops in on her way to bed. "I heard the wireless man say things are not good. We must be prepared, he said. This war is still a possibility if Mr Hitler doesn't see sense."

And it's not just on Dad's wireless either. Ingie says people in the street talk about nothing else. It's war, war, war, everywhere you go. "Surely you've heard?"

I tell her I saw a picture of some funny men marching across the front of Dad's newspaper, just like tin soldiers. Row upon row of them. "What do you think they're doing, Ingie?"

"Goose-stepping. Goose-stepping for Mr Hitler. And they're not funny, Little Brother... they're very serious."

"Well, Mr Bentham my teacher, said we should keep a scrapbook and I'm going to put Mr Hitler's goosy men in mine. They're going to be the first."

Dad's pub landlord says it's inevitable, I heard that too. Dad told Mum how the man was sure war was coming. "Everything's getting scarce, my shelves be half empty," he told Dad. "Them that know, knows." Dad had a double scotch to compensate. "You're a good customer, Perce, have this one on me."

Dad thought he would. A Bells is a Bells. Especially if it's the last. And especially if it's free.

War's crept into the church, Mr and Mrs Jenkins tell Mum, on the Monday, Mum's washing day, as they get all excited about Reverend Runcorn's prayer for peace in his Sunday sermon. It was a powerful sermon too, if you believed them.

"There'd be no war if it rested with him," they say as one voice, over the back fence.

"The Jenkinses are in a right old stupor," Mum says. "Just like two little squirrels with the winter coming on and no reserve of nuts to fall back on."

"Passionate about peace he was," Mrs Jenkins tells Mum, "passionate." They'd sung *Jerusalem*, hymn number 578 from *Ancient and Modern*, giving it their all. *This Green and Pleasant Land*, no-one sang better. Then knelt and prayed hard and put a whole half crown in the plate, it was the least they could do, Mr Jenkins being too old to enlist and fire a gun or anything.

"The reverend has done his bit, he can do no more," Mr Jenkins insists as Mum pegs the last of the washing on the line and the sky fills with clouds.

Mum nods in agreement. You might not be able to count on Reverend Runcorn for a good drying day but you could hardly blame him for the war.

* * * * *

Mum's reading Biggles every night now while Dad listens to the man on the wireless, but she doesn't have her heart in it, although I don't say. "Biggles-races-back-home-as-fast-as-his-plane-will-carry-him… " Mum rattles through it all with one ear cocked for Dad's voice.

The wireless man is finished now and I get a quick kiss as Mum dashes to get the bad news. But at least Biggles is down safely.

I lie there in the half dark wondering what is happening to my world. I hear Ingie come to bed, it seems ages later, as I watch the sunlight play tricks on the wall over my head and she tells me what she has heard about this evacuation.

"The man says we'll have to gather at our school to be sent off. Our teachers will come back from their holidays to organise it." Ingie is kind and concerned for both of us, standing there in the half-light. "Only if the government decides, of course," she says. "We'll be all right, Little Brother, you'll see," and goes off quietly, leaving me alone to think.

It seems only the other day that Dad was coming home from his bank with his tricks to make us laugh, Ingie and me. And Timmy, our cat, looking on, bemused. We couldn't wait to hear the sound of his footsteps on the gravel path, knowing we'd be in for a treat. Our favourite was when he played at being the Crumpet Man from the end of our street, calling out, "Get yer luverly crumpets 'ere", and ringing his pretend bell and stepping out like a guardsman with a pretend tray on his head.

And Mum saying how the wind would change one day and he'd get stuck like that. "Won't you be looking just a little bit silly, Father," she'd say. But there was always a twinkle in her eye.

"Going to Head Office with a pretend tray of crumpets on your head."

Now there are no more funny games, none of Dad's tricks. Now Ingie and me could be sent away, miles from anywhere, miles from Mum and Dad... Evacuees. That's what they'll call us.

I don't get much sleep, although I try hard. I close my eyes but nothing happens. I count sheep but they turn into soldiers, and they are being set upon by Mr Hitler's funny goose-stepping men coming across the fields to get them.

"Mum!" I'm calling out. "I'm having a bad dream, a nightmare. Mr Hitler's goosy men are getting my sheep..."

Richard's Scrapbook

Things are moving fast now.

One minute I'm playing with my Hornby trains, checking the signals, coupling the engine, drawing into the platform, and next I'm packing it up as quick as I can for Mum to wrap in tissue paper and bury deep down in our biggest tea chest. Saved for a better day, Mum says.

"Goodbye Flying Scotsman," I say, but Mum's not in the mood for jokes. And my five coaches: one first (for Posh people), three seconds (for ordinary people) and the buffet where the Posh people have their tea. Mum's not going to laugh about that either; I'm to hurry up if it's all to be packed ready for the day we escape the Red Brick House.

"There's only one goodbye round here," Mum says. "And it's goodbye to sanity while we wait for Mr Chamberlain and Mr Hitler to sort out their differences."

Dad's listened to his wireless for one last time and now he needs to talk to us urgently. He's going to tell us what he's decided. "Yes, all of you, gather round. Quickly, please."

"It must be bad news," Ingie whispers. "It's Thursday, normally Dad's night at the pub, winding down." Ingie says that's what Dad needs after he's had a bad day at the bank. "I heard him tell Mum the other day. A bit of winding down. That's what he called it."

Or he sometimes goes up there after his dinner, a plate of shepherd's pie warmed up with extra gravy and apple pie for afters. Tonight there's no afters and no winding down either. Just the left-overs and the bad news.

"I'm sure war's coming no matter how hard Mr Chamberlain tries to avoid it," Dad tells us. "Hitler's never going to stomach that silly treaty no matter how hard we dress it up."

He's standing at the fireplace like a sentry, knocking out his pipe on the grate, not just a gentle tapping either, he's giving it a real battering; something's up all right. Mum's sitting there on the sofa looking worried, her pinafore folded neatly at her side even though the washing up's still to be done. And Flying Scotsman to be saved for a better day.

Timmy slinks off as Dad gets going. "Cats are like that," Ingie says. "Sixth sense, nine lives."

"Anyone who wants to give peace a chance gets my vote," Dad tells us, still like a sentry, and Mum agrees. She remembers the last one with horror; Mum's brother killed as a young man. "It was in the trenches," she says. Ingie and me know the story inside out. How the telegram arrived, her mum and dad trying to hide their tears.

"It must have been terrible," Ingie says. "Arthur was Mum's only brother, one amongst five sisters. No wonder they cried."

"Chamberlain is walking a tightrope," Dad tells us. "Trying to see both sides... trying to avoid conflict. But I fear he's running out of friends."

"Arthur was only a lad," Mum says again. "Doing his bit by King and Country, just as Kitchener asked. Scarcely old enough to hold a razor, let alone a gun."

Lots of people will be killed, Dad tells us. "And not just in the trenches but innocent men, women and children in the streets. They have aeroplanes that can reach almost anywhere now." Dad knows such things.

And he tells us how they could reach Coulsdon, our street, even the Red Brick House; we'd be targets, he's sure. Sitting ducks, he calls us. Podgy and his mum and dad, pretty Isobel with her pigtails and Mr and Mrs Jenkins, the frightened squirrels. "Yes, them too. They're all sitting ducks." Even Postman Trimble, who escapes a mauling from Podgy's dog every day. He's a sitting duck, even when he gallops past.

"London would be the first to get it," Dad says. "Hitler's bombers would just take off, turn right, and make a beeline for our capital."

Mum's shaking her head. "Men and their wars."

Do we remember our Auntie Millie? Dad is asking now, drawing on his pipe as if it's a lifeline. Mum's saying we do, Ingie does anyway; Auntie Millie with the cottage in a little village miles away in the country. Dad has not been there himself, he admits, but Ingie went down there last summer to get some fresh air after a bout of 'flu and Dad is recounting her words now. "I'll send you off to Auntie's if I can," he says. "She might take you if she has the room."

Ingie remembers Auntie clearly. A tiny little lady with grey hair. Prim and proper, Ingie called her. And a husband who cut the firewood, set the fire, and then skulked off to the garden shed for a smoke and the rest of the day... "A Wills Woodbine is what Auntie called it," Ingie says. "A nasty old smell if ever there was."

Ingie had to eat her greens, not a scrap left, a guarantee of rosy cheeks to take back to London. "Severe looks if you didn't," Ingie says. But there were the rickety stairs and little windows looking out over fields full of animals. "Those were the bits I remember most. The bits I liked best."

Dad seems more relaxed now, standing there against the fireplace. The pipe is not being puffed so hard. The pouch of St Bruno untouched. Timmy slinks out from beneath the stairs as if nothing's happened. And Mum's definitely happier now Dad's made his decision.

It would be so much better if we could all go, Dad agrees, the Holdsworth family complete. "Mother and me. Our daughter and son." But it can't be. There's the bank to think about, the Kleinwarts' account to look after. And Dad says you just can't go off and leave the Red Brick House.

Mum doesn't like it one bit, Dad being left behind. "Are you sure, Father?" she says.

Dad will try to get a transfer. "But lots of others will too, I'm sure. I don't suppose it will be easy. No-one in their right mind wants to stay back and risk their lives." Take the punishment, as he calls it. "They'll all want to escape once they realise that war's inevitable."

Dad has written to Auntie asking if she could put us up, just the three of us. For a few weeks while he organises our own place, he hopes she will have enough room, even though it is a tiny cottage. Dad can't think of anything else. "Then I'll follow later, once I get my transfer."

Mum's praying it will be soon. I'm praying too and Ingie's eyes are closed so I'm sure she's asking God to do something if he can.

Auntie's reply arrives by return. "It's good news," Dad says.

"I'll be pleased to help," she writes. "It's the least I can do." Dad is holding Auntie's letter up to the light, peering at her tiny writing. Mum calls her a diamond. Dad's going to put on some Wagner. It'll be the first time he's enjoyed Siegfried in ages. "He's feeling much happier now," Ingie says.

Dad can't believe it and Mum is speechless but it has been made possible by Auntie's husband going off with a young gym mistress from the next village and him not coming back, from what Auntie can tell. "I have the space now," she says, near the top of the page, after the niceties. It seems the gym mistress was brilliant on the parallel bars and could do press-ups all day and Auntie couldn't compete even if she tried. "I'm just too old," she says halfway down the page. "I can manage the ironing. But not the trampoline. It's quite beyond me these days."

The letter, with its scratchy handwriting and smelling of lavender, was Auntie's the moment Mr Trimble popped it through the letterbox, Mum was sure. And the postmark, Bumblethorpe in deepest Berkshire: we didn't know anyone else from that part of the world. Perhaps no-one did. Not Hitler, anyway, Dad says. "He might be able to pinpoint London on his map in an instant but he'd be up all night trying to find Bumblethorpe."

So, there's no argument. Mum agrees.

"That's settled then, Mother. That's settled then, children."

The government is still telling everyone that war isn't a foregone conclusion. But as far as my Dad's concerned, it is.

Big Siss calls it the greatest upheaval of our lives.

Evacuation. Yes, *é văc'ü ātion.* Ingie explains.

Escape.

To safety.

That's Dad's plan.

Chapter 3

Far and Away

Dad says the taxi will be here any minute. And there's panic everywhere in the Red Brick House.

We're down to the last of the packing, but it's not going well; Mum and Dad seem to have been up all night although Mum wanted it all done in an "orderly fashion" and only a fresh white hanky to slip into her handbag as she walked out the door saying a sad farewell: "Goodbye old friend... Goodbye..."

"All the best laid plans of mice and men," Dad says, but there's no time for jokes. That's what Mum calls them anyway: "Your father's silly jokes."

As for Ingie and me, it's into our smartest clothes. Mum's shouts are ringing up the stairs, "I want you changed this minute!"

"Oh Mum! It's not Sunday School we're going to."

Prim and proper, that's what we've got to be. "Auntie doesn't want a couple of grubby street urchins in her little cottage." The shouts are still coming. "Do it *now* please children! N O W!"

There're beads of sweat trickling down Dad's brow, steaming up his glasses so he's missing half the things he can't afford to miss. Now where *did* he put the strap for securing the big brown case?

He's sure it will burst open if he doesn't find it and Mum's clothes and Ingie's and mine will rain down on some unsuspecting soul from the luggage rack of the train.

I didn't know trains had luggage racks and I'm looking forward to finding out what other surprises they have in store for me. It was just dark inside my Hornby LNER coaches when I'd knelt down and peered through the little windows to see what I could see. They are a good reproduction (Dad says the best) but I didn't find any luggage racks. Or seats, come to that.

We're up and about earlier than I can remember. Up with the birds, Ingie calls it, but I don't mind, it's the most exciting thing for ages, even pushing our holidays in Hastings into second place in my league table of Most Exciting Things To Do. There is the taxi journey (a first), the train (another first), and then there's Auntie's house in the country even though I'm sure I'll get one of those looks if I don't eat up my greens.

Mum's in a real tizz-wazz now. That's what Ingie says they're called. "Getting in a panic. A real tizz-wazz."

Dad has already announced the taxi will be here any moment and Mum still hasn't got all our things packed, Ingie's and mine, so there's this tizz-wazz thing going on. "I've told you before, children!" The shouts are still flying up the stairs. "If you want your things to go to Auntie's, I need them THIS MINUTE!"

I'm a good boy, I've got mine. My Biggles book and the Rupert Bear Annual and, most important of all, the box with my gas mask. Everyone has one, from the littlest babies right up to the oldest grannies and granddads. And it must go everywhere with us – 'DO NOT LET IT OUT OF YOUR SIGHT,' the OHMS man told Dad clearly. And my best friend, Podgy (whose dad is an expert on gas) reckons Hitler could easily drop a bit on us at any time, night or day, and how it would make us cough, clutch our throats and die an agonising death in an instant.

"That's distemper," I say. "My mum says so. Clutching your throat and calling out."

No, Podgy finks it's definitely gas. He really means thinks, but I don't say, just in case he gets angry. And his dog is an expert too, the way he barks. I bet he would fink too, if he could talk.

Most of our packing has been done in the days after Dad announced the Big Escape, standing bolt upright against the mantelpiece like a sentry, and Timmy taking cover under the stairs. Where is Timmy now? Ingie asks. "Wouldn't it be nice if he climbed into a case without us seeing and just climbed out again when we got to Auntie's, all smiles and purring, as if a trip on a train locked in a case was the most natural thing to do."

"Has a family ever moved house like this before?" Mum moans as Biggles and Rupert Bear get shoved deep down in the big brown case. Dad says we've been hoarding too much in the Red Brick House, that's where the trouble lies. Mum says she wouldn't have bought so much if she'd known we were going to have a war.

All our Worldly Possessions. That's what Mum calls them, Worldly Possessions, looking round sadly now, but there must be ten times as much left for Dad to bring with him, or put into Mr Carter Patterson's store, or sell off for what he can. "Fifty quid, perhaps, if we're lucky," he estimates. "A hundred at the most." It's the worst possible time to sell, with the house clearance man looking to snap up Worldly Possessions at a knock-down price. "He'll be giving your father a hard time," Mum's saying. "As if he doesn't have enough problems as it is."

I don't want to leave my red bike and Ingie wants to take her tennis racket, but she can't. There just isn't room, Mum insists, although Ingie and me can't imagine what it will be like without our favourites. We're sure there won't be anything to do in the country. "Just cows and pigs and fluffy things in the fields," Ingie remembers. "Even the fluffy things chase you down in the country," she says.

Mum is sure our toys will go to a good home. Other boys and girls. "Think how happy they'll be."

We do. But I'd still rather ride my bike than be chased by one of Auntie's fluffy things.

Now there's a horn tooting outside and it's the taxi driver. I run down the path to tell him "We're nearly ready." He's a chirpy little man with a waistcoat frayed round the edges and a flat cap to match. And a packet sticking out of his pocket with the word RIZLA on it. He loads the first cases in the space by the side of his seat and the rest go in the back. They stick out over the bumper and the lid won't shut down but not to worry, he has a bit of string to make it safe. "Is that the kitchen sink you got in the big brown case?" he asks, then says "Phew!", wipes his brow and reckons you could catch an Ernia lifting things like that.

"Biggles and Rupert Bear are in there," I tell him. "We can't leave them behind."

He's just looking for a tip, Mum thinks. Dad will probably give him a shilling if he helps with the cases when we get to Paddington. The big brown one alone could be worth a bob. Dad doesn't want to catch one of these Ernias either. Ingie says they get in your tummy and I wouldn't want one in mine.

The taxi driver pats me on my head and asks "Evacuating then, sonny?" And I tell him we're going to Auntie's to escape Mr Hitler's bombs. Podgy had said, "Don't tell no-one nuffink in case they're German spies." But I think our plans are safe with the taxi driver.

I say that my dad has to stay back and look after the bank, but I'm still a lucky boy and he rolls one of his Rizlas then licks the edge and lights up. He's staying put. He's not leaving London for no-one and blows a great puff of smoke and then coughs from right deep down. He says it's touch and go who'll get him first – the ones he rolls himself or Mr Hitler.

Timmy sits on the doorstep, not seeming to realise the full consequences of what he's seeing. Dad locks the door behind him and tells Timmy he will be back later. Ingie strokes him for the last time. He purrs and meows. "I wish we didn't have to leave Timmy behind," she says. I stroke him and wish too.

We climb in and the taxi chugs off down the road, past Isobel's, then the church. Reverend Runcorn has a sign hanging over the front porch saying MEET THY MAKER TODAY.

"Look, Ingie, Reverend Runcorn's meeting a maker," I say. "I wonder what he looks like?" Ingie says I'm not to worry. "All churches have makers, even Auntie's. You can see him when we get there."

Mum says I'm having my leg pulled.

The driver tells us he has never seen so many people leaving London before. He himself has taken five families to the station this very morning and that must be a record. "Some says there won't be no war, but I reckon they got it all wrong. That 'itler 'as 'ad the Sudatens. Now 'e's after the Poles. Our turn next." And he says through another puff of smoke, "Paddington Station it is then, Sir."

We look back at our house as we turn the corner, the only one I've ever known, and Podgy waving and his dog barking. The taxi driver thinks Podgy's dog would have a bit of Mr Hitler if he ventured this way. Somewhere between the front gate and the tradesman's entrance, if we were to ask him.

Ingie and me catch a last glimpse of Timmy. He doesn't seem very sad, I say.

"Cats don't understand," says Ingie. "Or he would be dabbing his eyes with his little hanky."

I think I'm having my leg pulled again as the taxi turns out of our street and heads towards Paddington. Dad tells us our train leaves at 1.30. Sharp, he calls it.

𝔇aily 𝔈xpress

Saturday, August 11, 1939

HOUR OF LIBERATION FOR DANZIG NEAR, SAYS HITLER

Hitler, through his Danzig leader, Albert Forster, continued the war of words with Poland last night and declared that the "hour of liberation" for Danzig was near.

In London, Forster's speech was regarded as "restrained"; in Paris it failed to arouse any excitement.

Paris opinion was that Danzig was safe "for the next few weeks at least".

And the reason for this confidence? It is because Forster, although claiming German support, merely hoped that their day of union with Germany might not be "too distant," a hope that has been expressed in Danzig for twenty years.

It was a busy day for the Polish Foreign Office, with Colonel Beck and Artichelki, Vice Minister of the Foreign Office, receiving envoys of Britain and France and also of Russia and Germany. Graf von Wuelich, German chargé d'affaires, protested against the expulsion of 400 German citizens for alleged propaganda for Germany.

It is believed, writes the Daily Express staff reporter in Berlin, that Forster's speech is the first shot in the more serious Nazi propaganda campaign Hitler is now planning to stage against Poland.

Paddington Station is probably the biggest in the world, only Kings Cross coming close. According to my dad, anyway.

"How do you know, Dad? Did someone measure it?"

"Well, not exactly," Dad says, looking round, a bit sheepish. "Not exactly."

"Fathers don't have to measure things to know," Mum says. "Especially *your* father. Now concentrate. What have you done with your gas mask? I don't want you to go losing it."

"It's in my hand, Mum."

"Anyway," Dad says, perking up a bit, "Paddington Station was built by Isambard Kingdom Brunel, the greatest engineer who ever lived. You can't argue with that. He was the best the world has seen."

Dad seems to be on safer ground with his man with the funny name. The engineer that was better than anyone else's.

And there's even more to this Mr Brunel, Dad says. Not only did he build the station but the railway as well, all the way to Bristol. And if *that* wasn't enough, he built the ships that sailed onwards to New York.

After all this I don't think I will ask about the station Dad doesn't have to measure. Even if it isn't the biggest, I bet it is the best.

"Well 'ow about getting this Brunel bloke to 'elp with the cases then." The taxi driver is only a little chap and has our luggage stacked in front of him and tells us he's not going to catch another Ernia for anyone. Dad finds a porter with his sleeves rolled up and it's soon into the guard's van with the help of the guard himself from our train, Paddington to Penzance, Reading first stop and then Newbury where we get off for Auntie's. "The Berks and Hants line," says the guard with authority; he's been doing it all his life and knows. Dad digs deep into his pocket and they each get a shilling.

It's the cost of escaping London, Mum says. "What did I tell you?"

Wherever you look there are people pushing and shoving; kids in prams, some being carried, some tugging along behind, all escaping the war, all confused. There are cases, bags and tea chests; it looks like the whole world is on the move, and it looks like the whole world is after a seat on our train.

The guard can't help, he has other things to do, but he'll make sure we get our cases unloaded when we get to Newbury. He's a Great Western Railway man. Dad calls him "the old school."

"Leave it to me, Sir," he's saying in his waistcoat and cap with his watch and chain swinging from his waistcoat pocket. "That's for telling whether we're on time or not," he booms out above the clatter of Mr Brunel's station. "And the letters GWR. You know what they stand for, children?" And we stand and stare up at him and say we don't. "God's Wonderful Railway... that's what." And he seems very pleased that we know what he knows about his railway.

Dad's found a compartment with a soldier, smart in his uniform and polished boots, who's going to give up his seat, and a sailor who doesn't mind standing either. "Stand and grow tall," he says, but now they just want to squabble over who's giving up a seat for my sister with her bouncy hair and pretty green eyes. I think I'll squeeze in beside Mum if a man as big as an elephant pushes up a bit. "Please, Sir, I think you've taken a bit of my seat."

Dad's lifting our smaller cases onto the luggage rack but the larger ones have to go in the corridor. They're making him puff, my dad.

"Look after yourselves," he's saying with the carriage door slammed shut and him on the platform. His silvery hair is all ruffled and his face looks tired.

"There's a steak and kidney pie in the larder," Mum tells him through the window, but he doesn't seem to hear in the commotion and she has to say it again, only louder. Everyone looks up at the idea of Dad's dinner in the larder, the steak and kidney pie that needs warming up, Reglo Five, the instructions are on the kitchen table. Mum has her hanky to her face now. "On the table," she repeats. "On the kitchen table…" Mum's voice trails off. It's getting too much. The hanky is damp with tears already.

"It's just a little bit of coal dust," Mum insists. "Just coal dust…"

Ingie wishes we didn't have to say goodbye.

I'm looking forward to the train ride but I don't want to leave Dad behind.

The soldier and sailor have left their loved ones already. "It were painful," the soldier tells us. The sailor said goodbye to his mum at a place called Broadstairs in Kent. His mum cried a lot. "Come back home safely, Son," she told him.

They are both going off to war but they can't say where or when. "It's more than my life is worth," the soldier says, and the sailor too. He can't tell us where he's sailing from in case the news gets to Mr Hitler and he uses it to his advantage.

Above the din the announcer is saying the Penzance train is about to leave, whistles are blowing, and we're on our way. We are doing a lot of waving today and here we are doing it again but this time it's to my dad and, suddenly, his face is getting smaller and smaller and then it's lost altogether in the crowd and I'm just left with a picture in my head to take to Auntie's.

"Well, at least we left on time." A cheery little man tucked away in the corner is holding up a book, a timetable book of train times is what he calls it. Everyone stops and looks at him. But they don't say anything. "Yes, we left Paddington bang on time," he says again, and points to a row of neat figures with his stubby little fingers and smiles and seems very happy about it. The bang on time bit especially.

The train is gathering speed now, clickatty-clack, clickatty-clack. I didn't know trains made that noise and I thought I'd do the same the next time I played with my Hornby trains. Clickatty-clacking. If there *is* a next time. The war might stop nice things like that. Nobody has said.

Now we're speeding past grimy buildings with tall chimneys trailing smoke across the people, heads down, going about their work. Getting ready for war. Clickatty-clack, clickatty-clack.

Then our first glimpse of the countryside. Fields full of golden corn sliced up by green hedgerows. "A patchwork," says a man with a tweed cap and smart jacket. The soldier tells us it's worth fighting for, "this country of ours." And the sailor says "We won't let 'itler 'ave so much as a sniff of it."

The man with the tweed cap seems to like this and gives a "Here, here," and looks as though he might shake them by the hand but goes back to his paper instead. "*The Times*," he says. "I always read *The Times*."

It's a King pulling the train, the Timetable Man tells us, not the one that wears a crown and sits on a throne, but an engine, number 6015 and it's King Richard the Third. "I went to see it specially before we left Paddington and wrote the number down in my book."

"That's a coincidence," Mum says, "my boy's name is Richard," and makes me stand up and introduce myself, and I say, "My name's Richard," which they know already because Mum just told them and everyone in the carriage is smiling and looking away because my face is turning red. Tweed Cap reads his paper, *The Times*.

The Timetable Man wants to tell us more about the engine and how the Kings are the finest in the world, but not many people seem interested. Not the sailor or soldier, anyway. They just want to get to where they are going, which is a secret.

We're arriving at Reading now; the train comes to a stop with a jolt while something called mayhem breaks out, with people fighting to get into our carriage with others fighting to get out.

We have forgotten the engine now, named after me, and the countryside that Mr Hitler won't get a sniff of. It's every man for himself. "Stand back and let them get out that wants to," says the guard in his booming voice while feet get trampled and ribs elbowed. Someone drags a case off the luggage rack and dislodges the sailor's kit bag, which falls on Tweed Cap. "I say!" he says, but no one takes much notice.

Then we're off again, bang on time, next stop Newbury, the nearest station to Auntie. "Just as I said," the Timetable Man tells us.

"I hope she has the kettle on," says Mum, who still hasn't got over the bit of coal dust in her eye.

Chapter 4

The Back of Beyond

Mr Alfie's the answer, Auntie had told Dad on the phone just a few days after he'd announced the Big Escape. "He'll pick you up at the station," she said, "I'm sure he will." And she wouldn't waste another moment making it happen. "I'll trot over to see him first thing in the morning."

Auntie's squeaky little voice was coming from the telephone box on the village green, just opposite the post office and general stores. "It's long distance," Dad said, when the phone rang and he'd rushed to pick it up. "I have a lady called Auntie for you," said the operator, "will you take the call?" And Dad did while we all stood round, excited, waiting to hear what she had to say.

Mum and Dad had already got Auntie's letter telling us she could put us up, of course. But Dad still had no idea how he would get us from the station to her little cottage, Mum, Ingie and me. All he knew it was miles and miles. And with that pile of luggage too.

Now Auntie was saying this man Mr Alfie was the answer. Her money might run out any minute, she warned, but not before Dad learnt just how valuable he was to her little village. As a handyman, especially. And part-time taxi driver, of course. "He will be ever so happy to help out," she said. "I'm sure he will."

"Auntie knows this helpful man," Dad said, putting his hand over the bit you speak into, so she wouldn't hear. "He does a bit of taxi driving on the side, apparently. I suppose he can be relied upon, this man Mr Alfie."

He'd taken the kids to school when the snow covered the ground last winter and the darts team to Yattenden the year before when the lower road flooded. And Mrs Hoddle's youngest to hospital with his head stuck in the chamber pot. "He couldn't 'ave his tea 'till it were off," Mr Alfie had told the villagers gathered round listening in the Red Lion that evening.

They all agreed it was the most exciting thing that had happened in the village for years and years.

"It's times like these that the village really values Mr Alfie," Auntie said. And as for the Big Occasion, weddings and funerals and the like, he had this smart cap with a polished peak and shiny badge. "It adds such a touch of decorum, don't you agree?"

And Dad was just about to when the phone started making a beeping noise and Auntie was gone... "Hello, Auntie. Hello... are you there...?"

But Auntie wasn't. Her sixpence had run out.

"Never mind," said Dad, he was sure the problem of getting us from the station was solved. This man Mr Alfie would be there. Auntie had said so. Just before the beep, beep, beeps...

The train is slowing. We must be coming to Newbury now. "It's your stop, isn't it?" says the Timetable Man. "We'll be there in two minutes and ten seconds exactly." He holds his hands up and counts on his stubby little fingers, "Ten, nine, eight...."

The soldier and sailor look at each other and say as one voice, "Bang on time, I bet."

"Newbury!" And then louder: "N-E-W-B-U-R-Y!" calls the Ticket Inspector, walking up and down the corridor. "All those for Newbury alight 'ere."

"... three, two, one," says the Timetable Man as we come to a halt. "Bang on time," he says, putting his stubby little fingers away.

Everyone's very good and helps out, getting our luggage off the train; the soldier lifting our cases from the luggage rack and the sailor carrying the two heaviest ones from the corridor where Dad left them when we got on the train at Paddington. He has them on the platform now.

"Don't forget your gas masks, children," says Mum, climbing over legs and feet to get to the door.

It's goodbye to the soldier and the sailor. The Timetable Man and Tweed Cap. "Goodbye," we say. "Goodbye, and good luck," they reply. Dad has always said to be polite to strangers. So I say "Thank you" to the Elephant Man I sat next to. "Thank you for squeezing up a bit."

The guard has the big brown case on the platform too. It's travelled all the way down with him in his guard's van. He's looked after it specially, knowing what it means to us, the kitchen sink and all that. The Great Western man, the Old School, as Dad called him at Paddington Station, waving his green flag and blowing his whistle to set the train going. And checking on the watch that swings from his waistcoat pocket.

"I wonder what Dad's doing now?" I say. And the soldier, leaning out of the window, says, "Don't you worry, sonny, you'll get your dad back, it's a dead cert."

And the big engine, King Richard the Third, starts to move off – slowly at first, and then gathering speed. Just like a great big dragon blowing big blasts of smoke and sparks into the sky.

There's only one porter on the platform, but he's just like the ones in London and he's ready to tackle our pile of luggage. "You movin' 'ouse?" he says, and laughs at his own joke. But it's not a problem. "Not a worry. I'll 'ave it shifted," and does. "Taxi for Bumblethorpe? That'll be Mr Alfie. 'e'll be 'ere in a jiffy. 'e won't let you down."

And then he says, "Mark my words." As if that helps too.

Outside the station there's a shiny bus resting in the shade of a giant conker tree. It's very peaceful here and the bus is different from ours in London; it's not red and it doesn't have a top bit where you sit.

"It's a single-decker," Mum tells us. "That's so it can get under the trees in the country lanes."

"Oh," I say, not knowing.

But it's a nice bus, with a tall, spindly driver sitting behind the steering wheel and the ticket collector leaning back in his seat with his cap pushed forwards over his eyes and he's dozing off. The bus is green and yellow and has Thames Valley Traction Company painted on the side in gold letters, and NEWBURY – TUFTON HARDWICK – BUMBLETHORPE – LITTLE PIDDLINGTON showing on the front. And that's it.

"Oi goes down there every mornin' and once again after I 'as my tea," says the thin driver in a funny way, with "Oi's" and "Ahh's", and Mum says it must be the way they talk in the country. "It's something we'll just have to get used to, children." Mum's saying it in a hush so the man can't hear.

But we're not going by bus even though it's sitting there and the driver wants to help. "Thank you," Mum says so the man can hear, "we're going by taxi today. My husband's treating us."

And here's Mr Alfie in his taxi now and he's stopping right beside our pile of luggage. And he's wearing the weddings and funerals cap too. "That's a good sign," Mum says.

He's a bit on the slow side though, Ingie thinks. And me too.

Mum shushes us. "The people down in the country probably take a long time to get going… as well as talking funny."

Mum's little joke is good to hear. Mum hasn't smiled once since we left Dad back in London, but she is now and it really bucks us up. Even the hanky is tucked away up Mum's sleeve.

Mr Alfie is clambering out of his taxi. He's a big, lolloping man with bushy eyebrows and a patchwork coat, and seems especially pleased to see us and asks "Mrs 'oldsworth, then?" And bows down like people do when the Queen pays a visit and says it isn't every day he meets someone off the London train and us with a pile of luggage the likes of which he's never seen before.

But it's all in a day's work, and has our cases lifted into the back of the taxi and some onto the roof where there is a roof rack; then tied down, side to side and front to back, as best he can, with hands like those of a great big bear. "'tis fiddly work this," he says and how he'd be lost without something called baler twine, the countryman's best friend, he says that's what it's called.

And then he goes to the front of his taxi, a black Austin with the numbers 10/4 on the bonnet, and a little "A" for Austin on the wheels, and winds it with a handle, just like Dad winding his gramophone.

It's making him puff, this winding, and tells Mum between puffs how the air is cleaner and fresher in the country and how Dad's done the right thing by sending us down here.

"By all accounts you only 'as fuggy old air up there in London," he says, and reckons a bit of rambling round the fields and meadows will soon see us right as long as we keep a sharp look out for the cow pats.

"What do they do then, Mr Alfie?" Ingie asks, not having come across a cow pat before.

"Why, they clings to your boots," Mr Alfie says, calling Ingie, Young Missie. If we go a-rambling round the fields, that is. And then tells us, "All aboard. Bumblethorpe next stop," and how standing around all day won't get the cows milked or the harvest harvested.

Mum's to sit in the front and Ingie and me in the back and we are not to mind the feathers left over from Farmer Millsom's hens taken to market that very morning. "And them making two and sixpence a pair, a fair return, who can argue with that?" he asks Mum. And Mum can't, not having had much experience of selling hens at market.

Now we're off, twenty miles an hour the most Mr Alfie will do, downhill included, speed only serving to get him where he's going before he wants. "And where's the sense in that?" he asks, though not seeming to expect an answer.

Ingie and me giggle. We can't imagine Mr Alfie ever arriving anywhere before he needs to.

Mum's looking forward to putting her feet up when we get to Auntie's. "A little faster, perhaps, Mr Alfie?" But Mr Alfie is happy with second gear. Auntie's will still be there when we get down to Bumblethorpe. "Everyone knows," he tells us over his shoulder.

Soon we're winding our way down little lanes, round corners and past signposts with the strangest names: Studdlecombe, Upton Bywater and the funniest of all, Little Piddlington. Ingie says it's just like Hampton Court Maze.

"You been there, Missie, that Maze?" Mr Alfie asks and says, "Well I never!" when Ingie says she has, with Miss Fosdyke and the rest of the history class last summer. And they did Hampton Court Palace in the afternoon, after they'd had the sandwiches their mums had packed specially.

He's funny, Mr Alfie, Ingie and me think. But nice funny with his bushy eyebrows and bits of his best friend, the baler twine, sticking out of his pockets.

"Well, I never!" he says again, chugging along in the Austin and marvelling at such things. "Packed lunch, eh. Whatever next?"

It's all cows, pigs and sheep in the fields where there had been people in streets just a few hours before, and horses turn their heads as we pass by. You can't say the countryside is deserted, Mr Alfie is saying, and knows more horses by their first name than those he doesn't, Flower and Dobbin for a start, and they probably know his too. Alfie the handyman and part-time taxi driver. "That's me," he says, and laughs again in his funny old way. "Can't keep no secrets down in the country."

Mum thinks it's something we will need to be wary of. "That and the cow pats," she says.

I've got my window open, smelling the smells of the countryside. The fresh country air Mr Alfie thinks is so good for our insides. Ingie has her window open too, her pretty hair blowing about in the breeze. "Ooh, what a pong!" she says.

Mum has never seen anything as lovely as this before, having been brought up in narrow streets and a little back yard in Clapham with Gran and her sisters and brother, Arthur, who went off to the war and never came back. "As pretty as a picture," Mum calls it, watching the countryside unfold, one beautiful bit after another. "Only an artist could do justice to this," she says.

And Mr Alfie tells Mum how there was one in the village until a few weeks back. "A real live artist, 'e was, with letters after 'is name and a little white beard, but no one ever recognised what 'e painted. And now 'e's gone, we'll never know."

"Gone?" Mum asks, wondering about their artist. "Gone where?"

"Dead," Mr Alfie says. "That's where 'e be gone, Mrs 'oldsworth. And never told a soul 'e were going neither."

Mum thinks it's awful. "In this beautiful countryside." And Ingie thinks so too, and me. And we go quiet for a bit.

It doesn't seem necessary for Mum to tell Mr Alfie we will be staying with Auntie in Rose Tree Cottage as he knows all about the husband running off with the gym mistress, and says how the news had gone round the village "like wildfire". There's nothing wrong with that, 'armless gossip, he calls it, as we pass a sign saying FARMER COLLINS FARM then a bit further on, MIND THE COWS.

We're in the village now, Bumblethorpe, passing the village green, a row of neat cottages and the Red Lion opposite, next to a little cluster of shops.

"Look, there's a pub for Dad," Ingie says, pointing. "Wait till he sees that."

Dad's new pub has a wooden seat with a table outside and a sign, SIMONDS BEERS ARE BEST FOR YOU, and a sloping roof, almost down to the ground.

And there's a meadow opposite and a horse called Champion that Mr Alfie knows, and a five-barred gate for him to look over. There's a pond and ducks and a willow tree with a rope and tyre on the end, hanging down, just out from the bank.

Mum calls it a picture postcard.

On the tyre swings a boy, shrieking with delight in case he gets tipped into the water, and there's another boy pushing him further and faster every time. "Something not right in the head with that lad," says Mr Alfie. "Can't put me finger on it... but there just isn't."

The country kids seem to be having fun I think to myself, even the one that's not quite right in the head. "Perhaps I can go and play later, Mum? If Ingie comes too."

Mum's not so sure. "They look a bit scruffy," she says.

Mum's scruffiest is Bobby White. With a middle name that spells trouble, according to Mr Alfie. "Won't do you no 'arm, tho'. Not like the lad doing the pushing. Just a bit of a scallywag, that's all."

Mr Alfie seems at home here. "There's the postman," he says, pointing to the postman on his bike with his trousers tied round his ankles with the baler twine Mr Alfie likes so much. "Afternoon, Dick."

"Afternoon, Alfie."

"And that's the goose that chases 'im every day. If Farmer Collins don't look out 'e'll 'ave that goose on 'is plate come Christmastime, surrounded by gravy and roast 'tatoes, and our postman sinking 'is teeth into one of 'is drumsticks."

But not today. There's letters to be delivered even though there aren't any for Mr Alfie. "Perhaps I shall be in luck tomorrow," he tells the horse.

We have pulled up alongside a neat garden with white fence and hollyhocks and lupins laid out in neat flower beds. "Rose Tree Cottage," Mr Alfie announces, satisfied. "Welcome to Bumblethorpe."

"Look, there's Auntie!" cries Ingie, and a little lady comes through a door surrounded by roses and a cat at her feet, like Timmy, but with more fluff. Mum waves and Ingie waves and I wave; it's Auntie all right, a tiny little lady with an apron and pink cheeks and lots of wrinkles like Gran.

Mr Alfie has the cases unloaded and carried upstairs before Mum even has time to ask, and pays him out of a handbag full of spare hankies. He looks more than happy. Perhaps Mum's given him extra for his trouble.

"Any time, Mrs 'oldsworth," he's saying and tips his cap and does another little bow like Mum's the Queen. "I'm off to fix the reverend's front gate now," he says, pats the Austin and calls it Old Girl. "Standing about won't do no good." And tells us again about getting the cows milked and the harvest harvested.

Auntie is so pleased to see us and says it has been ages, except for Ingie who she saw last year when she came down for her rosy cheeks. And then it's a case of "Well, well, who's this fine little man?" which is me, Richard, who she has only seen in pictures, just out of my pram. "My, how you've grown; quite the little gentleman now!"

"I'm going to be a beanpole when I grow up, Auntie, Dr

44

McGilligan said so," I say and hold out my hand like I'd been told and Auntie hangs on to it until it's Ingie's turn.

When I get my hand back I ask if I can stroke the cat as we have left ours in London and Auntie says I can. He's called Fluff and is too old to chase mice and has a plate of tripe that he doesn't have to catch.

I bend down and stroke Fluff and he purrs and I have made my first friend in the country, which is nice.

Auntie says we must be worn out coming from London and weighed down with luggage and has the kettle on, just as Mum had hoped. "Now there's mental telepathy for you," Mum's saying, which turns out to be when there's some people on a train in a packed compartment and some others miles away in a little cottage, yet still the kettle goes on.

And now Auntie wants to build us up with fresh food even before Mum has time to unpack. Ingie and me are poor mites coming from London with food that has been sitting in the delivery van or cold store and has lost its zest for life. Here it is now, this fresh food, a plum pie which Auntie has baked specially to make us into healthy grown ups. Mum's to have a slice too, even though she's a healthy grown up already.

The plums have come from the tree overhanging the fence at the bottom of the garden. We can see it now, if we look. "See children, right there, next to the swing and the bird table." And the garden shed where husbands spend their days having a smoke. "You can't get closer to a bowlful of goodness than that, now can you?" And all our heads are nodding. Mine especially, as all this time I'd been thinking plums came from Podgy's dad's shop in a paper bag.

Mum tells us we must tuck in as fresh foods will become scarce with war just around the corner. "People will be stocking up and then the shelves will become bare and that, in turn, will make people ask for more." Mum shakes her head and says it's a vicious circle, which happens every time there's a war with nothing but dog biscuits to eat and the dogs themselves with no choice but to go out and bite the postman.

"Well I never did!" says Auntie, and she probably didn't, living down in the country all her life.

Now it's time for bed. Mum says it's been a tiring day and we need our sleep. Soon I'm tucked up with a big fluffy pillow and Auntie's fresh-smelling eiderdown. "Aired with real country air," Auntie says. Ingie's in the bed next to me. Hers has been aired with proper air too.

"Goodnight, Ingie."

"Goodnight, Little Brother."

There's silence. No cars and no buses and no trains. No Podgy's dog to bark. No people walking home from Dad's pub. No Dad.

"It's very quiet in the country," I say.

"Go to sleep."

A cow moos in the distance. An owl makes a hooting sound.

It's our first night in the country. I wonder how many more there will be.

Chapter 5

So, It's War

Auntie is all of a lather.

It is a bright sunny day, a Sunday morning, and Ingie and me are taking turns on the swing. Mum is snipping the old flower heads from Auntie's roses – "dead heading," Mum calls it. Auntie has the Sunday roast on, a lamb shoulder from the village butcher, Mr Blenkinsop. "They're getting scarce," he'd told her the Thursday before, Auntie's shopping day. "But I can let you 'ave just this one, Auntie. Just the one."

"I wouldn't ask ordinarily," she told him. Except for it being a very special occasion – Mum, Ingie and me coming down from London. "To miss the bombs," she said.

It is more than two weeks since Dad sent us off on the Big Escape and we are getting used to living with Auntie in her little village; Mum goes up to the village stores, but she is not warmly welcomed, not yet. "It might take time," Auntie warns. "Just a bit of time." And Ingie and me have ventured to the stream and the pond, with the village kids, socks round their ankles, mop hair uncombed, looking on suspiciously.

One kid says, "Where you from?"

"From London," Ingie says.

Another kid, the one pushing the swing, says, "Townies... You're the Townies."

The others don't say anything. In a circle, around us, staring as if we've come from a strange planet. Townies, that's what we are. That's our new names.

"Why did they do that, Ingie?" I asked. "It's like we've got a smell or something..."

Ingie says, "Well, we haven't." But she thinks some of them could do with a good scrub. "Pongy country kids!"

And then it happened, just as Mum said, Auntie getting all of a lather, all of a froth. Rushing out of the house on this warm, sunny Sunday morning. "Goodness, whatever is the matter?" Mum says, dropping the snippers. "Whatever has happened?"

"It's Mr Chamberlain!" Auntie wails. "Our Prime Minister and he's on the wireless putting the fear of the Lord into the nation. Come quickly to hear!"

And we do come quickly to hear, Mum first, then Ingie, then me.

And here's Mr Chamberlain in Auntie's front parlour, on the mantelpiece, in his best suit voice and doing his Fear of the Lord bit and it's all because the Peace in Our Time piece of paper has failed and we are at war with Germany. Just like Dad said.

Auntie has seen a picture of Hitler with his little moustache and hair combed in a funny way. "I knew he was no good the moment I clapped eyes on the man." Auntie calls him a nasty piece of work and doesn't have much time for his paintings either. "The cat could do better, I do declare. And him with the name Schickelgruber."

We all look at each other. We thought Fluff was Fluff, and so he is too. It's Hitler who should have been Schickelgruber, but he didn't like it one bit so took his Mum's name, Mrs Hitler. Auntie has it all explained but it doesn't help Mr Chamberlain, who's in a dreadful state. "I informed Herr Hitler that unless he withdrew his forces from Poland by 11.00am today, a state of war would exist between our two countries..."

Mum has her ear glued to the wireless. Ingie and me stand quietly by. But Mr Hitler didn't even bother to reply to poor Mr Chamberlain.

"No wonder he's upset," Ingie says.

"Nasty piece of work," Auntie says again. She seems even more convinced now we're at war with him.

Mr Chamberlain tells us from the mantelpiece how his long struggle for peace has come to nothing. "You can imagine," his voice crackles over Auntie's wireless, "what a bitter blow it is for me. Everything that I have worked for, everything that I believe in, has crashed in ruins."

It is September the third, 1939, and it crashed in ruins just in time for elevenses.

"A fine time to have a war!" Auntie says.

Mum isn't waiting for elevenses, she's striding across the village green to the telephone box, and calling Dad. It is not easy; the phone lines are busy, very busy, and the girl at the telephone exchange says everyone is phoning everyone else. "You must be patient," she tells Mum. "There's a war on, you know." For the last five minutes, at least. Or maybe six. "Oh do hurry up!" Mum says.

When Mum does get through, Dad is worried but safe. He tells her he makes his sandwiches each day and feeds Timmy before going off to the bank and then again when he comes home in the evening. Are we all right? he asks. And when Mum says we are he does a bit more packing and waits for his transfer. Sirens had gone off just as Mr Chamberlain had finished his speech and Dad dusted off the instructions from the OHMS man telling him what to do when the bombers came. Some people had put on their tin hats and hidden under the stairs, but not my dad. Mum said he poured a whisky, lit his pipe and sat back and reflected on life.

"Nothing changes," she says.

Then he took out his records, wrapped them in brown paper, and put them in a packing case for safe keeping. It would be a long time before Siegfried stomped around the living room again, Dad told himself.

Dad just wished he was in the countryside with us. He was sure his transfer would come through one day, although he didn't know when. You have to be an optimist to work in a bank, he said.

The whisky helped. It usually did, Mum said.

We must be prepared, Auntie is saying, and puts the kettle on. A cup of tea won't stop the Germans coming but it will make it easier to bear. Mum is saying we must try on our gas masks, and we do. They steam up and Auntie can't find the teapot. She takes hers off and the tea is poured. "So far, so good," she tells us.

Then there's a chattering at the garden gate. A commotion, Mum calls it. It's Mr Alfie in his taxi, the Austin, him being one of Auntie's stalwarts and about to set off around the village bringing the news to the people who haven't got a wireless and don't know we're at war. Auntie tells him we listened to Mr Chamberlain, not a word missed, in the front parlour, but Mr Alfie still wants to tell us all about it. And Mr Lamplin the postman, and Mr Jiggins the roadsweeper. They are at Auntie's gate too, doing this chattering about Mr Chamberlain's news. Mum's commotion.

"I 'eard 'im when I were polishing the taxi," Mr Alfie tells us. He had the car half done, the roof and bonnet, and Farmer Millsom's feathers swept out from the back. "The wife said to come a-runnin'," he says. And he did as fast as his lolloping old legs would carry him.

"It be dreadful, this," he tells us, eyeing up the half-polished Austin. "Doubt it'll ever get done now."

Mr Jiggins is a stalwart too. But not as much as Mr Alfie, and says he's sure the war won't make much difference to the village. He's a nice little man and thinks it won't reach Bumblethorpe. "The first one didn't, anyway," he says, and he'd looked out for it specially. Then tells Auntie, "Nice garden you got there, Auntie," with his woolly hat pulled down tight over his head and a tiny bit of cigarette hanging from his mouth, just like our taxi driver in London.

The postman, Mr Lamplin, doesn't think Mr Jiggins knows what he is talking about and says how he should stick to roadsweeping. Mr Lamplin is a stalwart too, but with the OHMS envelopes in his bag he's an expert on wars. He delivered one to himself and read it over breakfast. "There it was, in black and white, this war," he tells Mr Jiggins. Between the toast and the second cup of tea is where he found it.

Mr Jiggins still thinks Auntie has one of the prettiest gardens around. "Just watch out for the green fly, Auntie," he tells her and calls them a right pestilence.

The police constable arrives now. He is PC Trendle, like Podgy only bigger round the middle and he is puffing, lots and lots. He was digging over his vegetable patch when Mr Chamberlain made his speech. He says it's a bad business but tells us not to worry – the chief constable will be working on a plan of action. "He'll know what to do," he says. Turning the clods to let in the frost was what he was doing when war broke out.

Mr Alfie worries about my dad still being up in London. The Big Smoke. "I wouldn't want to be up there," he says. "Fuggy old air and packed lunches…"

Mum is grateful for Mr Alfie saying what he is saying about Dad. We are all worried but it seems nice that Mr Alfie is too, one of Auntie's stalwarts, the village handyman for most of the time and taxi driver when he isn't.

Mum is wearing one of her most serious faces and tells them how Dad has put in for a transfer and how she hopes it will come through soon. Mum doesn't know when. "God forbid we will have to wait too long," she says. Mum's still wearing her serious face. "And the bombs about to drop."

Auntie tells them how it would work out so well if Dad could get this transfer to Newbury and catch the bus in the morning and the one back in the evening. "They leave promptly," she says, and at funny times. "Your Percy might end up doing a bit of running..."

Mum's not so sure about Dad doing a bit of running with his bowler hat and briefcase...

"Funny times," the stalwarts agree, heads nodding. Mr Alfie, Mr Jiggins, PC Tremble and Mr Lamplin the postman. "Funny times..." But don't know why.

Mr Alfie is going now. He tells us how he hasn't got time to stand about gossiping and is getting off down the Little Piddlington Road to tell the Little Piddlington people we're at war. "Tatt, ta," he says, and winds his Austin with a handle and a grunting noise. Mr Lamplin is cycling across the village green to Love Lane taking the news to Mr and Mrs Bishop and the others who haven't got a wireless. Not even a front parlour to put it in.

And Constable Trendle too. He'll go home and wait for the chief constable's instructions. "It's all about priorities," he tells us. "The clods will just have to wait until this war's over."

Mr Jiggins is going back to his gardening. He's going to make up some of his special green fly mixture for Auntie. "Give 'em a squirt every day and twice on Sundays... for good measure," he tells Auntie, "... that'll see to the little blighters." The little bit of cigarette is still stuck to his bottom lip and the woolly hat pulled down even tighter across his eyes.

Auntie's making another pot of tea. "What with all this talk of war the last one will be stone cold," she says.

Mum feels much happier now she's met Auntie's village stalwarts and calls them steadfast people. "People you can rely on."

Auntie is reaching for the biscuit tin. She tells us we need all the treats we can get with the problems ahead. "That awful man Hitler... and the green fly, of course."

In London, evacuation of the masses is in full swing. Dad tells Mum on the telephone how he struggled to get to work that morning and back again in the evening; there were so many people on the move, he said. People rushing to the safety of the country. He didn't get home until after dark, then fed Timmy, and made himself a sandwich and bowl of soup. Then listened to the man on the wireless. "I hope you're safe," he said, and when Mum said "We are" he went to bed.

"He's home safe," Mum tells us, "but worn out." Then says, "Yes, Timmy's safe too," after Ingie and me ask.

Bumblethorpe has a village hall. Auntie told us all about it our first evening in the country after she'd settled herself down on the sofa, leaving Ingie and me to curl up on the rug, listening, just before we were shoo'ed off to bed.

It must be something very special, Ingie thought. Even Mum didn't know about village halls when we asked as she said her goodnights. Mum hadn't seen one before. We didn't have them in Clapham, she said. Village halls.

"Oh, you'll be very impressed," Auntie told us next morning, after we'd woken up to strange noises from outside our window. Cows mooing and sheep baaing and another funny noise. "Horses neighing," Ingie said. "I remember when I came down last year."

"We'll do a conducted tour of the village," Auntie said. "Yes, that's what we'll do, a conducted tour... taking in the village hall." It would be straight after breakfast. "I know you'll be very impressed when you see it," she said again and seemed very pleased with herself. "Eggs in eggcups?" she asked cheerily after she'd said about the conducted tour. "With soldiers... you're in the country now... we can spare them. For the time being, anyway."

"It's very nice," Mum agreed on Auntie's conducted tour, as we stood in a little half circle and stared up at Auntie's village hall with a playground on one side and a merry-go-round on the other, the sort you pushed and jumped on and went round and round.

"I don't suppose you have those up in London," Auntie said to Ingie and me. She seemed very hopeful. But we did. In the park where Podgy and me found our football. We didn't think it right to say.

And we had eggs in eggcups too. Until people talked about the war, then they got scarce. We had thick butter on our soldiers too. But it didn't seem right to say about that either.

"It's the heart of the community, our village hall," Auntie was saying, looking very satisfied. "Where we have dances and the Bumblethorpe Players put on their Christmas pantomime for all to enjoy." That's the highlight of the year, Auntie told us, with Mr Framlington, the Scout Master, playing the prince and stealing a kiss from Teacher Peabody just before the curtain comes down. "She blushes and hopes he won't do it again… she always does," Auntie said. "Our Miss Peabody, kissed for all the world to see." And calls it "not right and proper."

And then there's the summer fete. Auntie's just as excited about that. With tents, gaily decorated, and Mr Pinchbeck turning up to give donkey rides, halfpenny a go, three for a penny.

"No-one puts on a better pantomime and no-one puts on a better fete," Auntie said on our conducted tour as we peeped in the village hall with its rows of seats stacked neatly at one end and a stage at the other. "No-one." And her squeaky little voice bounced around the empty hall and back out again.

But not now. Now the Thames Valley Traction Company bus is standing outside with the thin driver at the wheel and he has just arrived from Newbury Station with children from London like Ingie and me. They are the evacuees, and they are hoping to find families to take them in until the war is over.

"Come quickly and see the poor little mites," Auntie says, and we watch their reverend, just like ours, but theirs is Reverend Curd and he is skinny, like a scarecrow, with a wobbly head, and he's trying to find homes for the kids and won't give up till it's done. He has a plump lady to help, Teacher Pegg, very strict with the Infants, Auntie tells us, and Miss Peabody from the Juniors, and Mrs Pegg has a list that she is reading from. It has the names of the villagers who promised to take in the children and she is calling them out, just like morning assembly, and a scolding for any who might be thinking of changing their minds.

"Mrs Brown, do come forwards, dear, we haven't got all day." Teacher Pegg is having to shout above the din with all the other villagers, crammed in, wondering when it's their turn next.

𝔇𝔞𝔦𝔩𝔶 𝔈𝔵𝔭𝔯𝔢𝔰𝔰

Friday, September 1, 1939

FOUR-DAY MOVE BY RAIL – EVACUATION BEGINS

Trainloads of children and their mothers, hospital patients and blind people will begin streaming out of Britain's big cities early today to places of safety in country and seaside districts.

About 10,000 schools throughout the country are affected. One-hundred and fifty-one thousand of the women and children will go to East Sussex, 83,000 to West Sussex, 154,000 to Kent, 124,000 to Essex, 95,000 to Surrey, and 84,000 to Hertfordshire.

From Liverpool and Merseyside 216,000 people will go to Wales; 247,000 are to leave Manchester for places in Lancashire, Shropshire, Staffordshire, Cheshire and Derbyshire; and 127,000 from Newcastle and Gateshead will be dispersed over Cumberland, Durham, Northumberland and North Riding.

Expectant mothers to be evacuated will be accompanied by mid-wives. Teachers will also travel on trains to look after the children and they will be met at their destination points by local officials.

The immensity of the task is shown by the fact the time-table of the Southern Railway alone for the transfer of 475,000 persons from London runs to 130 closely-printed pages. Their trains will start running at 8.00am and continue to 5.00pm non-stop. Most of the Great Western's evacuation trains will start from Ealing Broadway. They will begin at 8.30am and will carry 5,600 children every hour until 5.00 p.m.

The schoolchildren to be evacuated will have to take with them gasmasks, underclothing, night-clothes, house shoes, or plimsolls, stockings or socks, toothbrush, comb, towel, soap, face-cloth, handkerchief, a warm coat, or mackintosh, if possible, and a packet of food for the day.

A million children in all are to be moved, and special printed postcards telling of their safe arrival will be awaiting them. The cards will be signed by them and posted to their parents – and this will be the first indication mothers and fathers will have of their new homes.

And Mrs Pettifer from Thatcher's End Lane. She has to come forwards too, getting her orders from the plump teacher. "I have you down here, Mrs Pettifer," Teacher Pegg says in her school marm voice. "You're taking some children from London, I believe?" And Mrs Tottle, pushing through the throng, trying to reach the front to stand next to Mrs Brown and Mrs Pettifer.

Then it's Farmer Collins's turn. He's hoping to take in one evacuee if he can. "A strong lad who'll 'elp with the 'arvest, if you 'aves one, Marm," he asks, with his cloddy old farmer's boots and battered old farmer's hat clutched at his side.

We watch and see how it is done. The kids assembled in the village hall with Mrs Pegg giving out her orders and Miss Peabody writing the names in her book while Reverend Curd says how he's praying for a happy outcome to the day. They come in all shapes and sizes, these kids from London: short ones and tall ones, fat ones and thin ones, and they all seem lost and forlorn. Some have teddies, and the girls their dollies, and it looks like some have been crying. They have name tags pinned to their coats and clutching their gas masks and the things their mums have packed for them – little cases or satchels, the lucky ones – and crumpled bags for those whose mums could find nothing better.

"Don't you worry," the reverend tells them kindly. "We'll find homes for you, and those that we can't will, I'm sure, find something in the next village. Or maybe the next...." He seems to be trying his hardest and the boys and girls haven't mentioned the wobbly old head once.

Now the mums and dads from the village are walking up and down the rows of children as if they are trying to pick the best ones. And Ingie and me, we wouldn't want to be in the queue, waiting to be picked out by a stranger, going to a strange house, maybe even different ones, Ingie in one and me in another. I hang on to Mum's coat and Ingie stays close, we don't want to get parted now. It could happen so easily. Even to Ingie, who's nearly a grown up.

The children have been on trains all day and then told to get on the bus for Bumblethorpe. Auntie says they'll be at the end of their tether. "I expect they thought it was an adventure when it started." But now she thinks it's just a bad dream. A little boy tells how they were given a bar of chocolate when they got on the train hours before, but now it's long gone. "I'm hungry," says a little girl with fair hair and chocolate all over her face; another little boy is hungry too. "Please sir, I need the toilet," says another sad little face.

Mrs Tottle with the big house and the unkempt garden is saying she'll take a couple to add to her own and Mrs Pettifer will have one, even though Mr Pettifer's gone down with a thing called The Gout which makes it hard to take evacuee children. Clandice Brown would have a pretty girl with a bow in her hair except she won't be parted from her little sister and isn't going anywhere without her. "Mum said not to let our Lizzie out of sight no matter what 'appens..."

"Perhaps we can take them both," says Mrs Brown kindly. She's one of Mum's Posh ladies, with a hat and feather; and Mr Brown doesn't have a say in it as he's away on his boat. They live next to the Artist's House, Auntie says, across the village green. "That's where he will be, Captain Brown, at sea, I expect. He always seems to be there these days."

Now Farmer Collins is getting his wish, a strong lad from Putney who always wanted to work on a farm. "I wants to drive a tractor," he tells them, and will. And stay in the room looking out over the farmyard with Farmer Collins's wife getting him up at the crack of dawn and a breakfast fit for two.

The rest have missed out and hope things will be better over in Little Piddlington. Bumblethorpe doesn't want them and Mrs Turvey is heard to say, "Over my dead body," and Mrs Pollard says she'll not be budged neither. Lots of people don't want these evacuees, it seems.

We watch as the kids climb back on the bus with their little bags and dollies and teddies and their names pinned to their coats, sad and forlorn, as it sets off for the next village where the reverend promises another village hall and another teacher with a list and more mums and dads to pick and choose.

"I'd love to take one if I could," Auntie says. "Two at a pinch." But not while she has us. Rose Tree Cottage is packed already and there's still Dad to fit in when he comes down. "Perhaps I can later," she's telling Teacher Pegg, the plump lady. "Keep my name on your list if you will..."

And then there's the reverend with the skinny neck and wobbly head who's quite upset by the whole affair. "I'm quite upset," he says, as the hall empties and the people make their way home.

"It's all been too much," he tells Miss Peabody as she makes him a cup of tea, a strong one, with two sugars and a biscuit.

"There," she says, "you deserve it." A pick-me-up when it's all been too much.

That's the excitement over for the day as we walk back to Auntie's house, and the lucky evacuees go off to their new homes: Mrs Brown, the Posh lady, the feather still sticking out of her hat and the two girls, Lydia and Lizzie at her side; and Mrs Tottle with the two boys traipsing along behind.

And then Farmer Collins and Mrs Farmer Collins setting off in the farm truck with the strong lad sitting on a bale of hay in the back. "You don't have fun like this in Putney," he tells them.

Mum hopes the other kids will fit into village life, but she can't be sure. Not if her experience is anything to go by, anyway. And me and Ingie too, by the village pond on the Sunday morning, with the village kids and us getting our new name, Townies. Mum says she has been getting the cold shoulder each time she goes up to the village stores or into Mr Blenkinsop's, the butcher's. "They could be a bit friendlier," Mum says.

"Oh, I'm sure they'll welcome you soon," Auntie is saying. "It just might take a week or two. A couple of months at the most."

"Auntie's only trying to convince," Ingie says. "Doing her best, that's what."

"Why can't they be more friendly, Ingie?" I can't think why they are being like that.

And time is passing by; hours become days and days become weeks and every week brings something new in Auntie's village.

Ingie is not going back to school. No, her education is ended. "The first casualty of this awful war," Mum declares. She cycles off to Little Piddlington and Harrington's Plastic Pipes and works for Mr Harrington, the owner with a bald head and big car and bags of letters for Ingie to do, and enjoys every minute of it although it is a pity her education is finished. "I'd like to stay on and get my diplomas," she says, "but I can't. The war has stopped all that."

She stays there all week, up at Little Piddlington, with Mr Plunkett the manager and his wife, Edna, who look after her as their own. "The bed's a bit lumpy," Ingie says, and Mrs Plunkett's cooking is not a patch on Mum's. But the shortages aren't helping. Ingie isn't complaining. "There's a war on now. It wouldn't do any good even if you did."

Then there's another change. I'm at school, the village school, where a man called Mr Williams with a fat tummy and tiny feet plays headmaster. There's Miss Peabody who takes the Juniors and who gets a kiss in the pantomime, or so Auntie says, and the Juniors includes me – a Junior, and a new Junior at that.

Lydia, the evacuee with the bow in her hair, is a new Junior too, and her younger sister, Lizzie, is in the Infants with Mrs Pegg's school marm voice and a harsh word for anyone who doesn't copy down the words from the blackboard properly.

In my new school are the village children, the boys and girls of the farmers, and farm workers and they're all looking at me and Lydia, the evacuees from London, and not concentrating one bit on what Miss Peabody is saying. Only Smith Junior, the Smartie, who listens to everything while the others would rather stare and call us by our new name, "Townies".

She doesn't have much control, Miss Peabody, not like Mr Bentham my teacher in London; but she must be doing her best, I think to myself, for a teacher in the country anyway. And there is always Lydia, who is the prettiest girl I have seen since Isobel with the pigtails, and Bobby White, who's best at cricket and football and is everyone's hero doing amazing tricks on his bike, better than anyone I know, even the cleverest kids in London.

Then there's Smith Junior with his round face and piggy ears who says he's Bobby's friend even though he's not much good at football or cricket and is not right in the head, according to Mr Alfie, even if Mr Alfie doesn't know why.

But Lydia's smiling at me and she's smiling at Bobby too. And most of the other boys. Which is the way of girls, it seems. The pretty ones, anyway.

If Ingie is settling in as an office girl and I am settling in at the village school, Mum is a bit happier and playing a thing called bridge on Thursday nights, at Posh Mrs Clandice Brown's house. You have a partner to play this bridge and Mrs Brown's partner is Mrs Pettifer from Thatcher's End Lane. Mum's partner is Auntie, who is an expert.

Sometimes I go up with them, across the village green, and there's me sitting quietly, or playing with Lydia, and Mum saying how it won't hurt for me to be up late one night a week.

Mum is only half an expert, but Auntie doesn't mind as the Good-for-Nothing husband was only half an expert in a game where you all have some cards and the one who guesses what the others have got wins the game. Then you put on your hat and coat and go home.

"How do you play that game, Mum?" I ask as we walk home across the village green. But Mum won't explain. "It's too complicated."

That's why people are only half experts, Ingie says.

And then there's the best news of all: Dad's got his transfer, he's coming soon, today even. Yes today. It's happened so suddenly, we can't believe it, off the morning train from Paddington and collected by Mr Alfie in the Austin. "The least I can do," he says. "For your 'usband, Mr 'oldsworth." Even if Dad has the same gut-bustin' luggage that Mum, Ingie and me had. Making Mr Alfie's eyes pop and the sweat run down his brow, under the weddings and funerals cap.

Dad is here now. A huge sigh of relief all round. Unpacked and then the Good-for-Nothing husband's chair for him to flop down into. Feet up, next to the fireplace, cup of tea in hand. Mental telepathy again. No pipe, of course, Auntie would say "tutt, tutt" and that wouldn't do at all. "It is *her* house when it's all boiled down," Mum says.

There's the garden shed for that.

The Red Brick House has been sold, Dad's found a buyer and our things have gone into store with Mr Carter Patterson's Removals. Dad's organised it all and a nice couple now live in our old house. They are in the Air Force and fly their planes at Croydon Airport and won't have time to dig Dad's garden. His hard work will be lost forever. It's a pity, Dad says, but he can't complain. He was lucky to find a buyer at all. Under the circumstances, is what Dad calls it.

Mum says it's all worked out so well. "You couldn't ask for better." Mum seems relieved. "A real weight off my mind."

Dad has brought what he could with him. The rest will come down later. "I had to leave Timmy with Isobel's mum and dad." Pretty Isobel – with the pigtails, the one I can't marry because she shows her knickers – would have looked after him but she's evacuated to Devon, or was it Dorset? Dad can't remember exactly where – he had other things on his mind, which is understandable.

But Gran is staying up in London, that's the worst bit. She's like the London taxi driver, Mum says – not that she rolls a Rizla and smokes it right down to the very last bit. No, she's not budging, Hitler or no Hitler.

"I was born in Clapham and that's where I stay," she's told the neighbours, full of determination, and Joey the budgie on the windowsill, next to a picture of Grandpa with an armful of greens he'd grown on his allotment.

Gran has a little house with a front door that opens onto the street; no garden, just a doorstep that she scrubs every day and makes it white with some stuff called whitewash. And a tiny back yard where Mum played, along with her sisters and Arthur before he went off to war and never came back. It's full of memories.

Gran is very set in her ways and Mum can't change her mind, not one bit. "She just won't listen." Mum still hopes she'll have second thoughts when the bombs start to fall; and Dad and Mr Alfie will go straight up to London to bring her back.

Mum writes Gran a letter and Ingie finds it on the table, half finished. "You shouldn't read other people's letters," Ingie says. "But this is special."

"*We might find a big house*," Mum writes. "*Then you must come down… I insist.*" And puts kisses at the bottom to help, she's being as persuasive as she can, Ingie's sure. And there are a couple of blotches on pages one and two. Where Mum's tears have landed, Ingie's sure about that too.

But Gran's still staying put.

"Old people are very intransigent," Dad says, which means if you like Clapham a lot it takes more than a few tears to change your mind.

And she has Joey the budgie, of course, who says Who's a Pretty Boy every time someone comes by.

Apparently Clapham suits him fine.

He's intransigent, too. Just like Gran, Dad reckons.

Chapter 6

Enter the Artist's House

The first thing to do would be to look for a house of our own, that's what Dad's thinking was. When we were up in London, in the Red Brick House, with Mum and Dad doing the packing and Ingie and me listening. Mum called it Dad's Master Plan.

"I'm sure we'll find something nice down in the country," Dad had said.

Ingie reckoned he was only trying to make Mum feel good about leaving London, putting a brave face on it, as Ingie called it. "Once we're all together again," Dad said. "A complete family as families should be."

But Mum didn't say anything. Apart from this Master Plan. And then about Gran being left behind in London. Mum didn't like that one bit. "If these bombs are going to fall."

"A little cottage near Auntie surrounded by meadows and trees, a stream at the bottom of the garden and a log fire keeping us warm in winter, you'll like that Mother." And gathering some things called chestnuts and roasting them on an open fire. It was what the country people did, Dad said. He'd heard it on good authority, he told Mum, spreading his hands out in front of him like he was warming them on a pretend fire and hoping Mum's unhappy looks would turn into happy ones.

But Mum was still wearing one of her worried looks. "I'm not sure I'll even like it down in the country. The only bit I've ever seen is on the way to Hastings on our holidays. The green bit out of the coach window."

"Oh, I'm sure you will, Mother," Dad said. "And if you're still worried about Gran, I'll go back straight away to get her. I can't say more than that."

Mum seemed happier when Dad said about going back to get Gran. "If you say so, Father. Before the bombs start dropping."

Ingie said, "Dad's doing his best... And if he gets us a house of our own... And Gran joins us... We couldn't be happier little bunnies."

* * * * *

I'm one of Ingie's happy little bunnies already. Now we're here. Especially now it's coming up to Christmastime.

"Can we go out and collect some of these chestnuts, Auntie? Dad says the ones you put on the fire at Christmastime."

"Not *on the fire*, silly," Auntie says. "On the hearth. You'll soon see... I'll show you."

Auntie promises we'll get rugged up the very next weekend and go out to gather the chestnuts. "We'll take the wicker basket... fill it to the brim... to overflowing..." And Auntie knows just the place – the woods next to Farmer Collins's Farm. With a little dab of butter and touch of salt they'll be a real treat, she says, "A real Christmas treat," smiling with her sparkly old eyes and whiskery old face and getting excited about Farmer Collins's chestnuts.

Ingie thinks it might not be very good this year, Christmastime. "What with the war spoiling everything."

"Oh, Christmas is going to be wonderful, "Auntie is saying. "All of us gathered round on Christmas Day. This silly old war won't spoil it for us... I won't let it."

And now she's saying how Ingie and me can make a start by gathering the holly from the bush at the end of the garden and stringing it up around the doors and picture frames and across the fireplace. Then making the paper chains. "It's not Christmastime till the paper chains go up," she says.

Auntie has bought the coloured paper already. From Mr Right-T-Ho in the village stores. "You're in luck, Auntie," Mr Right-T-Ho told her. "They're the very last ones and I dare say I won't be getting any more until that Hitler's sent packing and the war's over."

Auntie said she didn't need asking twice. She was getting her tuppence out of her purse and handing it over before he could change his mind. And the glue too. "They don't stick together by themselves, you know."

"Will we have a Christmas tree, Auntie? If you have them down in the country."

Auntie talks to the cat. "Of course we have Christmas trees in the country, don't we, Fluff?" And Fluff and Auntie say I'm a silly not knowing they're grown by Farmer Millsom, the hen farmer, as a sideline. Farmer Millsom who sells us the lovely brown eggs for breakfast every morning.

And then she's telling us how Farmer Millsom learnt his hen farming at farming college and how it taught him that hens don't lay many eggs when it gets cold and dark. "So he took up Christmas trees as a sideline."

Now it's time to ruffle my hair and smile into my face with her sparkly old eyes and all those wrinkles. "You see, there's so much to learn down in the country." Then giving Fluff a bowl of tripe, the dinner he doesn't have to catch, while I go off to tell Mum we're getting our Christmas tree from Farmer Millsom, the man who left his feathers in Mr Alfie's taxi.

"It's so kind of Auntie to teach you all these things about the country, Son," Mum says. "I hope you thanked her."

"I did, Mum," I say, and then wonder if Father Christmas will know his way to Bumblethorpe.

"Of course he will." Mum's helpful face is smiling and telling me I'm not to worry.

"Dad says Mr Hitler doesn't."

Mum thinks Father Christmas has something called "special powers" and eyes that are "all-seeing".

"I think Mum's right," I say to Ingie. "Biggles has them." And I tell how Dad was reading Biggles one night and how Biggles got lost in a thick fog, a pea-souper he called it, but found his way home with his special powers. And the all-seeing eyes, of course.

"What's wrong with a compass?" Ingie said. And then went "Hmmm," just like Mum does.

Mum says if it made me feel any better I could write to Father Christmas and explain how we've moved from the Red Brick House. In a thing called a PS, at the bottom of the letter, after my list of presents.

"Just a short list, mind," Mum thinks. "What with the war it would be unfair to ask Father Christmas for too much."

"Auntie says all the paper chains have gone already, Mum. And the last pot of glue. What do you think they do with paper chains and pots of glue in the war?"

Mum doesn't know. "Stupid war," she says.

"I could warn Father Christmas about Auntie's low beams as well," I say. "In my PS." Mum's sure that's a good idea too. I'd heard Dad bang his head on the one at the top of Auntie's rickety little stairs and thought Father Christmas would do the same, struggling with his sack of presents over his shoulder. And saying something he later regrets.

Not Father Christmas, of course. Mum says Father Christmas doesn't know any words you later regret. Dad knows a few although I'm not supposed to hear. And the tutt-tutts from Auntie when Dad gets caught. And Auntie saying how he has to wash his mouth out. I'm not supposed to hear that either.

Ingie says there's never been so many low beams and such a tiny house, even in fairytale books. "Mum and Dad aren't finding it easy," she says, and asks in a whisper if I can keep a secret about Mum and Dad arguing when Dad didn't have anywhere to hang his bank clothes. "But don't tell, will you."

I'm not going to tell, I say, in a whisper of my own.

Then I tell Ingie my secret. "Dad's got to wash his mouth out. I bet you didn't know that, Ingie."

At night, Mum and Dad have Auntie's room and she is in the little bedroom at the back, overlooking the back garden. The box room, Ingie calls it. And Ingie and me are sharing, which is a real treat. I never did like the dark and it was pitch black from the moment we arrived in the country, with only the moon and three little streetlights for the whole village to share. And now it's even darker, with the man in Dad's paper saying there's something called the Blackout and this Blackout stopping every single light, outdoor ones anyway.

Mum says how Dad finds the Blackout difficult when he comes home at night, across the village green. Getting off the bus in the dark. "You haven't stubbed your toe again, Father?"

"The KEEP OFF THE GRASS sign got me tonight," Dad says. He'd borrow Auntie's torch but he says that's against the Blackout laws. Dad can't even light his pipe in Auntie's back garden. That's against the law too.

"This government's going too far with all this," Mum thinks.

Mum and Auntie have made Blackout blinds to keep out the light. Dad tries them at the windows, standing on a chair with Mum holding it steady, and Auntie passes them up one by one, until every window is covered. "There're no bombers up there yet," Dad tells us, "but there will be. Prowling around looking for someone with a light to bomb."

Mum says, "Or your pipe."

I'm happy sharing my bedroom with Ingie with all this darkness around. When I was little, in the Red Brick House, I was sure there was a Bogeyman hiding in the dark just waiting to jump out. The moment Mum tucked me in and turned the light out.

"It's just your silly imagination, little Brother," Ingie had said. Being a bit helpful, like Big Sisters are supposed to be.

There could be a Bogeyman, I thought to myself, even with Ingie saying it was imagination. I thought I'd ask Podgy if he had seen a Bogeyman, but he wasn't much help, calling me a sissy and laughing his sides off fit to burst, and his face going red like a tomato. I wished I hadn't mentioned it.

"There might be a Bogeyman," pretty Isobel said when we were hiding from Podgy one day in a little cubby-hole, with us speaking in a hushed whisper so no-one else could hear and Isobel snuggling up closer and closer. "There could be one in here," she said in her soft voice, right into my ear. And then tickling me through my Rupert Bear pullover, the one Gran knitted for my birthday. Right by Rupert's left leg.

"There, the Bogeyman's getting you," breathing in my ear and making it all warm. And tickling Rupert's left leg again.

"I don't think the Bogeyman tickles you," I said.

"Well, *you* can tickle me a bit if you like."

I was just wondering how I could get out of this tickling, Isobel being a girl under her frock, when there was a voice and it belonged to Podgy.

"You in there?" it said. "Why don't you come out and play?" Podgy's face was still as red as a tomato and it looked like he was going to go pop. But he didn't say anything about the Bogeyman, anyway. Seeing pretty Isobel standing there put him off, I think.

Now it's time for Dad to look for a new house for us in Auntie's village, just as he's promised. If Dad said he'd do something, he always did. And Mum says I can have a little light of my own in my bedroom when Dad does find the new house... just a glimmer, Mum calls it. "What with our Blackout curtains, I'm sure the government won't mind."

"I've asked at Thimbleby and Thacket about the house," Dad announces in one of his family conferences, after his dinner. He'd popped into the agents in the High Street in his lunchtime. "Could you keep an eye open for something suitable?" he asked Mr Thimbleby. "For a family of four... five, perhaps, if Gran comes down."

"Well, I'm glad you've made a start, Father," Mum tells him.

Auntie had mentioned it to Mr Right-T-Ho in the village stores and Mr Right-T-Ho had passed it on to Mr Lamplin, the postman. Soon it had gone round the village. Mum said she heard little sniggers every time she went up to the shops. "Them Townies be looking to buy an 'ouse." And getting sideways glances to go with these sniggers, right behind her back.

"Only a bit of harmless village gossip," Auntie thinks. "I'm sure they'll make you very welcome once you've got a place of your own and settled in." Bumblethorpe regulars, is what Auntie says we'll be called. "And you'll not find a prettier village than ours. I'm sure of that... not for miles."

"So, I'll keep looking then?" Dad says, in his family conference. Ingie is nodding. "I like my new job."

"Bobby White's my new friend at school," I say.

"Well, we do enjoy our Thursday evenings at bridge, don't we, Auntie?" Mum seems a bit happier too and Dad's pleased with our answers. "A new house it is then... if I can find one, of course. It's not easy with the war on."

"I know you won't regret it," says Auntie again. And then telling us about the things in Bumblethorpe that we'll enjoy and listing them on her crinkly little fingers, counting them out, one by one, while we sit and listen.

"The village store and post office, with Mr Right-T-Ho behind the counter..." He's on Auntie's number one finger. A veritable mine of information, she calls him. "Then Mr Blenkinsop, the butcher, with pork sausages on his racks and sawdust on the floor..." He's finger number two. And Reverend Curd with his wibbly-wobbly head and his little church. He gets number three. Then there's the village hall for Christmas pantomimes and the recreation ground for summer shows – they get finger number four. Mr Cutler and the donkey, two goes a penny, they're on Auntie's crooked little thumb. "Mavis, the donkey," she says. "Kids can't do better."

Not Dad's new pub, though, the Red Lion; that gets nothing. Finger or thumb.

Now Auntie's having another idea, a brainwave it's called, and this brainwave comes in a flash to her, right there by the fireplace. "Why didn't I think of it before? The Artist's House – that's the perfect place for you to buy."

"The Artist's House?" Dad asks. "It's for sale, then?" Dad is putting his paper down now. "It hadn't crossed my mind."

"Well it wouldn't," Auntie says. There's no sign yet, no FOR SALE sign. But the house is empty, she knows that. "Ever since he passed on, without warning, going to a better place."

Auntie's even more excited now. Her cheeks are going all pink and her eyes sparkling, even more than usual. "The news went round the village like wildfire, what with him going so quick. Almost a mystery as to what got him," she says. "Then put to rest by Reverend Curd at the back of the churchyard amongst the others, the Cresswells and the Humphries, the true Bumblethorpe people." That's where he got lowered, Auntie says. "Round the back."

She's remembering it as if it was only yesterday. "A dark man, his brother, they said, with a beard and hat, came down from London to take care of the arrangements. And his sister, all in black too, with the black shawl." Auntie says they could scarcely make out her face, it was so well covered. "Some said how they were up to no good, that's what rumour had it. Creeping round the village like that."

And Auntie says they didn't stay. "Mr Alfie had instructions to take them back to Newbury for the Paddington train the moment they'd done all the arranging and had him put to rest."

"Died mysteriously?" Dad asks. "An illness, perhaps…?"

"He was as fit as the next."

"Old age?"

"With him not yet fifty?" Auntie doesn't think so.

"An accident, perhaps?"

Not that Auntie had heard…

Dad looks at Mum and Mum looks at Dad. "That only leaves foul play," Dad thinks, with Ingie and me looking on, wondering about foul play.

But Auntie says, "As if such a thing would happen in our quiet little village. Not down here in the country." Dad's getting a scolding now. "The Lord took him early, that's all, without warning." Auntie admits PC Trendle had investigated, writing it down in his notebook. *The artist has died all of a sudden.* That's all he wrote, Auntie's sure. Nothing more. "And even then he had to get a new pencil to write it down, crime not being solved in our village with pencils and notebooks, just clips round the ear."

"Well, what about this house," Mum insists, "the one you say is for sale… the one that has rooms for everyone, even Gran?"

"Yes," says Auntie, forgetting about the policeman and his pencil. "Lots of bedrooms, a bathroom and lounge, a nice kitchen too, south facing, and lovely wooden beams everywhere." Then Auntie's telling Dad about the garden, overgrown but large, and an outbuilding that had to be seen to be believed. "Not that I've been there, you understand, the house," she says. "That wouldn't be right at all."

Mum's happy about everything Auntie has said. "South facing, that's an advantage," she says, and then tells Auntie it wouldn't have been wise to be seen round there, a church-going lady like her and the Good-for-Nothing husband just run off. "That wouldn't be right. Not right at all."

"The artist was quite famous, apparently," Auntie's telling Mum and Dad now. "Some say he had pictures hanging on a wall... in London, in one of those galleries they have up there... People paid good money to see them although I have no idea why."

Auntie tells us how she'd bumped into the artist on the village green one summer's day. "With his easel in front of him... doing the cottage, he was." Not that Auntie recognized it, she tells us, even though she turned her head this way and that and asked all the right questions. Auntie said it would look nice when it was finished and he said it was. "Can you believe it?" Auntie says. "Finished, that's what he said." And tells us how it was called modern art. "Not nice at all."

After that Auntie went indoors and made herself a cup of tea and told Fluff to stay indoors too. There was no telling what would happen if he painted the cat.

"Well, the Artist's House does seem to have potential," Dad says when Auntie's finished her story. If he did buy it we'd be just across the village green. Over the stream and past the pond, just like the village hall, a stone's throw away. But in the opposite direction, of course.

"You could say we'd almost be neighbours," Auntie says. She thinks Ingie and me could pop in when we liked. "I'll have a slice of plum pie waiting. When they're in season, of course."

"Can we pop in, Auntie? Any time?"

Ingie agrees and Mum's head is nodding approvingly. She hasn't seen the house yet, of course, only glimpses through the overgrown hedge, but if it's like Auntie says, there'll be plenty of room for us all. Just the excuse Mum needs to persuade Gran to come down.

"Yes," Mum says. "Make enquiries, Father, and be as quick as you can."

There are no "Hmmms" now.

Chapter 7

Into the Lion's Den

Dad seems happy with Auntie's idea, the "brainwave", and tells us he might walk up to the pub right now, the Red Lion, for a pint and ask about the Artist's House while he's there. "Strike while the iron's hot," he says.

It's one of the things Mum loves about Dad. He might not like the mowing but he never lets the grass grow under his feet. It's Mum's favourite joke Ingie says.

One day, when we lived in the Red Brick House in London, I heard Dad talking to Mr Trimble, our postman, and Dad told Mr Trimble that in his opinion you could judge a place by its people and its pub, and if the people were any good they'd be in the pub. Dad said it was like killing two birds with one stone. Not real birds, my Dad told to Mr Trimble, who had some pigeons that raced against each other. "Just pretend ones."

And Mr Trimble nodded and replied, "Well, see you in the public bar tonight then Perce."

Now we're hearing Dad say that he could kill three of these pretend birds with his pretend stone by going to the Red Lion this evening, meeting the local people, and learning something about the Artist's House. "Perhaps you'd like to come too," he says to Mum.

But Auntie's smiley face has stopped being smiley, the thought of Mum walking into the pub; Auntie doesn't approve one bit. She's shaking her head as though pub is one of those words that Father Christmas doesn't know, and Dad later regrets.

"A den of iniquity," Auntie calls the Red Lion, "the ruination of my good husband," she tells us sadly. "Where he went to pieces, off the rails..." And as for the landlord, Old Joe by name, Auntie shakes her head so much that it looks like it might come off. "An evil man encouraging the taking of alcohol by all and sundry. That's what."

So Mum says to Dad, "Yes, Father, you go up – but by yourself, and just the one, mind. No dilly-dallying."

And while he's there, Dad has to find out everything he can about the Artist's House. "We'll be waiting to hear what you've learnt when you get back." Dad's to leave no stone unturned... the ups and downs... the good and the bad. Mum's keen for us to buy a house but doesn't want Dad to spend his money unwisely.

And here's Dad now, returned from his jaunt to the pub and asking "Are your sitting comfortably?", and when we say we are, telling us all about his adventure starting the minute he walked out of Auntie's front door, under the canopy of rose bushes, across the village green, turning right at the bus stop, then heading straight for the Red Lion.

"The KEEP OFF THE GRASS sign didn't get me tonight," Dad says.

The Red Lion is bang in front of him now, getting closer with every stride, a welcoming abode, Dad thinks, compared to the dark old Artist's House down on the left, behind the overgrown hedge. "I could almost taste the first pint," Dad says, looking a bit guilty about tasting a pint.

And Dad's telling it just as though we are actually with him, Mum, Ingie and me, ready for Mum's ups and downs, the good and the bad, on Auntie's sofa. And even Auntie seems to be enjoying it, but pretending not to. "Don't mind me and Fluff...

We'll just busy ourselves around the cottage," she says, "while you get on with your story."

And in his story, Dad's ducking through the porch and pushing past the blackout drape and into the hubbub and cosiness that is the public bar, the very place where Auntie's husband came off the rails.

"What happened next, Dad?" we're asking, as one voice. We can't wait a minute longer now he's through the front door.

"Don't keep us in suspense, " Mum tells him.

Silence comes down, that's what. "Quite off-putting, really," Dad admits, reflecting on what's just happened. "As if a shutter slammed in my face." It seems while Dad's wiping his feet, the locals, to a man, are stopping doing what they are doing and staring long and hard. "Anyone would think I was Adolf Hitler himself," Dad tells us, making a little joke of it.

Darts half darted, halfpennies half shoved, and lips pursed ready for the next sip, that's how Dad saw it. "You could have heard the proverbial pin drop," he tells us, and us on the edge of our seats wondering what happens when this funny pin did drop.

"Goodness, how did you get out of that, Dad?" Ingie asks.

"Well, I could have turned on my heel, of course. Or thought up some silly excuse about my wallet being left at home, on the mantelpiece, or in my other trousers..." It had crossed his mind, Dad admits to us. "It would be the easy way out," he says.

But it was ages since Dad had enjoyed a pint in the Dog and Duck with Mr Trimble, our postman, who raced pigeons as a hobby, so he gave one last wipe and stayed.

"Good old Dad," Ingie says. And gives a little clap.

"That's my man," Mum tells him.

Fluff has a purr. Auntie says nothing.

"I'm new round here," that's what Dad says to the man behind the bar, Old Joe, the shameful landlord who encouraged the taking of liquor by all and sundry, turning honest husbands into Good-for-Nothings. "Percy Holdsworth's the name." Dad tells us that's what he told Old Joe. "And I'll have a pint of your Best Bitter if I may." And Dad takes up a leaning position against an empty bit of bar, trying to look as though he belongs there.

"The Best be off," says the Landlord in a gruff voice like Dad's still Mr Hitler. "And that bit of bar be spoke for." Old Joe, tall and lanky with hair standing up like Beethoven, the great composer, and him without a comb to his name. Dad's relating it just as if Old Joe is standing there in front of us now, in Auntie's front lounge, and him saying how the Best be off.

Dad apologises and settles for a thing called Mild, and mentions, as a means of light conversation, that he is moving down from London with Mum and Ingie and me, having secured a transfer from the Overseas Office of the Midland Bank in the City of London to the Newbury Branch, and how he will be looking after local business accounts once he gets his feet under the desk. "I'll almost certainly be a regular in the evenings. If I get home in time, of course, and on Saturdays as soon as the mowing's behind me."

"Not *the* Midland Bank with the steps up and the solid oak door and brass knocker?" asks Old Joe.

"The very one," Dad replies. "You know it, then?"

"You can say I've 'ad the pleasure… if that's what you call it… mounting them steps and passing through that door…"

"Yes, I'll be responsible for raising overdrafts, or lowering them, and keeping an eye, especially, on those who don't make their repayments on time." It wasn't intentional, Dad tells us, but Old Joe was a changed man and from that moment onwards. "I wouldn't have believed it if I hadn't seen it with my own eyes, and heard it with my own ears," Dad tells us.

"Lean where you like, Perce," Old Joe's saying now. "If I can be so presumpchous as to call you that, or sit. Here, have that bar stool. Or another if you needs a padded one for your backside. I wants you comfortable when you're in here, in my pub, the Red Lion."

And Dad tells us how Old Joe suddenly finds a pint of Best from his taps, just as Dad had asked, moments before. "I always tries to keep a little back for my best customers."

Dad looks round, taking stock, as he calls it. There must be a dozen or so men crowding the bar, men of the land, in the main, with ruddy cheeks and barrel chests, and another, a dapper little man in waistcoat and tie. From an office, perhaps.

"Oh, that's our Mr Right-T-Ho," Auntie says. It seems she's been listening all along, but not saying. "He's the man who runs our post office and village stores. I'm sure he'll like you calling him dapper."

Mum has met him, of course, on shopping days. And when she posts letters to Gran. "He always seems very helpful."

"That's how he got his name," says Auntie. "Silly really, Mr Right-T-Ho. Always wanting to help... always cheerful. No matter what you need."

"I'll have one of your best brown loaves..."

"Right-T-Ho."

"And a couple of stamps for this letter..."

"Right-T-Ho."

"And a watering can from the top shelf there..."

"Right-T-Ho."

"Nothing's too much trouble, as I say," Auntie says. "Right-T-Ho. Yes, silly, really."

"'oldsworth, is it then?" says a man at the bar. Dad's a bit taken aback. The man's big with broad shoulders like an ox and a weather-worn face but a warm smile. And hands that look like they could crush the pint glass he's holding. "It's not a name from these parts," he says to Dad.

"It's a Yorkshire name. My father was from Scagglethorpe, in Yorkshire."

A man with a felt cap and a stoop, leaning forwards like he's walking into a gale, says, "I went there once." And calls Dad, Bank Manager.

Dad says he is taken aback again. "I'm not a bank manager," he tells the man, "not yet, anyway", and then wonders about Scagglethorpe. "You know Scagglethorpe then?"

"Not that exact place," says the leaning man. "But I been to Yorkshire on the train. I were visiting my sister in 'atfield, but got the wrong one." He says there were lots of platforms and he got confused. "I went up from Kings Cross, first stop York." He thought it looked nice with neatly clipped shrubs in pots on Platform One and flower baskets everywhere. "Prettying up the station," he says. But he wouldn't stay. He had never been that far from home and came back the first opportunity, on the next train. "I 'aven't gone since... never clapped eyes on that sister of mine since she moved to 'atfield. And probably never will."

Dad has not been to Yorkshire, not once, he tells them. "You've got me there," he says. Dad has been to Germany with Mum to a place called Bayreuth, to hear some of the music by Richard Wagner, the man who gave me his name, but with the war and still feeling his way with the locals thinks it best kept to himself.

Mum says from the edge of Auntie's sofa, "What's all this got to do with the Artist's House, Father? I hope you haven't forgotten why you went up there in the first place..."

And Dad says, "I'm getting round to that..."

The man with the broad shoulders is Dan Ledbetter, the squire's foreman from the big estate in the village. He'd been with him since he left school at fourteen and had heard what Dad was saying about the bank. He didn't think he could work there, shut up all day, he would rather be out in the fields, in the open.

So would the man who had gone to York, but shouldn't have. He is the cowman for Farmer Collins, Cowman Dance, and gets up every morning at five to milk the cows, Christmas Day and Boxing Day included, and Good Friday and Easter Monday too. He doesn't need an alarm, he just does it, every day, wakes up, goes out and milks the lot. Then comes back in the afternoon and does it all over again.

Dad tells him, "That's dedication for you..."

The cowman is well paid for his work and has free milk for him, his wife and kids, and a cottage as well, a Tied Cottage. And a pound of butter and tub of cream from time to time if Farmer Collins is having a good year. "I makes it myself, I does," the leaning cowman tells Dad. "In the little churn in the milking parlour, winding the handle till the milk turns to curd and the curd to butter."

Dad says he always wondered how they made butter.

Dan Ledbetter has a Tied Cottage too. "Where would me and the missus and our lad Tom be without it?" he asks Dad. "Where would any of us be without our Tied Cottages?" He couldn't afford a place of his own, not on a foreman's wages, and couldn't stand living on the council estate.... He said he'd lose spirit if he had to be there with kids screaming, dogs barking and rusty bikes everywhere.

Dad agrees. They are best off in a Tied Cottage, as a banker it makes sense, a roof over their heads, a good job and pay as well and thinks it's time to slip in a question about the Artist's House, behind the overgrown hedge, trying to make it seem like an afterthought.

Dad is the first to admit that he's from a big city, working in a big city bank, and doesn't have a knowledge of country people and their ways. He can tell a debit from a credit at ten paces (according to Mum) and when to give an overdraft and when not. But isn't up with the ways of country folk and how to ask a question and get an answer. A straight answer, anyway. One you can use and buy a house on.

"Yes, the Artist's House," he says as casually as he can. "I was wondering..."

"You know that house, then?" says Old Joe instantly, squeezing the last drops of Best from the barrel. "I told the brewery chappie I'd be out before 'e could deliver again. All 'e said was didn't I know there were a war on."

"Well, I was just wondering if it might be for sale," Dad says, "... and the price. It might be out of my reach, of course..."

"Of course," says Mr Ledbetter.

"Of course," says the leaning cowman, Cowman Dance.

Old Joe is getting more enthusiastic now. It is a good house to have even if it is a bit run-down and with a garden that hasn't seen a spade in years. "But Alfie, the handyman, will help you out there; 'e can't be beaten behind the spade."

Dad thanks him for the tip.

"There was the matter of the artist, of course," Old Joe says. "What with him dying so quick, kicking the bucket, in a manner of speaking." He thinks some people might see that as an impediment.

Dad has heard about that, he tells them. "This kicking the bucket."

"Thimbleby and Thackett be the agents," says Cowman Dance. "If you wants to know, that is. Just around the corner from that bank of yours… next to where Farmer Brown's horse went lame last Michaelmas."

Dad says he's popped in once already but would go in again on Monday, in his lunch break, and ask especially about the Artist's House. "I hope the horse is better," he says.

The farm foreman with shoulders like an ox, Dan Ledbetter, and the leaning cowman, Cowman Dance, agree. "Should suit you down to the ground, Mr 'oldsworth," they say. "Suit a man of your standing. That Artist's 'ouse."

Old Joe goes quiet and leans forwards across the bar, as if he is going to tell Dad a secret, and says in his ear, "Now, 'ow about my overdraft then, Perce?"

"And now you know all about my adventure," Dad says to Mum, Ingie and me, on Auntie's sofa. "And you also know what I know about the Artist's House."

Mum's not saying much… still thinking about what Dad has said, weighing up the pros and cons, the ups and downs.

Dad tells us how he's all in favour of putting in an offer as long as we aren't worried about the artist dying suddenly. "Kicking the bucket."

"It does seem a bit odd, doesn't it," Mum says eventually. "What could possibly be behind it all? And the brother and sister coming down from London, dressed in black. Strange people," she says. But on the face of it, Mum thinks it's a good idea. "Yes, Father, make an offer… as long as it's not a silly one… money doesn't grow on trees, you know."

And Auntie says from over by the fire, "Everyone's got to die somewhere," and takes up the poker and gives the fire a good prodding.

* * * * *

The village kids aren't that bad. They still call me Townie but it's just a tag. Like they call Minnow, Minnow, because he's little. And Smith Junior Smartie because he's the smartest around. Or Fatty because he's bursting out of his trousers. They don't mean any harm – it's just a tag. I'm Richard when some of them want to

82

be extra nice but even when they don't, they're not being nasty.

Bobby calls me Rich, which is really good. It's really good because Bobby's the leader of the gang and it's even better still to be called Rich. He makes a joke about it sometimes... "I bet you've got bags of money."

He says he'll show me round the village after school. The reccie, and the football ground and the village hall... "Tell your mum you'll be a bit late," he says. "We'll all cycle up there. It only takes a few minutes and you can see where we play footie."

I'm riding my new bike Dad got me. My birthday present come early, Mum tells me. A new second-hand one that a kid in Newbury doesn't want, grown out of it, Mum calls it, a Raleigh with Sturmy Archer gears and it looks pretty good after you've polished it with a bit of spit and an oily rag – even though it isn't as good as my bike in London and not nearly as good as Smith Junior's. He's got drop-down handlebars and racer's gears. And somewhere to put your drinks when you go on a long journey and can't stop even if you're thirsty.

Mum says I don't need racer's gears, not riding round country lanes. A saddlebag is much more useful. I've got one of them and a spanner to make my saddle go up and down: down when you're little with little legs and up when your legs grow a bit. And another for adjusting the brakes, front and back, so you stop quickly when you come across Farmer Collins's cows in the middle of the road like we did the other day when racing each other.

We're all gathering ready to go to the reccie, us kids, just as Bobby said, with Bobby leading. Then Smith Junior comes along and doesn't want to go to the recreation ground. "We can do that another day," he says, as if he runs everything. "Let's go to the Wishing Well. We can show Townie... I bet they don't have wishing wells up in London."

I don't think we did. Not that I'd seen, anyway.

"Well, you can see ours, it's great up there," Smith Junior says and sets off, with his drop-down handlebars and racing gears. "Race you!" he's shouting over his shoulder and changing gears without crunching even when he goes flat out, like now.

I'm pedalling as fast as I can to keep up, down Little Piddlington Road, turning off right, up Love Lane, past Farmer Millsom's hen farm, leaving the village green miles behind, till we all come out on a bit of flat ground with a tree that looks like it's about to fall over and a wall made in a little circle with a winding handle and a rope and bucket.

Smith Junior says, "The Wishing Well. I told you it's worth coming for."

We all rush to the edge and peer into the blackness below: me; Bobby; Colin, the postman's son; Minnow, the little lad; Fatty (out of breath) and Smith Junior. Minnow puts some bricks in a little pile and stands on them so he can look over. "You wouldn't want to fall in," he says.

I'm standing on my tip-toes, leaning over and peering down, but not too far. It looks really black and evil down there and has a smell like a dungeon. Smith Junior says you can call out and it comes back a bit later, an echo, he says. "And you can see the sky reflected in the bottom... but you've got to lean right over." He's getting really excited about his wishing well, the echo and what you can see. "It's like a little silver circle," he says, "and how you can drop a pebble and make a wish when you hear the splash."

Colin says a kid fell in the one at Little Piddlington when he did his wish and when they fished him out he was dead. "Dad told me," he says.

Fatty shouts: "Hello there, Fatty here," and it comes back again, only a few minutes later, and sounds like he's gone to the moon.

I say I can't see the sky reflected even when I lean over, which I don't want to do because it's too far down and I don't want to fall in like the kid in Little Piddlington. Bobby can see but he doesn't mind leaning right over and Colin holding his legs so he can't slip. "You've got to hang onto the wall!" he calls out. "Really hard. At the top..."

"The parapet," says Smith Junior.

"My Gran had one of those," says Fatty, "in a cage."

I'm not that bothered about a wish. Smith Junior says he'll give me a bunk up so I can get a good look over and make my wish. "You've got to," he says, "everyone does." And he tells me he'll hang on and make me safe. "I won't let you go," he says. "Only a nasty kid would do that."

But I'm still not that keen. He pushes me up, before I know it, and I'm hanging over the wall, the bricks pressing into my tummy so it hurts while he holds my legs and says I'm safe. But it doesn't feel like being safe.

"Can I come down now," I say, and add "please" because nothing changes and he doesn't get me down.

"Make your wish... Go on, make your wish," he's saying, like he really means it. "I won't let you slip... I told you..."

The blood's rushing to my head as it does when you are upside down and you think your head's going to burst and your eyes pop out of their sockets. And I can feel my legs slipping...

"Let Rich down," I hear Bobby shout at him. "You're not holding him properly... "

Everyone is looking over the edge of the wall at me hanging down and Smith Junior saying it's safe and Bobby saying it isn't. But I'm still hanging there with my head going to burst and tears coming into my eyes. And my legs slipping through his grasp...

I can just see a little silver circle of light, miles away at the bottom, like a shiny sixpence. I drop my stone and it takes ages and ages, then goes *plop* as it hits the water. "Get me down," I cry. "Get me down. I've made my wish."

"I didn't hear you... Do it again."

"I did," I plead. "I did, I promise."

And he pulls me back over the edge, just in time. But I don't tell him I wished he'd let me down. I said I wished I had a bike like his, with drop-down handlebars and racer's gears and somewhere to put your drinks...

And he says, "That's all right then," and tells me it's only a game. "Everyone has to make a wish..."

"Come on," says Minnow, the little kid. "Let's go and see the reccie now." He wants to show me where he scored a goal in a penalty shoot-out against Tufton Hardwick Juniors last year.

On the way back, Bobby cycles next to me, "You all right?" he says.

I nod.

"He doesn't mean any harm… He's okay when you get to know him… he's just a bit weird at times… Like the day he pushed a kid in the river at Pangbourne but said it was an accident so they didn't do anything."

Smith Junior stops on his racer bike so he's next to us, balancing on his pedals like smart kids do. "What you talking about?"

"Nothing," says Bobby.

And we go to the reccie and see where Minnow scored his penalty. Then home and Mum says, "You're late for your tea. I was getting worried."

"I was with Bobby and my friends, Mum."

"And you've got grubby marks all over the front of your new school shirt. If I didn't know better I'd say you've been climbing walls. I hope you haven't been doing anything silly."

Mum says she has enough to worry about without having to worry about me. Gran up in London, Dad finding his feet in his new job… and my sister. "The last thing I want is you getting into trouble."

I wonder if Mum might say something to Dad when he comes home from the bank… but she's still talking about Gran when he walks through the door.

"I agree, it's a real worry," Dad tells Mum. "If the war spreads to London." Then he's telling Mum about his day at the bank and how he saw Mr Broadbent, the village blacksmith, and how he needed extra on his overdraft because he didn't have as many horses to work on.

"'It makes me a bit short, you see, Bank Manager. 'aving no 'orses to shod.'"

"Tractors are the future," Dad says to Mum. "So I put my good deed hat on and gave him a bit extra. I think I did right… He seemed very pleased even though I said I'm not the bank manager. I told him that's Mr Snitchwell."

"I don't need to see Mr Snitchwell," the blacksmith said as he clumped out of Dad's office with his big boots and blacksmith's leather apron. "They said to see the Overdraft Man and that's what I did."

Dad breathed a sigh of relief. It was his first overdraft and it seemed to have gone all right.

But Mum's still worried about Gran being up in London and has forgotten about my shirt being messed up.

"I'm sure I did right," Dad says again, "with his overdraft."

Then telling Mum he might go to see Mr Alfie and if Mr Alfie could also be persuaded to put on his good deed hat, he might take Dad up to London and Dad could bring Gran back to Bumblethorpe.

Mum seems to brighten up with this news. "If anyone can make her change her mind, Father, it's you. It won't be easy though – you know what's she's like."

Dad says it wouldn't be a wasted journey even if she wouldn't budge. "There are lots of things I could bring back… things I really need." The banking books from Dad's college days, for a start. "They'll come in handy in my new bank job, giving out overdrafts." And Dad could collect his records, he tells Mum. "And my German phrase books too. I'd like to be able to tell the Germans 'I surrender' when they arrive. And wave my white flag, of course."

"You are joking, Father," Mum says.

Dad says, "I am joking."

But he's still going to bring back his German books. "You never know when a few words might come in handy."

"As long as you don't forget your umbrella," Mum says. Dad got soaked running for the bus the week before last. "And my comfy slippers… so many things got left behind in the rush…"

"And I could collect Timmy while I'm passing that way," Dad says. "He's got to get used to living in the country one day and now is as good as any." Isobel's mum and dad have been looking after him ever since Dad left the Red Brick House.

"Timmy's coming home!" Ingie says with glee when she hears. "What a treat." It's Saturday, and she's home from her job in Little Piddlington. It's the best news she's heard for ages, she says.

Mr Alfie agrees and they set out first thing Saturday. "I kept back some petrol coupons for emergencies like this," he tells Dad. "Like rescuing Gran." He's already announced to them in the Red Lion how he's going on a trek to foreign parts. "We'll be safe as long as we keep the doors locked and the windows wound up."

Mum, Ingie and me stand and watch. And Auntie and Fluff. "They're going to bring back a friend for you, Fluff," Auntie says. "One from London." Mr Alfie winds the Austin and leans against the bonnet as though it has worn him out. Then mops his brow and tells us, "Can't 'ang about 'ere all day..."

Dad says, "If we're not back before nightfall, you'd better send out the search party."

Ingie says we're not to worry – it's one of Dad's silly jokes.

It took them several hours. Dad read from the AA roadmap and pointed while Mr Alfie steered and didn't make many mistakes.

A bus driver shook his fist at them going round the Elephant and Castle and they were stuck behind a hearse on Streatham High Road. They reached the Red Brick House before mid-morning and then onto Gran's in Clapham an hour later. The little house with a white-washed doorstep and Joey the budgie in his cage by the front window. Gran was waiting with the kettle on.

"Who's a pretty boy, then," Joey said as Dad ducked in through the little doorway and Gran got out her best china. Mr Alfie stayed in the taxi to keep Timmy company. "I'll give a toot on the horn if I see them Germans a-coming..."

"Such a long way for you to journey," Gran told Dad, worrying about how he'd get back. "And you down there in the country, miles from anywhere." Dad could have a muffin, Gran had saved one specially. "And your friend in the shiny car. I saved one for him too."

Dad declined the muffin and said Mr Alfie was happy with a cup of tea, balanced on his knee, milk and one sugar. He'd never seen best china before.

"It's so risky up here in London," Dad told Gran. "I listen to the wireless every night and the threat's getting worse... there's the bombs and even talk about Hitler invading." Dad, onto his second cup, was using his most persuasive powers, but it still wasn't working.

Mr Alfie was telling Timmy how he was sure he'd like it down in Bumblethorpe. "And it be a lot safer," he told him, between slurps. "And the country mice be the plumpest you'll ever see."

"We're thinking of buying a house in Bumblethorpe," Dad was explaining to Gran. "And there's sure to be a bedroom for you... Mother says you'll have first choice – and space for Joey too, of course." It would be perfect, he said. But Dad didn't mention the artist dying without warning. The mysterious death. He didn't think that the thing to do at all.

"Let him come, that Hitler," Gran replied with jaw set, her spare teeth grinning at Dad from the jar on the mantelpiece. "I'll be waiting. And the surprise of a lifetime if he pokes his head round my door."

Dad was disappointed, of course, but not surprised. Gran was intransigent, he'd always said, and he was doing his best.

"You can always change your mind," he told her, on the way out. "Mother will be very upset if you don't."

"Who's a pretty boy, then," was all Dad and Mr Alfie heard as they set off back home with Timmy in a box on the back seat. Dad had made it specially with little holes cut in the sides so he could get some fresh air.

Mr Alfie was sure Timmy was looking forward to getting to the country. "I told 'im about the mice – the plumpest ones 'e'll ever see."

* * * * *

"We didn't get her, I'm afraid," Dad tells Mum when they get home. "There's Joey to keep her company and a broom handle for Hitler. But we got your slippers."

Mum is very quiet for a while, getting our dinner. "Well, at least you tried," she tells Dad eventually, warming the dinner plates. "And she might change her mind. There's still time, isn't there?"

That seems to make Mum a bit happier, but only for a day or two. Dad says a man's going to ration our food and we've got to tune into his wireless and find out all about it.

"Would you believe it?" Mum says.

Dad says, "I would." And we sit down and listen to a man called Mr Morrison, from the government, and Mr Morrison seems very nice although what he says makes Mum very angry.

89

The Rt. Hon. W S Morrison, M.P, Minister for Food. November 11, 1939

"When I spoke on our food supplies a month ago, I promised to speak to you again before rationing began. So here I am this evening. The plain story is this – the scheme will apply to bacon and butter only, and even for these articles there is no great urgency. They will be rationed on a date to be announced shortly and I expect the ration will be a quarter of a pound of bacon each week, and the same of butter. And now I'll tell you the main reasons for this action.

The ration books which you will receive were printed long ago as part of our normal defence preparations. In them we had to prepare for anything. That is why the books contain coupons for meat, sugar and cooking fats and also some spare coupons in case they were needed.

I don't want to impose restrictions but I believe it is the duty of Government to make rules in the common interest for all to observe. It is our duty to see that supplies are shared by all of us alike, by all equally. That is done by rationing and that is why we have now decided to issue the books. They may be a bit troublesome at first. Forms always are. But I am confident that, as in the last war, housewives will soon get used to the business and be glad of the assurance – each of her fair share, without waiting and uncertainty.

And what – I think you are asking – of the other, unrationed foods. Take meat. Well, we draw about one-half of our meat supplies from overseas and these imports were delayed as the first result of war. We have had to supply greatly increased amounts of imported meat to the armed forces of the Crown. That accounts for the temporary shortages that have occurred in some places. But I can tell you this, on a longer view I see no reason to expect any shortages of meat, and I do not see any reason why we should impose rationing.

All of us have our own tastes and ways of living. Some of us eat more of one thing, and some more of another. Each of us must do our utmost to avoid waste.

On sugar I shall be more definite, and my proposition is this – that we should set ourselves a voluntary limit of 1lb a week – 1 lb of sugar to cover for everything for each person and no more buying for household storage or preserves.

Now I want to tell you what to do. The ration books will be delivered through the post. There is a General Ration Book, a Child's Book for children under six years of age, and a Travellers' Book for persons who are constantly moving about the country. When you receive your book, you should choose the retail shops from which you wish to buy bacon and butter. You should fill in your name and address on the two counterfoils. The retailer will cut them out and send them to the local Food Offices, to show his list of customers and so the amount of supplies he needs. After rationing has begun, you must take your book when you go to buy bacon and butter. There will be one coupon each for bacon and butter; he will sell you your ration in exchange for the coupon.

On your side, I know I can count on every one of you to co-operate willingly with us so as to reduce our difficulties as far as possible.

We are in this together.

Good night."

Chapter 8

The Ghostly Apparition

We've got Timmy back and it's a real treat, all of us agree.

Dad says he looks none the worse for wear. Auntie declares he's as fit as a fiddle.

Mum agrees. "I always knew Isobel's mother and father would treat him like their own." Right royally, Mum calls it. "I always knew they would." Mum thinks we'll be lucky to get such good neighbours again.

Ingie gives him an extra big cuddle. "It's lovely to see you again, dear Timmy." Ingie smiles and Timmy purrs; it's almost like the old days in the Red Brick House. Everyone agrees about that too.

Some mornings he ventures into Auntie's front garden and waits for Mr Lamplin, the postman, and Mr Lamplin says, "Is it as bad up there in London as Mr Alfie says?" Then he trots off to sit on Auntie's back fence. Sometimes he jumps down into Farmer Collins's field, which he is allowed to do, of course. That's where you find Mr Alfie's plumpest mice. "Just as long as you don't bring them in here," Auntie tells him. "I've had enough of that with Fluff."

* * * * *

And that's it. Just as Timmy is getting used to living in Rose Tree Cottage, he has to think all over again. Dad's bought the Artist's House and we're moving in the moment Mr Carter Patterson's big green lorry arrives with Mum's Worldly Possessions. It's a bright and frosty morning and Dad's looking anxiously up and down the lane, tapping his watch and saying, "They should be here by now."

"I bet they be stuck behind that 'earse on the Streatham High Road," says Mr Alfie, who's come over to give a hand.

But they aren't. It's the overhanging trees that have done it. And the hump backed bridges and tiny lanes. "I bet Hitler's seen nothing like this," says the driver as he jumps down from his cab. "He'll need a good compass if 'e's going to do 'is invading round 'ere and get back in time for 'is 'orliks."

And there's a man called The Mate and he says he's seen nothing like it either. "And tuck 'is long johns in if 'e wants to keep Jack Frost at bay."

They laugh between themselves, roll up their sleeves and tell Dad not to worry. We'll soon 'ave it done, they say at a canter.

"There's no stopping 'em now," says Mr Alfie. He calls them 'uman dynamos and asks why Townies go at everything like a bull at a gate. "It ain't 'ealthy."

Carrying tables and chairs, beds and cupboards, and all the things Mum packed in crates and boxes before we left the Red Brick House. Mum's telling them where everything should go. "That in there, this in here..." There's a tick on each box in a different colour; red for the kitchen and orange for the lounge. Ingie's bedroom is green and mine blue.

"You got it all organized, Mrs H," says the driver, and tells Mum he'd doff his cap if he had one.

The Mate says, "That's my girl," then calls Dad Squire. "Where do you want this then, Squire?" He's carrying Dad's big leather chair, all by himself. "I'll bust a gut if I don't find an 'ome for it soon."

Mr Alfie tells them he's not helping just for the beer money. "The 'oldsworths be new down 'ere... they needs 'elp setting up 'ouse, you see."

Ingie and me are darting backwards and forwards with our smaller things, our prized possessions. I've found my Biggles books at the bottom of the big brown case and Ingie has discovered her tennis racket. Mum made space after all.

"What's a long john, Ingie?" I say.

Ingie says it's something you put on to keep warm in winter.

Sounds funny to me. "On your head, Ingie?"

"On your legs, silly!"

Now everything's unloaded and Dad announces, "Time for a breather."

Mum's got the kettle on ready.

It's a smoke-o, Mr Carter Patterson's men call it. The Mate has a red hanky and mops his brow. "'ot work this..." He's going to take the weight off his pins, stretching out on Dad's big, fat, lazy leather chair and singing...

"Lord of the Manor, I am, I am."

Dad doesn't look pleased.

Ingie and me have the Artist's House to explore. We're not having a smoke-o.

"It's much bigger than I thought," Ingie says. "From the pictures Dad got from the agent people, anyway. Thimbleby and something." Ingie says it's much larger than an ordinary house but not like a mansion. "That's for rich people, of course, and Mum and Dad aren't rich." Ingie's eyes light up, she's remembering an adventure story in *The Girls' Crystal* when she was little. "It's just like an old Hunting Lodge... there was one in there."

I say I don't know what a hunting lodge looks like.

"Well, there's one in front of you, Little Brother, just open your eyes and look around you. Come on, race you up the front steps."

We're dashing through our new hallway and into the lounge. It's much bigger than the one we had in the Red Brick House. Doors lead out onto the garden and there's an open fireplace with lots of black roof beams, just as Auntie promised. A huge kitchen for Mum and a pantry that Dad says is large enough to "swing a cat... but don't tell Timmy." And another big room at the front. "They call that the parlour." Ingie pulls a face. "Where you serve tea when the vicar calls."

We're exploring upstairs now. A landing and six bedrooms – they seem to go on and on forever, just like Mrs Lillywhite's guest house in Hastings. We're racing from one to another... choosing our favourite... our feet rattling on the bare wooden floors.

I've found one with masses of shelves for my Biggles books. "And look, Ingie, someone's put an old fireplace in this bedroom."

Ingie's has a fireplace too. "People did that in olden days. And wait till you see the view from my window..." Ingie can see right to the end of our new garden.

"And I can see the Posh lady's house from mine," I say. "Where the evacuee girls are staying."

At the end of the landing we discover some rickety little steps and a little door that squeaks when Ingie pushes it open. "Gosh, how spooky!" Our voices echo back from the darkness beyond.

"Biggles escaped through a doorway like that," I say, and tell Ingie how it was pitch black too. "Bats whizzed past his head and cobwebs clogged up his goggles. But he still escaped."

"You and your Biggles!"

Dad has forbidden us to go in there. "It goes up to the loft," he said. "Very dangerous and definitely not the place for children."

There's a way up to this loft from the outside too. It's a spiral staircase, Dad calls it, rusty and half hidden behind overgrown bushes. "I don't want you two trying that either." Dad saw it when the man from the house agents showed him round.

We're keen to investigate through the doorway and up to the loft. Even with Dad saying we can't. "Just a little peep, perhaps, when no-one's looking," Ingie thinks. "A few steps, anyway. If we're very careful."

"We could borrow a box of matches, as long as we're not caught. To light the way."

"Just like the adventure in *The Girls' Crystal*."

"Just like Biggles. He had a box of matches. And the all-seeing eyes, of course."

Dad doesn't want us to go up to the loft because the floor is old and worn out. Mr Alfie said the artist had told the people in the village it was unsafe and best kept out of. "You falls through if you don't look out."

Mum's calling to us. "Have you chosen your bedrooms yet, children?"

"Yes, Mum…"

"Me too…"

The biggest bedroom is at the front, and it's also the nicest. Mum and Dad are having that, Ingie says, but they should, mums and dads always have the best. There are two more bedrooms looking over the village green. "Gran has a choice when she comes down." Mum's determined it'll be only the best for Gran.

"I can see Mrs Clandice Brown's house from mine, Mum," I say. "Where the evacuee girls are staying, Lydia and Lizzie. Do you think they'll come out to play now we're neighbours?"

Mum's sure they will.

"The garden's very overgrown," Ingie says. "All I can see are loads of weeds… lots of work for poor old Dad, I'm afraid." There's a pond and fountain with a lady holding a torch and that's where the water is supposed to come from, but it isn't today. "I bet it's all clogged up," Ingie says, but she's sure Dad will be able to make it work if we promise to help him clean out the pond.

There's a thing like a plate with a pointer. Ingie calls it a sundial and says how it tells the time – but only when the sun's out. "We'll go to see it after we've finished exploring upstairs. I'll show you how it works."

"And the overgrown garden?"

"And explore the overgrown garden, Little Brother, if you're brave enough."

"Of course I am," I say, and tell Ingie I think this must be the best house anyone ever had.

"Ever?"

"Yes, ever… Even if the artist died here somewhere. Remember? That's a bit scary isn't it?"

Ingie thinks he might have fallen through Mr Alfie's rotten old floor. "Then bashed his head on the fireplace."

"Perhaps it was in your bedroom, Ingie, with loads of blood everywhere."

"Yuk!"

"Come on, don't think about him, let's get downstairs and explore the garden."

We're rushing down the stairs, two at a time, sometimes three, forgetting all about the spooky artist. Ingie's going to show me how to tell the time – sundial time. While the sun's still out, she says.

"You're our first guest," Mum's saying to Auntie, on the Sunday morning. "If you don't mind the mess... I've scarcely had time to start the unpacking." Mum's no idea where half the things are. Our best cups and saucers are still buried somewhere in a packing case. And the frying pan's vanished too.

Auntie's crinkly little fingers clutch an old mug. "I don't need best china... a cup of tea is a cup of tea any time." And tells Mum how lucky we are with our new house, even if it could do with a bit of tidying up. Lick of paint and a scrub, is what she calls it. "I wouldn't be surprised if Gran changed her mind and came down after all."

Mum's not so sure. "Father tried to persuade her, you know."

"And the children with a bedroom each and the huge garden all to themselves."

There's no stopping Auntie now. Except for the war hanging over our heads; apart from that we're the luckiest people alive, she tells Mum. "Like a black cloud, it is, although I have the feeling it could be over soon. In my bones." Auntie says there's scarcely a thing about it on the wireless these days... "I wouldn't be surprised if that dreadful Hitler is happy with what he's got and has given up."

Mum and Auntie are having a chin-wag, as Ingie calls it. Mum shakes her head while she's unpacking and chin-wagging. "I wish you were right... men and their wars."

Auntie says it's always men who are to blame. "Always," she says, still chin-wagging while I'm on my Biggles book and Timmy's stretched out on his warm spot in front of the fire. "If women were in charge we wouldn't have wars."

Mum's found the frying pan. It had hidden itself away in the tea chest. "Stupid men. Stupid wars. Stupid frying pan..."

Now Auntie wants to know where's Dad. "Haven't seen him all morning..."

Mum says he's outside sizing up the garden. "I think he has a battle on his hands out there..."

"Everywhere I look I see weeds and yet more weeds, " Dad told Mum when he first went out. It's like a jungle, he said, just after breakfast. "Still, it's got to be done." Dad's spade was at the ready.

"Well, don't overdo it," Mum told him. "Remember your lumbago."

Dad makes a start. The ground's like concrete... "Old Joe was right, it hasn't seen a spade in ages.... Definitely a job for Mr Alfie." The spade gets put away. "I think I'll pop over to see him after elevenses. I hope the kettle's on."

Ingie is upstairs, sorting out her room. Timmy's enjoying his warm spot. Biggles has taken off on a sortie. A bombing sortie. I'm glad we have wars, I think to myself, or Biggles wouldn't have anything to do.

Auntie goes home. Wrapped up against the chill wind. "Mind

the frosty patches," Mum tells her from the doorway.

Dad comes in for his break. "Auntie gone already?"

"Been chin-wagging," I say.

Mum looks disapproving.

"Something smells nice," Dad says. Mum tells him she's trying a new recipe – a Berkshire hotpot that Auntie recommended. Mum says Auntie cut it out of the paper specially. "It's very popular with the locals, apparently. It's very nourishing, she says."

"I could do with a treat," Dad says. "All this gardening makes you hungry."

* * * * *

Tomorrow I have my new school with my new friend Bobby White. And Minnow, the little lad, and Colin whose dad's the village postman. And Fatty and Smith Junior, the Smartie. And the girls from next door... now we're neighbours they'll come round to play. Mum's sure they will.

Ingie says she likes working in her office in Little Piddlington – her first job. She cycles off every Monday. The thin driver takes Dad to the bank each morning and brings him back in the evening. Dad's got his pub on Tuesday and Thursdays and Saturdays, if Mum lets him. Mum's got her bridge to look forward to on Thursdays.

It's nice down here in the country, I think to myself. Then it gets even nicer.

It's a Thursday evening and Mum has gone off for her hand of bridge and Dad is home with his "thirsty look" (as Mum calls it), having had a bad day at the bank, and Dad's saying how it would do no harm if he went up to the pub for a pint, "a bit of winding down" he calls it.

And Dad can either leave me at home in the dark old Artist's House with Timmy for company and the fire casting shadows over the blackened roof beams, or he can take me along with him. And that is no contest, as Dad says. So, here I am, trotting along beside him, trying to keep up, with the blackness all around us, and rugged up against the cold winter, not minding it one bit.

"Just half an hour, Son," Dad says. "No more." As long as we don't let on to Mum. "She'll only worry."

And before I know it, I'm sitting next to a roaring log fire in Dad's smoky old bar, in a little cubby-hole, and the men saying, "Well, well, if it isn't Master 'oldsworth, the Bank Manager's boy," and being nice as pie and even Old Joe, the landlord, telling everyone it's all right, that I'm "not doing no 'arm," while Dad has his pint.

"Half hour, mind, Son. No more."

Which will be a bit longer if the day has been an especially bad one and Dad needs more than one glass of beer to help his winding down. .

And that's how it is. Me going up there to sit in my little corner, not harming anyone, and only speaking when spoken to, while Mum is playing her bridge with Auntie and Mrs Pettifer at Mrs Clandice Brown's house.

And not much of the war that made us rush away from London in the first place, leaving Gran behind. Apart from the Blackout and Mr Right-T-Ho running out of pots of glue and paper chains. Apart from that I haven't seen any war.

But that doesn't worry me. I like it down in the country.

* * * * *

"I've 'ad a couple of bob on it being over by Easter," I hear Mr Jiggins, the Roadsweeper say from my little cubby hole, next to the fire, in Dad's pub.

It is Thursday and Dad is making his regular visit to the Red Lion and listening to the opinions from each side, the chit-chat, as he calls it, on how the war is going and Mr Jiggins is convinced it will be over almost before it has begun.

He seems very sure. "And my two bob," he tells them, all standing around listening, "be as safe as 'ouses."

I don't understand about war unless Dad gives me one of his explanations on the way home, down the little path to the Artist's House. About what's happening and why Mr Jiggins has made a bet.

Then I hear Old Joe, the landlord, say how it will not be over as quickly as Mr Jiggins thinks and Mr Blenkinsop, our butcher, tells them how he has seen something called action in the first war

PHONEY WAR

"How's yours doing Fred?"
"My bloke only wants sixteen and double top for out."

and is convinced Mr Jiggins has got it all wrong. "It will be a long one, this one," he says to poor Mr Jiggins, who is lost for words, this action seeming to give Mr Blenkinsop the advantage of knowing when wars are coming to an end and when they are not.

"I've not fixed bayonet and run at Germans for nothing," he tells them, and they listen in silence as he tells them about a place called the Somme where he did this running and how it made a man of him. "In pitched battle," he says, seeming very pleased with himself.

"What was Mr Blenkinsop before he was a man, Dad?" I ask on the way home. "And why was he running about in the Somme?"

Dad says the Somme is in France and making a man of Mr Blenkinson is only an expression he likes to use. "It was one of the worst battles in the First World War, the Somme." And Dad explains how bayonets have pointy bits and how Mr Blenkinsop ran at the Germans with this pointy bit shouting nasty things. "It's all part of these terrible wars, Son."

"He's very good at shouting," I say, "Mr Blenkinsop, our butcher."

"Shouting, Son?"

"Yes, when I'm walking past his shop after school with Bobby White and Colin Lamplin, the postman's son, and Minnow, the little kid, and the others. We're always hearing him shouting out for people to come and get their meat rations. "I got lovely pork chops, 'ere," he says, 'I'll give you the chops if you give me the coupons'." Things like that, I say.

And I tell Dad how Bobby White sometimes makes fun of him, calling out "Get your luvly pork chops 'ere!" That's what Bobby shouts. Taking him off. Then we all run away.

Dad says, "Oh, do you, Son?" and his eyebrows go up a bit, behind his glasses. But I don't think Dad minds too much about Bobby shouting out. At Mr Blenkinson, anyway. And us all running away as fast as we can.

* * * * *

And then a few days later something funny happens. I'm tucked up in bed, half awake and half asleep, and in the half asleep bit dreaming about Mr Blenkinsop chasing Bobby and me with his pointy bit, when I hear Mum call out, "Are you out of bed, Son?"

"No, Mum," I say. "I'm having a bad dream at the moment. The sort you have in bed."

Mum is soon at my bedroom door. "I was sure I heard footsteps coming from upstairs..."

Mum's shaking her head now, not so sure. "Perhaps it's the pipes... the pipes cooling down in the loft; we had that in the Red Brick House, I remember." Or Mum thinks it might be squirrels on the roof. "I've heard Auntie talk about squirrels getting everywhere." Mum says she'll ask Dad when he gets home. "He'll know, I'm sure."

Mum even admits it could be her imagination. "Nothing more than that," she says. "I don't want to alarm anyone..."

I'm getting another tucking in. "Try to get some sleep, Son... and no more nasty Mr Blenkinsop dreams... and don't worry about the noises."

I do my best, but can't. I'm wide awake, wondering about Mum's noises. The water pipes cooling down. Or the squirrels... Even Mum's imagination. She admitted she might have imagined the whole thing.

And then it happened again, about a week later, and this time I am hearing some of these noises, not exactly over my bedroom but Ingie's, perhaps, just down the passageway by the squeaky little door, and it's like someone's moving around, not pipes or squirrels, and definitely not imagination either.

"Well, it's not the squirrels, Mother," Dad said next day. "You can cross them off your list." He'd checked with Mr Leadbetter and Mr Leadbetter had said they went to bed at night. "Responsible for eating the squire's crops, maybe, but not walking about on our roof. That's what Mr Leadbetter said, and he knows."

That only left the water pipes... "Must be them," Dad says, and leaves it at that.

* * * * *

Just when Mum and Dad were getting used to the noise from our roof there was something else to make them wonder about the house we'd just bought and this time it was Cowman Dance telling Dad how he had seen Dad darting about in our garden, late at night. "Looking furtive," he said. He was checking the cows, just before he went off to bed, when he saw what he thought was Dad doing this furtive bit. "You were some way off," Cowman Dance admitted, calling Dad Bank Manager, as he did, and saying how it was only a glimpse – caught in the glow of the moon, he said.

"Well, I were sure it was you, Bank Manager, with your 'at pulled down tight against the chill of the evening. Who else would it be," he asked, "in your back garden, at that time? No-one I know."

And none of the others had any idea who it could be either, so it just had to be my Dad. And there was lots of silence as they all had a good think.

Yes, it had to be Dad, they agreed, after this silence.

"Or a ghostly apparition," said Cowman Dance eventually, after he had done some thinking of his own. "'ave you considered that, Bank Manager?"

And this made Mum and Dad worry even more about the house they had just bought with funny noises in the roof and Cowman Dance's ghostly apparition scurrying about in our garden with its hat pulled down against the cold.

"Goodness," says Mum.

And Dad says "Goodness" too, because he was supposed to be on his way back from the pub, down our little path with its overgrown hedge, not darting about in our garden at all. That's what he tells Mum.

And Mum says, "If that's so, Father, it only leaves the cowman's ghostly apparition..."

Dad agrees.

"What next can we expect from this house of ours?" Mum asks, looking even more worried.

"What about meat rationing? Mr Morrison said he was not going to ration our meat, now he is. That will worry you."

𝕯𝖆𝖎𝖑𝖞 𝕰𝖝𝖕𝖗𝖊𝖘𝖘

Monday, March 11, 1940

ANNOUNCEMENT FROM THE MINISTRY OF FOOD

MEAT RATIONING BEGINS TODAY

From today, Monday, March 11, the full meat ration is 1/10d. worth per week, or 11d. for young children with a Child's Ration Book.

Start with Meat Coupon No. 10 – coupons Nos. 1 to 9 should therefore be cut out and destroyed. If for any reason you have not Registered – do so at once.

No coupons are required for liver, kidney, tripe, heart, ox-tail, etc., or for poultry or game. Sausages, meat pies and galantines containing not more than 50% meat are not to be rationed at present.

No coupons are required for meat served by Canteens, Schools, Restaurants and Catering establishments – which are all rationed at sources of supply.

WHEN SHOPPING REMEMBER:

1 During the war our meat supplies are bound to vary from time to time. When you cannot get just what you want in a particular week, be ready to take something else – your butcher will be glad to advise you.

2 When you cannot get Imported Beef, bear in mind that our Fighting Forces, whose needs must come first, consume a large proportion of our supplies. Remember that the eating of Home-killed instead of Imported meat saves shipping space and foreign exchange.

RATIONING IS PART OF NATIONAL DEFENCE

THE MINISTRY OF FOOD, GT. WESTMINSTER HOUSE. LONDON. S.W.1

Chapter 9

It Never Rains but...

"It never rains but it pours," Auntie tells us, shaking the snow from her coat and stamping her feet on the doormat. And dabbing her nose with a tiny lace hanky, her pink cheeks peeping out from under her bonnet. "I could kill for one of your Mum's cuppas, and that's the truth of it."

Auntie's hoping to bring some life back to her feet with this stamping. "Frozen to the marrow," she says, and calls them trotters. "My poor little trotters."

Ingie says it must be chin-wag time again. "Mum and Auntie love a chin-wag," she says. Over one of the cups of tea Auntie could kill some poor person for.

"You really shouldn't have come out this morning," Mum's saying, taking Auntie's coat and hanging it by the fire and scolding her all at the same time. "You could have slipped and broken something. I warned you not to."

She wouldn't have normally, Auntie tells us. But she has brought a book for Ingie to read. "I knew you'd be stuck indoors with this dreadful weather and wanting something to do." I'm stuck indoors and get a barley sugar to suck, "a little treat" and a pat on the head, and told to brush my teeth afterwards in case they fall out. "There's a good boy."

It's only been a couple of months since Father Christmas came with his little handful of presents; not even a handful, really. Mum had warned he'd have trouble what with the war. "Don't be too hard on him," she said, in a knowing sort of way. "I'm sure he'll do his best." Then the New Year and Mum and Dad sitting up to see the New Year come in with Auntie on the sofa and Timmy sound asleep by the fire not seeing in anything.

This seeing in was something grown ups had to do before the New Year arrived, Ingie said when I asked her.

"What do they do, Ingie?" Mum and Dad used to do some seeing in when we lived in the Red Brick House, I remembered that and I remembered their friends popping round and Ingie and me lying awake wondering if we should creep downstairs, hoping to catch a glimpse of what happened. But never being brave enough to venture past the first landing, of course.

This time Mum had said to Ingie, "Now you're old enough to earn a wage, your father says you're old enough to enjoy some grown ups' treats... like sitting up and waiting for the New Year to come in." I was still only old enough to be in bed but lying awake, waiting to hear Ingie's footsteps, hoping she'd come into my bedroom to tell me what really happened.

"Nothing," Ingie said, in the half dark. "Nothing at all... that's what happened. It was a big let-down, really." Apparently Auntie had said White Rabbits just as the grandfather clock struck twelve, but as she did that every month it wasn't anything special. And how it would bring us good luck. Auntie announced that too, Ingie said, so that wasn't much of a surprise either. "So you see, Little Brother, you didn't miss much."

They had all sat around the log fire and Auntie took a little sip of her home-made elderberry wine and went a bit giggly. And then telling them how the villagers usually rang the church bells... But how they couldn't this year in case Mr Hitler heard and came and bombed the church.

"So, you don't have to worry about missing anything," Ingie said in a quiet whisper, landing a kiss on my cheek, leaving a wet patch. "There wasn't anything to miss."

"That's sissy…" I said, about the kiss.

"It's a present for not being able to sit up… to see nothing."

Next morning, Dad went off to his bank and Ingie cycled to her work at Little Piddlington; then a few days later I had to go back to school, and I asked in the playground if any mums and dads had seen in the New Year and any had said White Rabbits. But they all looked at me as if I was daft. Except pretty Lydia, who said, "It makes yer lucky, dunnit."

Mum says to Dad, "Have you seen this in your newspaper, Father. The headlines." Dad says he has. "I read it on the bus coming home, Mother. More call ups."

"They'll want you next."

Dad goes, "Hmmm…" And reads his paper again. He says he wants to study the detail, from his big fat, lazy, leather chair. And

Daily Express

Saturday, March 16, 1940

CALL-UP OF 600,000 IN APRIL

Two age-groups, totalling more than 600,000 men, are to be registered for the armed forces next month. There will be no registration in May, but the last of the groups covered by the "omnibus" Royal Proclamation will be registered by June at the latest.

These are the latest Government plans announced last night.

They mean that the next Royal Proclamation can be expected in July and it will probably cover the age groups up to thirty-five. Last night's announcement affects primarily men who reach the age of twenty between March 10 and April 8, and those who became twenty-five in 1939. They will register on April 27.

All that follows after registration, including medical examination, operation of the reserved scheme and appeals before the Hardship Committees, will in future be completed before calling-up. It is expected a start will be made by about May 14 on the calling-up of those who register on April 6. Those registered on April 27 will be joining the Services in the first days of June.

puffing on his pipe too. "They have been doing this calling up ever since Mr Chamberlain came back from Munich telling us about peace in our time."

"Some peace," Mum says and Dad goes "Hmmm..." again and tells us its called drafting. "They've already drafted more than one-and-a-half million. I read the figure somewhere. The Army, Navy and Air Force. And now some more."

"What's drafting, Dad?"

Dad says it's to fight Mr Hitler... nothing to do with the wind blowing under our front door. "It's not for little boys to worry about," he says. "Not till you get to fighting age, Son. And by that time I hope it will all be over."

Mum says she could be drafted if she didn't have me to look after, and the house to run. "Mrs Fuller has gone in. Helping the men fly the planes, or something," Mum says.

Dad knows this too. "The Waafs," he calls it. "Women's Auxiliary Air Force." And tells us Mr Snitchley's daughter has gone in the Auxiliary Territorials. "They call them the Ats. Forty thousand altogether, I read that somewhere, too. Forty thousand women for the Waafs and Ats and even more for nursing."

Mum repeats what Dad has just said, but she doesn't like it. "Forty thousand women. And a million men. No wonder there's no one left to run the country."

Dad says, "One-and-a-half million... not just a million, Mother. And there's the thousands who will be looking out for bombs if they fall, they call them the ARP, and then those who will be putting out fires, the AFS. There's thousands of them too."

Mum doesn't think she will read the headlines again. "They're too gloomy," she says. "It's bad enough trying to put a decent plate of food on the table each evening."

* * * * *

Christmas and New Year seems ages ago. Now there's this really bad weather and Auntie's standing at our front door shaking the snow from her coat and giving me my barley sugar and Ingie her book, which is called *Black Beauty* and has been written by a horse. Then saying how it never rains but it pours.

"The worst spell of weather in living memory," she says. "Mr Lamplin told me and he should know, him being the postman, postmen knowing these things." Auntie had been on her way to buy a pair of woolly booties from Mr Right-T-Ho in the village stores when he told her.

"I can't ever remember a winter like it," he said, pushing his bike through the snow, a foot deep on the village green and even deeper out in the country lanes. "Some places the 'edges 'ave vanished altogether with the drifting…" Mr Lamplin was sure. "I 'aven't seen nothing like it in all my years."

And it's bitterly cold. Mum says it's a mercy we've got log fires in the Artist's House and tells us we'd freeze if we didn't. Dad had got a huge pile of logs from Mr Alfie and they're stacked outside our back door. Mum says about them being a mercy too.

"Can't rely on the electric now," Auntie tells us. "What with the government restrictions."

And Auntie never did get her booties. "Even though there were lots on the shelves just a week before," she says. "That Mrs Mimms had the last ones." Auntie wrings her hands. "And Mr Right-T-Ho won't be getting any more as they've gone for soldiers and sailors… and the men up there in their aeroplanes." Auntie points to our ceiling. Our brave men, she calls them.

Lydia, Lizzie and me tried to build a snowman but the wind blew his head off even though we fixed it as hard as we could. It blew and blew and soon there was nothing left but a bump in the middle of the lawn where our Mr Snowman had been.

Lizzie said, "I'm cold… I'm going indoors." And Lydia followed.

I went in and warmed up by the fire. "I think you were fighting a losing battle out there," Mum said. "You and your snowman." My fingers hurt when they warmed up and I stuck them in my pockets and hoped the hurting would go away. But it wouldn't. "They're frozen, that's what," Mum said, and made some warm milk and I wrapped my fingers round the mug… which made them better.

Next morning, Mum and Auntie listen to Dad's wireless after Dad has gone off early saying he wouldn't be surprised if the bus couldn't get through and how he would have to walk, and the man on the wireless tells Mum and Auntie how it's right across the country, this weather, not just Berkshire or Auntie's little village. Mum turns him up and tells us to be shushed so we won't miss the details. And the man says how the trains can't run and roads are blocked in his stiff voice, like a headmaster, and makes Auntie and Mum amazed at what is happening out there.

When Auntie stops being amazed she says, "The whole country's coming to a halt, that's what."

Mum says I have to eat up my porridge. "In case."

"In case what, Mum?"

"In case the trains can't bring your porridge."

Mum pours another coffee. "Here Auntie, warm yourself with this, by the fire. And a biscuit? I can spare just the one."

Auntie is not going to have our biscuits, not with the rationing taking hold. "I'd have baked my own if my ingredients hadn't run out. It's desperate in my larder."

"The government must take us for fools," Mum says. "The sugar allowance is nowhere near enough, not for a growing family, anyway. Six tiny spoons a day for tea, coffee, baking and preserves. Everything." Bacon and ham have joined sugar and butter on Mum's Ration Books. "They say milk will be next." Mum throws a log at the fire. "They'll be rationing them next."

Auntie shakes her head. "It never rains but it pours. The war, the rationing and now this dreadful weather."

Dad has ventured up to the Red Lion a few times, but not as often as he would have liked. Slipping and sliding all the way, he said. Mum wasn't going to risk going to her game of bridge so I couldn't go up with Dad.

"You'll break your neck one day going for that pint of yours," Mum tells Dad.

But Dad is pulling on his coat already. "I need to bring Old Joe some business. He's one of my best customers. I can't see him starve." Dad says there were only two others in the pub when he went up last time. After the slipping and sliding bit. And one of them, Cowman Dance, shouldn't have been there at all but at

Don't use **TWO** make **ONE** do

SAVE ELECTRICITY & GAS they both come from **COAL**

ISSUED BY THE MINISTRY OF FUEL AND POWER

Printed by Greycaines, Watford and London. 51-43

home with his feet up in front of the fire with Mrs Cowman Dance.

"I 'ad to go out and check Betsy and her new-born calf and as she were just up the road it didn't seem right not to pop in." There was just him and Mr Lamplin, the postman, who'd left his bike at home. "I haven't seen nothing like it, Perce. Me pedals won't go round, you see. I've been on Shankies all week."

"They be in the winter byre, the cow and her calf, Bank Manager," Cowman Dance said to Dad, leaning forwards, fixed like that from milking his cows all day. "Not a stone's throw away." And he checked the water troughs while he was at it. "They freezes up you see, in minutes, in this weather." And he looked round the empty bar as if seeking out some sympathy and saying how he had his work cut out just keeping the water flowing.

"Some people might think the cows don't get thirsty when it's cold; but they be wrong," the cowman told Dad, who didn't know much about looking after cows in winter, this not being needed for the Overseas Branch of the Midland Bank in London.

"Well, Cowman Dance seems to have it all worked out, looking after the cows," Dad told Mum when he got back, hanging his coat and taking himself off to the fire. "I'm sure Farmer Collins is safe with him in charge, and Farmer Collins's overdraft is, in turn, safe with me."

Mum was listening but said, "You'll scorch your trousers standing that close."

And in the trousers that could get scorched, Dad told Mum that Farmer Collins was coming to see him the very next day. "About his overdraft, I expect." Dad thought he'd be wanting a bit extra. "In my office at 10.30."

"I just need something to tide me over this bad spell, Perce," the farmer explained when he got in there with his stubbly old face and battered old hat and some sums on a few scraps of paper spread out in front of him, on Dad's desk. "What with this bitterly cold spell the cows aren't filling the buckets and the bullocks not putting fat on the bone."

Dad said he was happy to help where he could, although Dad could never make it too easy in case the locals started asking for lots more (as had been known) and Head Office turning them down without seeming to give it a second thought.

Then the next time he saw them in the Red Lion they would be all huffetty and saying how Dad was a Townie and how he did not understand country ways and country people's needs and, anyway, he could buy his own liquor if that was going to be his attitude.

That's what huffetty meant, it seemed.

"If you could just come up with some extra reasons and some extra sums it would be a great help," Dad said. "In case Head Office asks awkward questions."

"If you say so, Perce," said Farmer Collins, who was happy to oblige, Dad said, especially where money was involved.

And without further ado Farmer Collins was soon writing out in his best handwriting how his cows were "not filling the buckets proper" and the bullocks "not putting meat on the bone" and all this because the farm was "all froze up". And doing some sums, helped by Dad, of course, him needing all his fingers just to get to ten, and Dad being able to count in his sleep, or so Mum said.

And when they were finished, Dad told him "I think I can raise your limit to five hundred pounds, Farmer Collins," and the Farmer seemed satisfied enough to say that if Dad ever wanted an extra pint of milk for us kids, Ingie and me, he only had to ask.

"As long as you don't dob me in to the authorities, Bank Manager, what with the milk being on the rations sooner rather than later and the government chappies risking my licence, you see…."

Dad did see.

"… and me ending up in jail. Then where would we be?" he said, gathering up his papers and pulling on his battered old hat and weary old coat against the bitter cold and asking, before he left, "You 'eard them funny noises lately?"

And Dad saying, "No, I haven't."

"Funny, them noises, " said the farmer, and went out into the bitter cold wind and driving snow again. "I be grateful for the bit extra," he said, "on the overdraft."

"Well, at least that's one happy customer," Dad told Mum when he got home, enjoying the fire and his slippers. "Oh yes, don't forget the pint of milk. Farmer Collins says as long as we don't tell the authorities."

Mum said, "As if I would. I've been waiting long enough to get something out of these farmer friends of yours."

And that was the matter closed.

"Spring has sprung," Dad announces as he marches through the front door, home early from his work, his jacket over his arm, tie loosened.

"Very un-gentlemanly," Mum says.

The snow has melted and the spring sunshine has arrived so that the green of the farmer's fields really hurts your eyes. Much more than in London, even the park where Podgy and me found our football, Greenhill Park, with bushes to hide under and trees to climb and Mr Herbert, the park keeper, shouting out "You kids get yourselfs off them trees..."

Mum says it's the spring that's put Dad in such good spirits and Mum gets a peck on the cheek as a reward.

"Oh, I like that Father..." Mum's still in her pinafore, making one of her steak and kidney pies (slaving more like, is what Mum calls it) but with only a couple of kidneys and scraps in place of steak.

Dad's hanging his coat in the hallway and is off to the garden for some mouthfuls of this fresh air that Mr Alfie says is so good for our insides. And saying again how spring has sprung. "Better than being cooped up inside that stuffy old bank all day," he says, in between these mouthfuls.

Mum seems to have forgotten the peck and says in a sort of scolding voice, "Never mind all that, Father. Couldn't you get one of those farmers to provide me with some meat for my pie?" Mum says a bit of stewing steak would make such a difference, even some things she calls off-cuts. "On the side, Father, if the needs be. Anything to make it more tasty."

I am building a Wellington bomber with my Meccano outfit, unpacked from the Red Brick House, but without the parts a Wellington bomber really needs. Wheels and propellers, for a start. Father Christmas always brought everything I asked for up in London, but he couldn't this year. Put it down to the war, Mum said. Even though I'd written my list clearly and done a neat letter, spelling all the words properly, even 'reinder'. *"I'd like some wheels for my plane, Father Christmas, if you have them. And some propellers would come in handy. I can't take off without them."*

My PS told him how to find us, so that wasn't the problem. *"I'm staying with Auntie in her little cottage, with Mum and Dad and my Big Sister. It's opposite the telephone box, you can't miss us. Just mind the beams at the top of Auntie's stairs. And while you're at it, Ingie needs a pencil sharpener for her work if you can spare one."*

Mum had said, "You can't do better than that, Son. So neat and tidy. Just remember 'reindeer' has two 'e's…"

Dad shakes his head. "It's not that easy," he tells Mum. He's still enjoying the fresh air, then saying about the problems in getting this extra bit of meat for the steak and kidney pie, even the off-cuts. "It's against the law now," Dad tells Mum, through the kitchen window. "The government people are on the look-out everywhere for this 'bit on the side' of yours. That's why they give you Ration Books and coupons. Anything more and it's Black Market, and you'll get arrested."

Mum's not happy hearing about this Black Market, even if it's not Dad's fault. "Well, what about a bit under the counter, then? You know what I mean, Father. *Under the counter...* Surely no-one would notice."

Dad says he'll drop a hint the next time he bumps into Farmer Collins, although he can't promise anything. "Milk is one thing, meat another."

"Well, this is the only steak and kidney pie in the world that's only got a couple of kidneys and if you find a bit of steak... you get a prize." Though Mum doesn't say what sort of prize Dad would get.

All Mum's food coupons have been used up on last week's chops and a rasher of bacon. "You've had your lot for the month, Mrs 'oldsworth," Mr Blenkinsop told Mum, and Mum told Dad.

Dad's onto something new now. A surprise for Mum and it's one Mum will like even though it doesn't help with the steak and kidney pie. Dad's telling how he's going to dig the vegetable patch, just like he did at the Red Brick House. And it's come right out of the blue, this digging of his.

"And this time I'm going to do it properly," he tells Mum. "There'll be no carrots for the likes of Mr Higgins to laugh at." Dad's been listening to the country people who know a thing or two about vegetables, the Wise Old Owls, Dad calls them.

Mr Jiggins best of all, apparently. He's been giving Dad useful tips in the pub, especially about chitting the seed potatoes.

"What did you say, Mr Jiggins?" Dad asked, looking a bit surprised, a City banker who had only grown funny carrots up till now.

"Chitting, I said," said Mr Jiggins, seeming pleased to be telling Dad twice. "So they gets off to a good start."

And then telling Dad where he could get them. "Mr Right-T-Ho's, of course," he said, with lots of this vegetable-growing information in his head, just under his woolly hat. "It's a known fact, Mr Right-T-Ho 'ave got the best for miles around."

And that's where we're off, Dad and me, this Saturday afternoon, Dad in his gardening clothes, sleeves rolled up, and keen to get a good start with his chitting. "Come on, Son, let's get down to

Mr Right-T-Ho's before they're all gone, the seed potatoes Mr Jiggins says are the best that money can buy."

And I roll my sleeves up just like Dad and trot along beside him. Dad calls me his assistant as we go. The Assistant Gardener, he tells me. And then says, "What a team!"

"You're in luck, Perce," Mr Right-T-Ho says. "I got one sack left, the King Edwards, good for mashing and roasting, you'll be thanking me come Christmastime when you come across them on your plate snuggling up to your parsnips." And he helps load us up in Dad's new wheelbarrow, and Dad wheels them home for Mum to see, through our side gate.

"I'm proud of you, Father," Mum says. "And our son helping too."

"I'm Dad's assistant, Mum," I say.

"Assistant Head Gardener," Dad tells Mum. And we smile together, with our sleeves rolled up. And go indoors for a cup of tea so Dad can think of what to do next.

"We're doing the right thing, this vegetable growing," Dad tells Mum, tucking into a slice of cake. The one he's allowed for the month. It seems the OHMS man who told Dad about evacuating is now telling him to dig his garden. "It's on posters everywhere and in a little booklet – grow your own – there's no clearer message." Mr Hitler has lots of submarines and these are sinking our food boats and this means we must fend for ourselves… or starve, Dad says. "It's all here, in black and white. You can read it yourself if you don't believe me."

Mr Lamplin, the postman, brought the booklet and Dad put it on the mantelpiece, with a picture of a man holding a spade and a lady with a basket filled to the brim with beans and other nice things and the words 'Dig for Victory' and Mr Churchill doing a V with his fingers.

"That could be me with the spade," Dad says. "And you, Mother, with the basket of beans. You never know."

"And who's doing the rude sign with the fingers, then?" Mum asks. "Not our son, I hope. Teaching him bad habits."

Now Dad's thinking where he'll put our potatoes, the King Edwards that will be snuggling up to the parsnips when

Christmastime comes. "Over there by the hedge, Son, out of the cold wind, that's where we'll do our sowing," he tells me after he's done his thinking and a second cup. "And the cabbage patch will be to the left, the other side, with the carrots that won't get laughed at." Dad's drawn it all up on a piece of paper, neat and tidy, and it's in the empty bit of space on the mantelpiece, next to the OHMS booklet.

"I'll get Mr Alfie to help dig over the vegetable patch," Dad says. "My assistant and me can't do everything."

If this isn't enough of a surprise for Mum, Dad's got another; he's buying some chickens from Farmer Millsom, the hen farmer, so we will have eggs to go with our vegetables. The OHMS man told Dad about them too, in another booklet, and that's up there on the mantelpiece with the first one and Mr Churchill doing another V but this time he's saying *Rear Your Own Livestock*, which is what chickens are. Livestock with feathers, Dad says.

Mum can scarcely believe her ears. "First home-grown vegetables, now home-grown eggs. Are you sure, Father?"

eggs bacon fats

MORE OF THEM FROM YOUR

KITCHEN SCRAPS

If 250 housewives regularly contributed their kitchen scraps they would provide sufficient feeding stuffs to feed 500 poultry or 30 pigs for one week. This shows how important it is to put your potato and apple peelings, table scraps and vegetable leaves in the nearest pig bin.

★ Do NOT include orange, lemon, banana or grapefruit skins. And no salt, soap or soda please.

Issued by the Board of Trade

PIG BIN

Dad's sure he's sure. He's spoken to Farmer Millsom the day the hen farmer came striding into the bank with his tweed jacket and accounts book tucked under his arm like he was carrying a cane. "My figures do not show me up in a good light, I fear," he told Dad. "The bad weather has blown me off course."

And Dad nodded sympathetically about being blown off course and asked about keeping some hens himself.

"The Light Sussex is the best for your needs," said Farmer Millsom in his authoritative way, and Dad noted down

120

about these Light Sussex being the best layers, and raised his overdraft by two hundred pounds without giving it another thought. "Can't have you blown off course, Farmer Millsom," he said. "And I'll allow you another hundred on top, if you wish, during these difficult times."

And the hen farmer agreed, Dad said, in the manner of a man realising that difficult times called for another hundred on top. "Anything can happen the way the price of hen feed is escalating," he told Dad, with his book open on Dad's desk and lots of figures in red, which were the ones that were doing this escalating.

Then they both nodded their heads in knowing sorts of ways, Dad having gone to college to study money and Farmer Millson having gone to college to study hens.

And Dad asked about buying five of these Light Sussex layers, if the hen farmer could spare them, of course, and Dad would ask Mr Alfie to come round and build a hen run and a hen house to keep them in.

That is what Farmer Millsom said they wanted, these Light Sussex. "You'll need separate laying boxes when they go broody," said the farmer, lowering his voice (so Dad said) in case Miss Perriwinkle (in accounts) might overhear and get embarrassed about hens going broody.

Mr Alfie came round in the afternoon with planks of wood and a roll of chicken wire in the back of his taxi and made our chicken shed and chicken run. And when it was done the two of them went up to Farmer Millsom's, Mr Alfie and Dad, and brought back our hens in a crate, with Mum, Ingie and me at home waiting. Five of them making worried clucking noises until Dad let them out into the new chicken run. Then they went for a little walk and started making a different noise.

"A happy clucking noise," Ingie calls it.

"They'll be even happier," Dad tells us, "once they have the run of the back garden… once they know their way around." And, best of all, Dad says they will enjoy the scraps from our dinner plates. And from Mum's kitchen. "There will be nothing wasted in the Holdsworth household now we have our chickens."

"Don't forget to pen them every night," Mr Alfie tells us. "Pen 'em or lose 'em to wily Mr Fox. 'e'll be waiting. And being a greedy begger , 'e don't take one – 'e takes the lot."

Ingie says, "Mr Alfie's a real countryman, he knows." And we take it in turns to lock them up. Every night, as Mr Alfie said. Me and Mum. And Dad if he gets home in time from the bank. And Ingie on Saturdays and Sundays when she's back from her job in Little Piddlington.

Now all Dad has to do is make sure his vegetables won't be laughed at. "Mr Jiggins told me that a pile of manure is the answer. The bigger the better," he says.

"That's where the horses' doings come in," Mum agrees, seeming pleased to be able to contribute. "My old Dad always swore by them."

Dad asks in the Red Lion about horses' doings, with me in my little cubby hole listening to the Wise Old Owls. "The Wise Old Owls in the Red Lion will know, Son," Dad says, and gets the shock of his life when they tell him he needs cow dung for the best results.

"'orses doings be too sharp ," they say. Sharp meaning they're all right if that's all you have (as up in London) but not a patch on the cow dung as used in the country by the country people.

"They reckon cow manure beats your dad's horses' doings," Dad tells Mum when she gets back from her hand of bridge, and Mum says, "I've been living under a misunderstanding all these years."

Better still, Farmer Collins will gladly bring some cow manure for Dad next weekend with his Fordson tractor and trailer piled high, and muck fork to fork it off with. And Mr Alfie standing by to help.

"I can't let you 'ave a shoulder of lamb nor side of beef," said Farmer Collins, sadly, after Dad had asked about the cow manure. "Because of them government regilations. But I can let you 'ave as much cow dung as you want. Cow dung ain't rationed... yet."

And as good as his word, when next Saturday came, Farmer Collins was at our front door with the tractor and his muck fork and soon Dad had a heap to be proud of. "Beat that for two bob," said the Farmer and set off back to his farm again. "One good turn deserves another," he said, meaning the overdraft, Dad thought.

Dad's dashing through the front door, making straight for the wireless… There have been some dramatic developments, he tells Mum, doing his dashing. "Quickly, we must hear… We'll catch the end of the news if we're lucky…"

Dad's all ears. Mum's not daring to breathe. Timmy's taking cover. I've got to go to bed.

> **"Here are the news headlines from the BBC for May 10, 1940**
>
> *Mr Chamberlain has stepped down as Prime Minister. Mr Churchill has succeeded him.*
> *The invasion of the Low Countries – Holland, Belgium and Luxembourg – by Germany is being fiercely resisted. French and British troops have crossed the frontier into Belgium to lend support.*
> *There have been widespread raids over France.*
> *In this country, the Defence Services are on the alert, and work is to go on during Whitsun.*
> *The Dutch Foreign Minister, Dr. van Kleffens, will be speaking after the News about the situation in his country…"*

Mum is dumbfounded. "Mr Chamberlain stepping down? I can't believe it. "

Dad says, "Stepped down… Mr Chamberlain *has* stepped down… Churchill has taken over. That's what it says…"

Mum is still dumbfounded. She says Mr Chamberlain worked so hard for peace… "And the poor people in these Low Countries…"

Dad takes to his big, fat, lazy leather chair. He isn't even asking for a glass of whisky. It must be bad.

It's not my fault, I think.

But I've still got to go to bed.

Timmy still hasn't broken cover. You can't blame him really.

Chapter 10

Time for Action

must be understood that this is, so to speak, a spare-time job, so there will be no need for any volunteer to abandon his present occupation.

Now a word for those who propose to volunteer. When on duty you will form part of the armed forces, and your period of service will be for the duration of the war. You will not be paid, but you will receive uniform and be armed. You will be entrusted with certain vital duties for which reasonable fitness and knowledge of firearms is necessary. These duties will not require you to live away from your home...

Here, then, is the opportunity for which so many of you have been waiting. Your loyal help, added to the arrangements which already exist, will make and keep your country safe."

"Well, how did it go?" Mum asks, wearing a pinny and one of her worried looks, having tackled the oven with determination and a thing called a Brillo pad while Dad has been to a meeting called by Mr Blenkinsop, the butcher, in Dad's pub. I'm in front of the fire, building my Lancaster bomber and thinking it best to pretend I'm not here while Mum asks questions and Dad tries to find answers.

"Well, how did it go?" The oven gets one final scrub so it gleams like the day it was born, so Dad reckons. "A real credit to you, Mother."

But Mum says, "I'd rather hear about your meeting."

"Well, it went on for some time," Dad says, seeming to be quite cheery about his meeting as he takes to his big, fat, lazy leather chair for a quick puff on his pipe. "Do you have a spare hour or two?"

Mum doesn't. "And I'm not interested in your silly jokes, Father, if that's what you call them."

Mum says scrubbing the oven is bad enough without having to laugh while you're doing it. "Well go on then, tell us what happened."

126

The night before, Mum and Dad listened to Mr Eden on Dad's wireless after Mum had cleared away our dinner plates, and Mr Eden had asked for lots of people to join an army he had invented to fight Mr Hitler if he invaded. Not the proper army, he said in his dull tones, the one that Mr Potter in the village had joined and marched off to proudly with a smart uniform and moustache Dad called bristling. Or Tommy Ledbetter, Dan Ledbetter's son, who wanted to march off as soon as he was old enough to get one of these uniforms and a moustache to go with it.

"It's for people who have to stay back with important jobs to do." Mr Eden's voice droned on while Mum and Dad listened and I stayed hushed. Like my dad's job, I thought to myself, in his bank – that's important. "… or for those who are, perhaps, too old for normal fighting duties." Mr Eden said he wanted them all. "Lots of volunteers," he told Mum and Dad. "From all walks of life."

"Sounds like a good idea to me," Dad said to Mum when Mr Eden had finished. "This new army of his."

"Sounds more like an excuse for an Old Timers' get-together," Mum replied. "I hope you're not thinking of joining up Father, you and your lumbago would make an unlikely pair." And Mum reckoned Dad could do this joining up without even knowing it, raising his hand at the wrong moment or scratching his ear or doing something equally silly, as he did at an auction last year when he ended up with a mahogany table and a chair with a wobbly leg.

My dad hadn't ended up with a chair with a wobbly leg or anything but he had ended up in Mr Eden's army after Mr Blenkinsop made himself leader and called for these volunteers.

Mum says, "Just what I feared."

"Does it mean you will have to go off and fight, Dad?" I didn't want that one bit. Ingie had said how lots of dads had gone off and some were not coming back because they were dead. I thought that Dad might end up on one of Mr Blenkinsop's pointy bits…

"There," says Mum, "see what you've done. Already your son is worried about what you've let yourself in for."

"These are desperate times, Mother," Dad is saying, getting up from his chair and heading for the kitchen. "You heard what Mr Eden said; as many men as possible and I thought I'd better be one of them." Dad's lifting saucepan lids and peering in to see what he can see while Mum's saying how she's unhappy with Mr Eden's army – Dad being part of it, anyway. "This looks tasty," Dad tells Mum, finding the rabbit stew Mum's had on the go all day.

"Mr Right-T-Ho from the village stores has joined," Dad says, his glasses steaming up with rabbit stew steam. "And Mr Lamplin, the postman and Mr Jiggins, the roadsweeper. Nearly everyone from the village is in Mr Eden's new army." And Dad seems pleased about his new army, especially now he's found something tasty to put on his plate.

"Don't worry, Son, I won't have to go off and fight," Dad tells me. "I've volunteered for the stores... where I can do my bit and be safe." Dad says that's where he was in the last one, in these stores, and he didn't get stuck on the end of a pointy bit once. "In fact," Dad says, "the only ones I ever saw were the ones I counted."

All this seems to make Mum happier too. "I'll serve it up, then," she says, sounding a bit relieved. "The rabbit stew. If you'll lay the table, Father."

Bobby White and Colin Lamplin and the others are sure to talk about what their dads will be doing for Mr Eden when we're playing in the playground or walking home or having a game on the reccie, and I'd like to tell them that my dad will be doing something important. Bobby especially, the leader of the gang.

"Will it help win the war in these stores, Dad?" I ask.

Dad says it will be "vital" but I'm thinking it might be another of his little jokes because he's bending down tickling Timmy under his chin and saying, "Vital, isn't it, Timmy?" as if Timmy knows about winning wars. "I'll be counting all the guns and bullets and making a list," Dad says. "You can't go into battle without a list, Son – just tell your friends that. Lists make all the difference."

Dad's finished talking to Timmy now and heading for the dining room, tucking his serviette under his chin as he goes. "Mr Right-T-Ho was the first to join," he tells Mum as she serves him a plateful. "And then Mr Jiggins, the roadsweeper and Mr Lamplin, the postman. They joined very quickly too." Dad's ticking them off, just like teacher in morning assembly.

But Mum says, "You've told us about them already, Father. Haven't you got anyone else in this army of yours? Apart from the store-keeper, the roadsweeper and the postman? And led by the man who sells lamb chops... when he can get them, that is."

And Mum wonders why the people she calls The Big Names haven't joined up and asks about the squire first. A man of standing, Mum calls him. Striding around the village, a smart gentleman if ever you saw one, doffing his hat to the ladies, and with shoes polished so you can see your face in them. "He should be the first to join this army of yours."

But Dad says that the squire has his estate to look after and a desk piled high with forms for filling in and letters for signing. "That's what squires are for, Mother, not armies." And organising committees for gathering pots and pans and old bits of tin for melting down and making into tanks and guns as called for by our government. Dad tells Mum he's even had the gates and fences around the estate dismantled and melted down. "The squire is taking this war very seriously, Mother. Twenty-four hours a day."

"I 'as to admit 'e don't come in the Red Lion much these days," Old Joe, the landlord, had told Dad. "Not once since the last time."

He'd come marching in, telling the villagers what fine people they were, then marching out again, into the sunshine with his shoes that you could see your face in, and hat that got doffed and a tie from a place called Eton that did the talking for him. "In a manner of speaking," said Old Joe, being pleased he had come in at all.

Then Dad says to Mum how the police constable, P.C. Trendle, and the ARP officer, Mr Pickering, had not joined either, seeming to want to get in before Mum could ask. "They have other things to do for the war effort, Mother. Just like the squire."

I know Mr Pickering is doing something special. I saw him in Dad's pub when Mum was playing her hand of cards and he told me how he was doing his bit, the village ARP officer, an important man. "ARP stands for Air Raid Precaution," he said, taking it seriously, and calling me lad, not smiling one bit. "Doing the rounds of the village, and stopping the light escaping so you can sleep safely in your bed at night and not get bombed. That's what it means, lad."

And I told him I knew, Dad had said all about the drafting, and he knelt down in front of me, on his haunches Mum calls it when she makes me smart for school, and Mr Pickering looked me straight in the face: "… not getting bombed," he said again, eagle-eyed, just like teacher when you've done something wrong. "You wouldn't want that now, would you, lad?"

I said that I wouldn't and called him Sir because it seemed the thing to do.

Then Dad's landlord called over to him, "Ahh, there you are, Alf" (that seeming to be his name as well as Mr Pickering). "You aren't going out in the chill tonight to do your checking when you could be a-sitting in my warm pub enjoying some small mercies and a pint of my Best Bitter."

Then I saw them all looking at Mr Pickering drinking up, as Dad called it, and Mr Pickering said he had no alternative but to go out in the cold, small mercies not coming into it, and seemed a bit annoyed at being asked in the first place, him still in the middle of talking to me.

"I'm just telling the lad 'ere that you wouldn't like it if some light was to escape and them German bombers started giving us a fair old pasting." And the others started muttering among themselves about not wanting a pasting of any sort, a fair old one anyway, which seemed to be the worst sort.

And Mr Pickering, up from his haunches now, told them all about his rounds and how he started on the village green, by the bus shelter, and then down by the council houses where the people had been known to call out "Sod off!" when he shouted to them to snuff out that light!

"Well, they do…" he said, with Old Joe and the others listening to what happened when Mr Pickering went down to the council houses, "them being ignorant buggers down there."

Then Mr Right-T-Ho came out with some tutt-tutts. "Tutt-tutt, Mr Pickering," he said. "Not in front of the boy", which was me, and how Mr Pickering should not use swear words when I was sitting there. "Even if they're being used to a good purpose."

Mr Pickering didn't seem to like Mr Right-T-Ho tutt-tutting him and told him so, right into his face. "I'll be paying particular attention to your blackout when I do my rounds tonight, Mr Right-T-Ho, and I won't like it one bit if I see some light escaping." Then stared at him again with his eagle eye. And poor Mr Right-T-Ho got taken aback, him seeming to be a nice little man and not used to being taken aback.

"Our ARP officer doesn't seem very popular in the village, anyway," Dad told Mum that evening when Mum got back from her hand of bridge.

And Mum said how Auntie had heard much the same sort of thing and, more than that, how PC Trendle, the police constable, had been asking himself why Mr Pickering's rounds always seemed to end up outside Mrs Clandice Brown's house, with him finding a chink of light when the husband was away on the high seas, and not finding one when he wasn't. And then popping in to help her solve the problem. "The chink of light problem, that is," he said.

"It must be the warm cocoa," Auntie told Mum by way of explanation, with Dad listening. "A warm mug from Mrs Brown to thank him."

And Mum looked at Dad with a look that said "If you believe that, you'll believe anything."

Daily Express

Friday, May 31, 1940

Ships of all sizes dare inferno of shells and bombs to bring the British Army back across the Channel from Dunkirk

TENS OF THOUSANDS SAFELY HOME ALREADY

Under the guns of the allied navies, under the wings of the Royal Air Force, a large proportion of the B.E.F. who for three days had been fighting their way back to the Flanders Coast have now been brought safely to England.

First to return were the wounded. An armada of ships – all sizes and shapes – were used for crossing the Channel. The weather which helped Hitler's tanks to advance also smoothed the Channel for the British troops to return.

Many more men than was expected have already been extricated from their perilous position around Dunkirk, thanks to the devotion of merchant seamen who have ferried backwards and forwards again and again, careless of the danger to themselves.

All last night, until dawn this morning, troops who had left Flanders fields to fire and flood were being landed along the south coast of England.

A midnight message from Paris brought dramatic news which suggested that the withdrawal was nearly at its end...

Bobby says, "Your dad's got a nice stick."

Me and the village lads, and the evacuee girls, Lydia and Lizzie, are on the village green watching our dads on their parade.

"It'll be our first one," Dad had said when he came home from his bank. He seemed very pleased to be going.

"Playing soldiers in this Old Timers' army of yours." Mum was using her not-so-happy voice. "I hope you know what you're doing..." Mum found a bit of fluff on Dad's jacket and didn't like that either. "... when you could be at home with your family..."

"It's going to be the backbone of the country," Dad told Mum, saying how Mr Eden's army would save us from Mr Hitler if he marched up the Little Piddlington Road and captured the bus shelter.

Mum straightened Dad's tie and brushed off the bit of fluff. "Well, try to come home in one piece... if only for the children's sake." Mum had made some sandwiches, wrapped neatly in greaseproof paper, for Dad to take with him. "No doubt you'll get peckish doing all this soldiering."

Then Dad had gone off, taking his sandwiches with him, and a stick he'd found in the garden shed. And I'd run up alongside him, to see what happened when Dad got there.

Bobby thinks they are a funny-looking lot. "Except for my dad, and yours," he says. "And some others," looking round at our dads lined up, standing shoulder to shoulder, like the School Inspector's coming.

Colin says, "Mine doesn't look funny." His dad is wearing his postman's uniform and had cycled up to the village green straight after his tea. He couldn't wait, Colin reckons. "Dad polished the badge on his cap specially. I watched him Brasso it like billy-o. You can see it shining from here." And Colin reckons his dad's stick is as good as anyone's. "Blooming well is," he says when Smith Junior says it isn't.

Minnow, the little boy, thinks his dad looks pretty good too. Minnow says he's not as big as the others but he packs a punch. "My dad does," he says, drawing himself up to his full height, which is still only little. "I bet he'll give Hitler something to think about if he comes this way." And he tells us how his helmet was his granddad's helmet from a war they had years ago. "Before Granddad got a beard and a wonky leg." His dad keeps his bike clips in it now, he tells us. "On the kitchen table. It's very useful for that."

Mr Blenkinsop is walking up and down now, looking at our dads just like he's doing his School Inspector bit.

"A fine body of men," we hear him say, and how he's put in a thing called a requisition. "A requisition for some guns, that is. We should have a response soon. Then we'll be a real fighting force."

"My Dad doesn't have any medals," I say, thinking how best I can explain why Dad doesn't have anything to pin on his jacket and nothing to put on his head. Just his glasses, which don't count. "You don't get medals and a helmet when you're in charge of the stores," I tell them. "But he's still very important... counting things... and making a list..."

They are all listening, even Smith Junior, so I think I'll keep going. "... my Dad says lists make all the difference... About winning the war..."

Mr Blenkinsop shouts "Attention, men!"

And our dads shuffle their feet and do things with their sticks. Mr Jiggins has brought his roadsweeper's broom. He's taken the end off, the bristly bit. And Mr Right-T-Ho has a garden fork from his shop window. Mr Spatchcock, the gamekeeper, has a real gun that he slaps to his shoulder, and shouts "Sir".

We all giggle: me, Bobby, Minnow, Colin Lamplin and the evacuee girls. Fatty Tucker giggles a bit but not so Mr Spatchcock can hear. "'e could kill you with that thing," he says.

Mr Blenkinsop turns and shouts, "'aven't you kids got nothing better to do?" And we think we'd better go off and play.

"Come on," says Bobby, "race you up to the reccie... Last one there is a sissy."

And we race off as fast as we can. Leaving our dads to save us from Mr Hitler if he marches up the Little Piddlington Road and captures the bus shelter.

Vroomm!

An aeroplane roars over the village green, missing the church and skimming the clump of trees on the top of the hill above Farmer Millsom's hen farm, scattering the hens and frightening his black and white dog. We all duck, it's so low.

"Let us brace ourselves to our duty"

"Upon this battle depends the survival of Christian civilisation... We shall do our duty and so bear ourselves that, if the British Commonwealth and Empire lasts for a thousand years, men will still say, 'This was their finest hour'."

The RT. HON. WINSTON CHURCHILL, C.H., M.P.
Prime Minister

"A Spitfire!" shouts Bobby. He's the leader of the gang and knows for sure.

"A Hawker Hurricane" says Smith Junior, the Smartie.

"No, a Spitfire..."

"I tell you it's a Hurricane. You only have to look at the wing tips. And there's a big air scoop under the engine... My brother's a pilot, he tells me everything there is to know about planes."

Bobby's not so sure now. "Well, it's one of ours, anyway..." We all feel guilty about it being a Hurricane and not a Spitfire, except Smith Junior who looks pretty smug about planes.

It's a Saturday afternoon and we're playing cricket on the recreation ground. Bobby's our captain, then there's Colin Lamplin, the postman's son, Minnow, the little boy and Henry, the lanky lad from the council houses. The girls, Lydia and Lizzie, are fielding and sometimes they are allowed to bowl their silly underarm ones that are really easy to hit.

And Smith Junior, the Smartie, of course. He's the captain of the other side but only because he's got a proper ball that you polish on your pants and make whiz through the air like real bowlers do. Henry, the lanky lad, is mostly the captain but Smith Junior's going home and taking his proper ball unless he's made captain today.

And he's got his posh bat with rubber on the handle and Len Hutton written on the front, in grown-up writing. He'll take that home too.

I knew the aeroplane was one of ours. In my Biggles book all our planes have red, white and blue colours on the wings and the sides and the Germans just black crosses. But I don't say. Smith Junior says he knows everything and I don't want to make Bobby feel more rotten than he does already.

"How do you know?" I ask, hoping it might make him feel a bit better.

Bobby says, "Ours have little circles in different colours, some red, some white and some blue. The red one's the littlest. I knew it was one of ours. Anyway, it's gone now, whatever it was."

"A Hawker Hurricane," Smith Junior, the Smartie, says again, doing a practice hit with his posh bat.

"Anyway, it's not Len Hutton's real writing," says Henry, the lanky lad who's not the captain any more. "Someone did it for him."

"Crikey," says Minnow, about the plane that went over. "It nearly got the church." He's still half ducked down.

All we got was a glimpse, on the reccie in the sunshine, roaring in one end of the village and out over Farmer Millsom's hen farm at the other. "I bet he was doing a million miles an hour," says Fatty.

"Anyway, if your brother is so clever," Henry says, "why isn't he up there in the sky fighting the Germans?"

"He is... I expect he'll fly over in a minute and give us a wave."

Farmer Millsom's hens are gathering themselves together again, in little groups, and starting to peck at the ground and his black and white dog has come out of hiding. He's standing outside the hen house, hands resting on his hips, looking up into the sky like Biggles's Commanding Officer does when he's waiting for his planes to come back after a raid.

"I expect he's swearing now," Bobbie says. "My brother says you're allowed to swear when an aeroplane frightens your chickens or your motorbike breaks down."

Dad told me to expect lots of aeroplanes over our village because there's a battle going on. The Battle of Britain, Dad called it, and how I was to stay hushed while he listened to the man on the wireless say how many had been shot down, ours and theirs. A bit like our cricket scores, I said. Dad said it was a lot more serious than that and even Mum had to stay hushed. The outcome of the war could depend on it, Dad told us.

Yesterday the man said we got 57 and they got 32. And today it is 66 and they got 45. "Hmmmm..." says Dad, and thinks it is something called government propaganda. But it's still worth going up to the pub to celebrate.

It's very exciting and I tell Mum all about it. "The planes will be coming over our village, Mum. That's what Dad said. I bet that's what he was doing today. Searching for a German to shoot at."

Mum tells me I must run indoors and hide under the table next time I see an aeroplane. "Promise me, you will."

I promise, but I don't want to miss the Battle of Britain. "I'd really like to have a look at it Mum. It's very exciting."

"And get yourself riddled?"

"What's riddled, Mum?"

"You'll be dead, that's what. And what would your father say then?"

In Dad's pub, Mr Jiggins told them he had seen lots of aeroplanes chasing each other. He stopped and leant on his broom and watched until Mr Trendle the roly-poly policeman told him to "get down before me 'ead were blown off".

He did get down under the hedge by the Little Piddlington Road and stayed there till they had gone, even though he was in a nettle patch.

"It was a dogfight," said Mr Blenkinsop, who is like Smith Junior, the Smartie, only grown up. He also knows everything. "I haven't fought the Germans in hand-to-hand combat without knowing a dogfight when I see one." He was looking round with satisfaction when he said it. "Yes, a dogfight. I can tell."

"Looked like aeriplanes to me," Mr Jiggins said. He'd seen nothing like it in his entire life and told them the nettles didn't bother him because they were good for your joints. "I don't mind getting a bit of a stingin'."

"I hope Mrs Lillywhite's in Hastings is safe," I say to Mum after Dad had told me about the Battle of Britain. "Dad says it's over the seaside as well as over Farmer Millsom's farm. And the man who sells ice creams on the pier. I hope he doesn't get bombed. I'd like a strawberry one next time, Mum." I'd only got a vanilla one last year and Ingie had most of it after she'd finished hers in double-quick time.

"That's what Big Sisters are for," she said. "To help Little Brothers eat up their ice creams."

Mum says, "If there is a next time."

Bobby digs deep in his pocket and brings out his special penny that's thin and flat and has been on the railway line at Newbury and run over by lots of trains. "Heads or tails?" he calls.

Minnow tells us that a German aeroplane has crashed in Little Piddlington. It has gone into a haystack. His dad told him, although no-one else had seen it.

"Hasn't your dad got a bit of the aeroplane?" asks Smith Junior, the Smartie. "Everyone gets a bit of a German plane when it crashes. As a prize."

Minnow says his dad didn't have time to get a prize, he was cycling to work and didn't want to be late. "Anyway, there was a policeman standing by it," he tells us. A very big one. And Minnow draws an invisible line miles above his head and says "This high." Then tells us they always put a big policeman next to a German plane when it crashes in case Hitler's in it. "Then he arrests him," he says.

Smith Junior still thinks Minnow's dad should have a bit of the plane to prove it. "Or we might think he made it up."

Minnow has a good point, I think, about the policeman. Anyway, I didn't want to pick on him, he was only little. And it wasn't his fault his dad hadn't pinched a bit of the German aeroplane, with Hitler sitting in it, in a haystack.

Smith Junior calls heads, but it's tails and we're batting.

"My turn to open," says Colin, the postman's son. "I haven't opened for ages." And then it's Minnow's turn, then mine. Henry, the lanky boy, is going to bowl. Really fast ones, not silly under-arm ones like the girls'. Fast over-arm ones that are the hardest to hit. With the proper ball that you polish on your pants and make it whiz through the air.

Colin gets lot of runs and Bobby gets lots more, fours mostly and a six that goes up and up until it comes down in Farmer Collins's field. I get ten, then Henry bowls a really fast one that hits me on the shin, which hurts a lot.

"Give him a bouncer!" shouts Smith Junior, then whispers something to Henry and his next one nearly knocks my head off and the one after that skittles my stumps, which is good because I don't want my head nearly knocked off.

"Sissy," cries Smith junior, but I don't mind. Mum always says it's better to be out than dead. "I don't know why you play that silly game..."

We've got sixty altogether and Smith Junior's team only makes thirty-three and he's going home, taking the posh ball with him and the proper bat, with Len Hutton's name on it, under his arm, saying we didn't play fair.

Minnow calls out, "Spoilsport."

And Smith Junior calls Minnow a pea brain and me a sissy and says he'll get me one day. "You just see, Townie."

"Come on, let's go home," says Bobby. "Before we get riddled like your mum says."

"Here is the 8 o'clock News from the BBC for September 9, 1940,

Air raids even more widespread than those of Saturday were carried out on London and the London area last night and almost until daylight this morning – the longest of the war so far.

The alarm was sounded at eight o'clock yesterday evening and was followed quickly by the sound of bomb explosions and heavy anti-aircraft gunfire as the German aircraft began their attack. The number of enemy machines which penetrated the defence was fewer than in the previous big raid but their activity appears to have been greater – and some flew over Central London dropping bombs.

Very little news is available so far about the effects of the bombing but it seems that the dock area in the east of London, which was considerably affected in Saturday's raid, was again attacked. The German airmen were apparently able to make use of the still smouldering fires as a guide to their targets. In one part of this area another big fire was started and among the buildings hit by high explosive bombs was a nurses' home attached to a hospital...

Bombs dropped in other areas are reported to have caused damage to house property and have caused several fires to break out. Six bombs fell outside the offices of a London newspaper..."

Dad's glued to his wireless just like the days in the Red Brick House.

Ingie had said I'd better keep out of Dad's way and not get under Mum's feet either. "Mr Hitler is bombing London now," she said, when she came home from her work on Saturday afternoon. "And Gran's house might be one of them."

They were all talking about it in the office, Ingie said, and called it the Blitz. "Now the Battle of Britain's over, Hitler's bombing London... and our other places... but mostly London. I think you'd better make yourself scarce, Little Brother. While this bombing's going on."

Summer holidays are over and school is back and I'm walking home with the others, dawdling along and they are dawdling too. We're keeping out of the way of our mums and dads, trying to be scarce, like Ingie says. Our mums and dads aren't interested in us kids at the moment, just the bombing.

"My older sister works in Southampton," Colin, the postman's son, tells us. "Hitler's bombing it now... Mum can't stop wondering if she's all right..."

Bobby has an uncle in a place called Coventry. "That's getting bombed too. Dad reckons Uncle Ben could cop it any time."

Lydia says, "We lives in London... Just Mum and Dad, anyway, now Lizzie and me are down 'ere. Our 'ouse, in Lewisham, round the corner from the Empire. I bet that gets bombed."

In the school holidays Lydia and Lizzie's mum had come down by train and said she was going to take them back. But their dad said it wasn't safe so she changed her mind and went back by herself. "Anyway we don't mind it in the country. Do we, Lizzie?" says Lydia.

Lizzie doesn't say yes or no.

"She's shy," Lydia says. "And she misses our mum. Specially at bed-time. Don't you, Lizzie?"

"'ope Mum and Dad don't get bombed," says Lizzie quietly, looking at the ground as we dawdle along.

Lydia says their mum waved to them from the train and Lizzie cried when she had to say goodbye. "You're not to worry, now," she told them, leaning out the window. "And don't give that nice

Mrs Brown no trouble, will you. And wash your 'ands before you 'ave yer tea."

Then Mr Right-T-Ho peddles past on his red bike. "Is your mum and dad at home?" he calls out to me, peddling along, ringing the bell on his handlebars. "I've got a telegram for them."

"Mum's home," I call back. "I expect Dad's still at work."

"What do yer want a telegram for?" says Fatty Tucker.

Bobby says telegrams are for people when they have birthdays... or get married... "Things like that," he says.

"And when they have babies," says Minnow. "Our mum got one when Auntie Ida had a nipper." Minnow says his dad read it out in the kitchen and it was full of stops. *Ida had a baby* **STOP** *Six pounds five ounces* **STOP** *A boy* **STOP** *We've named him Horace* **STOP**.*"

"And you gets one from the King when you get to a hundred," Colin tells us. His dad took one to old Mr Plunkett on Thatcher's End Lane. That's how he knows. "The King didn't put any stops in his," he says. "Just: *'Well done, Mr Plunkett. From your King.' "* His dad read it out on the doorstep and they asked him in for tea. "They never had a telegram from the King before."

I know how telegrams can bring bad news. "My gran had a son called Arthur who got killed in the war," I say. "The last one, not the one they're having now. My mum said my gran cried when they brought the telegram and she read it. And Granddad went to his allotment so they wouldn't see him crying either."

"Cripes!" says Minnow.

"Crikey!" says Fatty.

Bobby says, "I hope your telegram doesn't mean someone's dead."

Everyone goes very quiet for a bit. Lizzie picks a flower from the hedge. It has white petals and a yellow middle bit. "It's for teacher in the morning," she tells us quietly.

Smith Junior snatches it from her hand and scrunches it up. "It's a weed," he says.

"What did you do that for?" says Bobby.

"It's a weed... I told you... "

"Well, you didn't have to do that," says Lydia. "She wasn't doing you no 'arm."

Lizzie is in tears. They flood down her cheeks and she wipes them off with her sleeve like girls do. Lydia has a hanky. "'ere 'ave this... and don't worry, we'll pick another flower for teacher."

"It's not a flower. It's a weed. I told you."

There is silence. Except for Lizzie sobbing.

Bobby says, "We can't stand around here all day. Let's get up the reccie and have a game of footie."

I say I'm going home to find out what Mum and Dad's telegram says. "I'll tell you tomorrow... on the way to school."

Mum's anxious when I get home, after she's read her telegram, and when Dad arrives from the bank, he's anxious too. He says he's going to go down the road to find Mr Alfie. "Your mother and I might have to go to London, Son... to make sure Gran's all right." Dad says the telegram is from Reverend Runcorn and is about the Blitz and how Gran's house might have been bombed. "Come straight away," Reverend Runcorn said to them. "Urgent..."

"It's very good of the reverend to let us know," Dad says, still being anxious. "A kind man if ever there was."

Mum packs a little bag and tells me I'll have to stay with Auntie. "Auntie will get you ready for school and have your tea on the table when you get home."

"How long will you be away, Mum?"

Mum doesn't know... not for sure, anyway. "A day, perhaps. Maybe two at the most... just to check Gran's safe and well."

And I hear Dad say to Mum, "I tried to warn her about the bombing when I went up there... but she wouldn't listen."

And Mum says she told her too, in her letters. "'*Why don't you come down to the country and stay with us? It's so much safer down here.*'" Mum told Gran there was room in the Artist's House, a nice bedroom looking out over the village green, in fact, a choice of two. "I underlined it," Mum says. "'*And you can bring Joey, he doesn't have to be left behind.*'"

Dad says to me, "Gran could have changed her mind by now, Son. We might be bringing her back. Wouldn't that be a treat?"

143

Now Mum and Dad are waving goodbye from Mr Alfie's taxi, and Auntie's crinkly little fingers are squeezing my hand and we're waving and Mum calling out, "Back soon. Be a good boy..." And fluttering a hanky out of the window.

And then they're gone and it's very quiet in Auntie's house, Rose Tree Cottage, except for Auntie chatting away saying how it will be all right and there's the biscuit she's saved for a rainy day and how the rainy day has come and there's the porridge to look forward to in the morning, followed by school, and how Mum and Dad will be back before you can say Jack Robinson. "Yes, Jack Robinson," she says. "You see, they'll be back before you know it."

"Before Jack Robinson, Auntie?"

"Yes, before him. "

Next morning Auntie gets me up early. "What on earth would your Mum and Dad say if you were late for school? And me responsible."

I skip along to school. "My gran's coming to stay," I tell Bobby and the others. "She lives in a tiny little house in Clapham but Mr Hitler's bombed it now so she can't. She's coming back in Mr Alfie's taxi with Mum and Dad and Joey the budgie."

The kids stand and stare. None of them have heard of a house that only has a step for a front garden.

"You can come and talk to my gran's budgie if you like," I tell them.

"I bet he knows lots of swear words," Bobbie says.

I say I don't think he does. "He only says 'Who's a Pretty Boy then?' From his cage. When the milkman comes, and Gran's postman. But not the rent collector."

It's dark now and Auntie is reading *Rupert Bear and the Chinese Dragon,* my bedtime story, when there's the sound of a car outside. It must be Mr Alfie with Mum and Dad and Gran... "I'll see," says Auntie, rushing to the window. Auntie has forgotten the Blackout curtains and can't see a thing. "Oh, drat this Blackout!"

144

I'm jumping out of bed and rushing down Auntie's rickety little stairs as fast as I can.

The door is pushed open, it's Dad with Joey, chirping merrily in his cage, which is a bit dented. And Mum following, her hanky clutched in her hand. Mr Alfie is following behind with Mum's little bag.

"Where's Gran, Mum?"

Auntie says, "Is she staying in London after all?"

Mum has the hanky to her face now. "It's so nice to see you," she says. "Auntie, and my lovely son." She's been crying, I can tell.

Auntie's putting the kettle on. Dad says we could all do with a cup of tea. "It's been a wearisome couple of days," he says.

Mr Alfie looks awkward. "I'll be off if that's all right, Mr 'oldsworth. You can settle up later."

Dad sees him to the door and is grateful for his help. And then wants us to sit down, Auntie and me. The tea can wait for a moment, he has something important to tell us. We have to "brace" ourselves. "Gran won't be coming home... not today... not ever... She's no longer with us. It was in the bombing..."

Auntie says, "Oh dear, oh dear... This dreadful war..." and tells us Mr Hitler has a lot to answer for.

The door's shut behind Mr Alfie. Joey's cage is on the table. Auntie's on her sofa, her crinkly little hands clasped on her lap. Her face has gone crinkly too.

Dad says, "You mustn't worry, Son. She'll be in Heaven now..."

I wonder how she got there. Reverend Runcorn said you drifted upwards, with angels helping you along. Sort of floating up, I suppose.

Auntie is getting the cup of tea and telling Joey it's a dreadful war...

I'll say a prayer tonight, I think to myself. I'm sure Gran will hear if she's got to Heaven by then; even though it's dark with the Blackout, the angels will know the way. Reverend Runcorn said some people take a long time. "Some never make it," he said. "The bad people."

We hear Mr Alfie wind the taxi with a grunting noise. It coughs into life.

We have our cup of tea and then walk home across the village green. Without Gran.

But with Joey.

Chapter 11

Your Dad's an Enermie Spy

The war has been going for nearly two years now. Ingie works it out, counting the months, September 1939 to June 1941, 21 in all. Then she tells me there's no end in sight. That's what they said in her office, anyway, in Little Piddlington. And Mr Harrington reckoned it would get a lot worse before it got any better. The way things were going, he said.

It's hard to remember when we didn't have a war. I can remember when Mum went up to the shops and got some sweets and I compared what I'd got with Podgy and him saying his were the best and not wanting to trade except when I had gum drops, which everyone wanted. And I can remember going to Hastings for our holidays with Ingie and Mum and Dad. And having ice creams (if Ingie didn't finish them off first) and going on the pier and other exciting things.

Mum says they have cut the pier in half so that when Mr Hitler invades it will be difficult for him to jump from one side to the other. That was the main reason he hadn't invaded already, Mum said. The pier being cut in half.

"Will they join it together again, Mum, when the war's over?"

Mum doesn't answer. I don't think Mum's an expert on joining piers together.

Ingie says the war may never end. "There was one that lasted a hundred years, Little Brother. Haven't you learnt about that at school?" Ingie says the people in that war thought it would never end.

I asked Auntie but she just said, "Hitler's got a lot to answer for," as she always does and went off and gave Fluff his dinner.

I'd like to ask Dad but he's too busy with his bank and then listening to his wireless. I'm lucky to get any Biggles these days.

"Here is the 9 o'clock News from the BBC for Sunday, June 22, 1941

In a proclamation broadcast early this morning, Hitler announced that the German army was marching against Russia to preserve Europe from the Bolshevist menace. The German army is helped by the Finns in the north and the Romanians in the south. There are no reports, as yet, of any fighting.

The proclamation ended with these words: 'I have today decided to put the fate and the future of the German Reich and the German people in the hands of our soldiers. May God help us in this battle.'

Other headlines tonight. Two German bombers were destroyed during last night's raids on towns in the south of England. And it is now known that 28 enemy fighters were shot down during yesterday's daylight operations."

Dad goes up to the pub to "think it over" and tells Mum when he gets back how Mr Jiggins had said he predicted something like this would happen. "That 'itler and that Stalin," he told Dad. "Sleep with dogs and you catches fleas."

And Mr Alfie said, "Birds of a feather flock together."

Then Old Joe said from behind the bar, "Live by the sword, die by the sword..."

Dad says he just nodded. He didn't want to commit himself. Anyway, he wasn't certain what all these fleas and feathers and swords had got to do with Hitler marching on Russia.

Then Mr Jiggins said, "You're a clever bloke, Perce, coming from that bank of yours. You expected this, I reckon. That 'itler attacking 'is friends, them Russians."

Dad nodded again. "There is a lot of this war to run yet, Mr Jiggins," he said. "A lot to run yet..." And downed his pint and came home telling Mum that was enough thinking things over for one night.

Dad seems a bit perkier after Hitler's invaded Russia and he's even got some time for a few pages of Biggles. "Are we sitting comfortably?" he asks.

"You bet, Dad!"

Dad perches himself on the edge of my bed. "Then I shall begin..." And before I know it, Biggles is shouting "Two Huns are bombing Ramsgate – I'm going for them." His C.O. protests but Biggles is already on his way, taking a flying leap into the cockpit.

"Switches off, petrol on," sings out the ack-emma.

"Petrol on," echoes Biggles.

"Contact!"

"Contact!"

The Bentley aero engine starts with a roar and sends a cloud of smoke whirling aft into the slipstream. Biggles adjusts his goggles, waves his chocks away, and in a few minutes is in the air..."

Dad is very good with technical terms like Contact and Chocks Away and stops every now and again and explains (in his ordinary voice, of course) what they mean.

Chocks Away and Contact; they're easy now. Even the difficult ones like ack-emma (short for air mechanic) and C.O. (Commanding Officer). I'm up with them too. And then Dad's straight back to being Biggles and his chums. His Flying Officer Kite voices, Mum calls them.

"I say, chaps, let's get up there and get after the Hun," and things like that, and I am up there with him, in the cockpit, gripping the joystick and ready for action. "By Jove, I'll wager we'll bag a few today...."

I'm just saying how I bet Biggles would shoot down lots if he was in the Battle of Britain when there's a sharp knocking on our front door and Mum from downstairs, calling out, "I wonder who on earth that could be at this time of night?"

Biggles has swung his fighter plane around and is taxiing down the runway, waiting for the signal that will give him the "off". Any minute now and the battle will be on – and me with him – ducking and weaving, guns blazing, machine gun bullets flying. Thanks to Dad, I've not missed a single dogfight (lots of aeroplanes chasing each other, Mr Blenkinsop says) and I don't want to miss this one. "Come on, Dad, can't wait to see what happens next."

It's PC Trendle, Mum's saying, with a police sergeant from Reading she hasn't seen before and a man in ordinary clothes she doesn't recognize either. Dark raincoat and hat pulled down across his eyes. Shady character if ever I saw one, Mum said after it was all over.

"It must be something to do with the bank," Dad says, putting down Biggles with a sigh and making his way to the bedroom door. "I'll be back in a moment, Son. Shouldn't take too long."

Dad has the keys to the bank these days, what with Mr Snitchley being off with a sickness – nerves is what Mum calls it. Dad could get some of these nerves too, Mum warns him; as the assistant manager he's having to make lots of decisions and solve lots of bank problems. And making sure it's open in the morning and locked up at night and overseeing all the transactions in-between. The "goings on," Dad calls them.

"Come back soon, Dad," I say. "Biggles is taking off this very minute. We don't want to miss anything..."

I could read Biggles myself, I suppose, but it's not the same without Dad. And my machine gun *ratta-tat-tats* are not a patch on his. Then there's my Bentley aero engines, they're hopeless. "I can't do them, Dad," I say, "not like you."

"There's nothing wrong with your machine guns, Son." And

Dad says my engines are coming along a treat. "Anyone would be proud of them."

But I bet he's only being nice. Anyway, I'd much rather Dad does the noises while I concentrate on what's happening to Biggles and his chums. "The sound effects," Mum calls them. "I'm sure the neighbours must think we're living in a war zone." But Mum's smiling when she says it so I know she's only joking... about this war zone thing.

I'll just pop out of bed and wait for Dad to come back – on our landing, it can't do any harm. Just out of sight of Mum. You can get a telling off if you're spotted. "Back into bed with you this minute!" Things like that if you're caught.

I just want to know why PC Trendle and two strange men have come to see Dad; the one in a dark coat and hat pulled down across his eyes, just like Mr X in one of Biggles stories when he had to meet Mr X in a dark alleyway with just a pin-prick of light from his cigarette to guide him and a password only Biggles knew. "Is that you, Mr X?" Biggles said in a hoarse voice, and the man with his collar turned up and not able to look Biggles in the eye, not once. The man in our lounge is just like that, but without the pin-prick of light, of course.

"It's not about the bank, not even the keys," I hear PC Trendle say. "We've come... err... as a result of information received." And he doesn't call Dad, Dad, or Perce, or anything like he usually does. Just "Mr 'oldsworth". He's not being nearly as nice as he normally is. What's made him change? I wonder.

"Make yourselves at home, gentlemen," Dad says, being friendly. "On our comfy sofa." But they're not making themselves comfy on the sofa or anywhere else. Even when Mum says she'll put the kettle on, there's still no reply. It's this information received they're interested in, not Dad's sofa or Mum's kettle.

"Information received?" I hear Dad ask in a puzzled voice. "How do you mean, information received?" He's repeating it like it's a question. PC Trendle's not making much sense tonight. I can't think what's going on.

"I'll take over now, Constable, thank you," says the sergeant, and I watch him step forward, a big man with a moustache and smart stripes and a notebook for writing things down like they do in films. The shady character in the raincoat and hat is keeping back, saying nothing, while PC Trendle's going over to our bookcase, peering at our books one by one, looking at the covers: *Oliver Twist*, the orphan boy, and then the atlas Mum and Dad bought me for my school learning.

"Have you ever been to Germany?" I hear the sergeant ask, and when Dad says he has, he seems to grow a bit taller and when Dad tells him that he's been twice, he's stretching his legs, like he's exercising, up on his toes looking at my dad with satisfaction, just like Smith Junior when he wins at conkers, or comes top in sums.

"You never told me you went to Germany," PC Trendle says. He's got Dad's gardening book in his hand: Mum's Christmas present. *The Beginner's Book of Vegetable Growing*. "Germany," he's repeating, "you never said nothing about going to Germany..."

Dad says, "I didn't think it was important."

"Perhaps it isn't," comes the reply from PC Trendle, slipping Dad's vegetable book back in our bookcase next to the long plays by Mr Shakespeare.

"Quite to the contrary, Constable," replies the sergeant, in his booming voice with a thing called a smirk, "it is important, very important." And he's stretching up again, on his toes, looking down on Dad with Mum going pale. He's so tall his sergeant's cap nearly touches the frilly bits on our lampshade in the middle of our lounge. And he's writing something down now: *Gone to Germany*. I bet that's what he's writing. Then he does some more of these ups and downs on his toes. And another of his smirks.

Mum is at Dad's side now. "Well really..." Mum says.

"Yes, in 1929 and then again in 1932," Dad's explaining. "We went to hear Richard Wagner..."

But Dad can't finish, the sergeant isn't letting him. "Oh, so you're not denying you went to see a German?" Just as though you need permission to hear the music of the man you like the most.

And then PC Trendle calls out from over by our bookcase, "What's this 'ere, then, Mr 'oldsworth?" And holds up a map. It's

Dad's map of Germany. PC Trendle's making it seem like having a map is another thing you need to ask a policeman about.

Dad says, "It's best to have a map when you're travelling around a strange country, especially if you go by train like we did... it's invaluable."

Anyone knows that, I think to myself, and if PC Trendle was a proper policeman he'd know it too. Without a map Mum and Dad could have got on the wrong train or got off at the wrong place; it's easily done, Mum said so.

But it doesn't help, any of this, getting on a train or getting off again. The sergeant turns to the man in the dark coat and he's nodding now and the sergeant's saying, "I'm afraid you'll have to come with us, Sir. For further questioning... down at the station..."

There's the five of them standing there in our lounge like they're doing a play in Auntie's village hall, but it's all going horribly wrong. Mum's hanging onto Dad's arm as if she's trying to stop him being taken away. "What on earth do you mean?" Mum says. "For further questioning...?"

But there's no answer. Like the cup of tea.

The sergeant isn't budging; the shady man in the coat still hasn't said a thing, just the nod, and poor PC Trendle's looking as if he wishes he wasn't there. It was him who found Dad's map but now he's wishing he hadn't, but was in the pub with Dad, and him saying "'ave one on me, Perce" and Dad replying, "I don't mind if I do."

"I'll take that map if you don't mind, Constable," says the sergeant, still exercising his legs, up and down, looking round, showing us his smirk.

And PC Trendle's wishing the floor would open up and swallow him complete, map and all. "It's an old one," he says, as if that's going to help. "It's probably out of date by now."

"It's not of consequence whether it's out of date, or not, Constable. It's a map of Germany," says the sergeant, holding it up for all to see. "It's a map and it's evidence, with places on it, like Berlin where Hitler's got a house, a big one, I'll be bound. Huge garden and ride-on mower with his Master Plan tucked in his back pocket. The trappings of power," he says.

It's all he needs, these trappings. And the map and Dad having gone to Germany. "Twice," he says triumphantly, just like Smith Junior when his conker whacks ours.

I wish Ingie was here, she might think of something to say, or something to do – like slipping out through the back door and letting their tyres down or throwing their starting handle over the hedge. But there's no Ingie and there's no handle over the hedge, and now Mum's showing how upset she can be, saying, "I've never heard such rubbish in all my life" and telling them, "You can't do this."

But they can.

"It's war, Mrs Holdsworth," says the sergeant. "And we have the authority." And now Dad's got to get his things, toothbrush and toothpaste. And pyjamas in a little bag. "This could be a long one, this one," the sergeant's saying.

"Dad!" I call out from the top of the landing. "Dad...."

But it makes no difference. The sergeant's still going to lead Dad away. He could make a dash for it, I think, but he wouldn't get far in his slippers and those little elastic braces that hold up his trousers.

"You'd best get along to bed, my boy," says PC Trendle, looking up to where I am standing in the dressing gown poor Gran bought me before she got bombed. "You can't do your dad no good now."

And to Mum he says about the keys to Dad's bank, "I'll make sure the keys get to them in the morning... so they can open up. Mr 'oldsworth won't be needing them for a while yet."

And then Dad's gone. I hear car doors slam, an engine start up and there's a crunch of gears. Mum sits down at the foot of the stairs, and out comes her hanky and she has a little cry. Mum can't believe what's happened... Her arms are round me and I get a big cuddle. "It's ridiculous, a terrible mistake," she's insisting. But then there are the tears too. Lots of them.

Mum doesn't get any sleep. I only get a little bit, lying there listening to the hootie old owl out there in the dark, wondering where they've taken Dad. A cold, damp cell, I expect, with rats scurrying around his feet and a hard bed; that's where they always take Biggles when he falls into enemy hands.

Half a potato for dinner and bit of meat with some fluff growing on it. A tin plate and bent fork. And I bet they won't be giving Dad a knife so he can saw his way through the bars and make his escape.

And I'm thinking deep thoughts about why Dad has been taken off. There's got to be a reason.

He's not a German spy, I know that, so why is he in a prison cell now, Mum crying and me getting no sleep? Someone's dobbed him in… that's it, an informer – that's who got Biggles. "Don't trust anyone, even your best friends," Biggles said. Not counting Algy and Ginger, of course. "I can trust them with my life."

But Dad hasn't got an Algy or Ginger. Someone must have said something, someone in the village, perhaps, if Dad let it slip about his German maps and being in Germany with Mum for some German music, all innocent, but now used as evidence to lock him up in that cold, damp cell with those horrid rats scurrying around his feet.

Next morning Mum is up early and rushes out to see Auntie, straight across the village green, only stopping to telephone Ingie with the dreadful news, and hoping Auntie might in some way be able to help.

And Mum's told me it might have got to my school, this news; I must prepare myself for "some unpleasantness" Mum calls it. "You know how Mr Alfie said gossip goes round the village like wildfire." And Mum thinks there might be a bit of this gossip and some wildfire already. "Keep your chin up, Son, we're going to stick together as a family no matter what the policeman said." There's a fresh hanky for my top pocket. And the chin up bit too. "For Dad's sake."

I arrive at school a bit late, on purpose, and quietly slip into my seat next to Lydia, not noticed by Miss Peabody, who is about to start on some *Treasure Island*, when I see a little note pushed on my desk: *Your dad's an Enermie Spy*, it reads, and then there are giggles all round the class and these get louder until Miss Peabody from the parlour of the Admiral Benbow looks up and says, "What is all this noise, children?"

And Smith Junior, the Smartie, puts his hand up and blurts out, "Miss, they say the evacuee's dad's a German spy!" And they all have their hands up (except Bobby and Colin and pretty Lydia), and calling out how they are more interested in German spies than stuffy old *Treasure Island*, even some pieces of eight.

Smith Junior says, "I'm sure it's not true," and he's got a silly smile on his face specially for me – "but on the other hand it might be. You never know."

And me not finding it easy to keep my chin up at all, but just trying to fight back the tears and wanting to shout out, "You've got it all wrong! My Dad's not a spy. I know he's not…"

Miss Peabody raps the desk with her ruler and everyone stops in surprise; prim Miss Peabody, with the rosy cheeks and buttoned-up dress, is angry now. "You don't know at all, children," she's saying. "It could all be a dreadful mistake", and she's back into *Treasure Island,* with Black Spot slinking in through the front door of the Admiral Benbow and putting the fear of the devil into the Captain – not to mention young Jim Boy – and this making the children sit up and take notice, and I am mighty grateful for Black Spot and his slinking bit and praying he will do some slinking every day until Dad is safely back home again and proved to be innocent.

And after morning break there are sums, which are a bit like Black Spot, and then dinner when I run home to see Mum and back again to keep out of the other kids' way. Then at the end of the day there's another bit of luck when Mr Williams, our headmaster with his fat tummy and tiny feet, calls me over and tells me I'm not to worry as it will all be sorted out soon and how I'll look back on it one day like a bad dream.

And he's hoping to see Dad around the village, and in the post office, and places like that, although he doesn't say anything about seeing Dad in the Red Lion and sharing a pint with him, which I know is his favourite, as I've seen him there from my little cubby hole – not that I say so, of course.

Three days pass and no news of Dad. Mum is getting more worried by the minute and Auntie's beside herself and Ingie, in Little Piddlington, wondering what is going on and I'm lying awake at night thinking about Dad on his hard bed and even when I'm asleep I'm having horrid dreams about Dad being tortured on a thing called a rack, which makes your arms and legs go long and sometimes drop off altogether.

When suddenly, in the afternoon, a car draws up outside and Dad is home again, as if by magic.

It is the Thursday and Mum and me are having our tea, with Uncle Mac on Children's Hour as company, when the handle turns on the door and in walks Dad, wearily, as if from another world.

"Thank goodness you're home safely!" Mum's first to say. "I was beside myself... and your son... neither of us got any sleep."

Dad was beside himself too, in his prison cell. "The questions," he says. "There was no stopping them. I'm sure they were convinced I was a Nazi spy."

Mum's got the kettle on. "Or perhaps something stronger?"

It's got to be something stronger, much stronger. "Time to bring out the whisky, Mother." Mum's reaching for the Bells, kept for special occasions, like being locked up as a Nazi spy. And a glass, an extra big one, that's called for too.

Dad's taking a gulp and telling us he can't believe what has happened since they took him off in the car with slammed doors and a crunch of gears, on that awful Monday night.

Then there were those questions, Dad says, hour after hour from the sinister man in the raincoat with a bright light shone in Dad's face (at times), and the man wanting to know why he had maps of Germany and a picture postcard of a place called Bayreuth sent to Ingie, saying "Having a wonderful time." And kisses too.

They were convinced it was some sort of code, and even asked Dad if he swallowed the messages when they arrived from Germany. All sorts of silly stuff like that... Dad couldn't believe it.

"How ridiculous!" says Mum. "Swallowing your messages... They'd stick in your throat... You'd never whistle again."

Dad insisted he was just an ordinary dad working for the bank and digging his vegetable patch on Sundays and going to the Red Lion two evenings a week and once on Saturday... if he had the mowing done. And that was it.

Dad said he thought Hitler was a lunatic and would have told him so if he'd bumped into him in the street.

"That seemed to keep them happy," Dad says, "for the moment anyway." Although they told him his file was still open and he could be taken in for questioning any time. "At the drop of a hat," they said.

Mum is delighted to have Dad home, of course, but not so keen on this "drop of a hat" bit that could take him away again. "The villagers have never been friendly from the moment we arrived – this can only make it worse." Mum still gets funny looks and sideways glances when she goes up to the shops, even though the villagers are cheerful enough to her face. And now Mum's telling Dad how the kids at school had made my life a misery from the moment he was taken off.

"Miss Peabody rapped her desk, Dad," I say. "Then told them it was all wrong what they were doing. Then we had some more *Treasure Island* and they forgot about it till we got in the playground."

"Life isn't easy, Son," Dad says, and tells us he will dip his toe in the water himself at the Red Lion on Tuesday, his regular, and see how he gets on. Dad will tell us all about it. "A blow by blow account," he says.

And Dad does venture in, standing there quietly by the bar, saying a cheery "Good Evening" to Old Joe and Farmer Collins and Mr Right-T-Ho, but only getting silence in reply, as if they hadn't seen him and even if they had, making out they hadn't.

And he's treated to "Best be off," just like the first time he went in there, all those years ago, and soon an empty circle forms around him as though he has a bad smell and isn't nice to stand next to.

"I better slink off home," Dad says to himself, with no-one else to say it to. "I don't know what's got into them," he tells Mum after he gets home. "Old Joe and Mr Blenkinsop and Mr Pickering. I thought they were my friends."

I can't believe all this is happening. I'm lying here, in my bed, thinking about Dad and how his life has become a misery. And Mum too, the people in the village tittle-tattling behind her back. And lots of the kids saying nasty things to my face and shutting

158

me out of their games. Even Bobby's not so sure he wants to be a friend any more. I think Smith Junior might be whispering things in his ear.

Only Ingie is out of it. Although she did say how Mr Harrington had told her that people who spied against their country should be locked up. "And that's a sight too good for them," he said, out loud, in front of the others. Ingie said she thought he meant being hanged. Hanged at dawn!

My Dad, hanged!

I must do something, I think to myself, I can't lie here doing nothing... Somehow I must try to prove Dad's innocence. Like the Secret Service man in Biggles who got Biggles's name cleared. Doing some phone tapping (Dad had said how it didn't really mean tapping on the phone but listening to what was being said without the other person knowing). That's what phone tapping meant, Dad said. Then catching the culprit red handed with his notebook in his hand and his binoculars round his neck spying on Biggles's new plane, the one that goes faster than anything else... Then writing it down in his notebook: "I've seen the plane that goes faster than anything else."

What's needed is real evidence, not like the silly old map that PC Trendle found in Dad's bookcase. "What's this 'ere then, Mr 'oldsworth?" And holding it up like it was very hot and burning his fingers, as detectives do when they don't want to smudge the fingerprints.

But what can I do? I don't know anyone who might be spying on Dad's aeroplane, even if he had one, and I can't tap Dad's phone because he hasn't got one of those either.

I'm thinking and thinking, lots and lots, until my head aches, then suddenly it comes to me in a flash and this flash says how the loft and the spiral stairs outside, hidden behind the bushes, might have something to do with the funny noises in the roof, not Mum's pipes cooling down at all.

"NOT THE PIPES AT ALL," I say out loud, before I can stop myself, suddenly stumbling on the answer... realizing it might be someone creeping up the stairs at night, no-one would know, going to the loft and sending their secret messages to Germany for Mr Hitler to use.

My silly Mum and Dad – why didn't they think of it? Dad should have realized this long ago and told PC Trendle and the sergeant and the sinister man with the collar turned up and hat turned down, so he was not locked up for days and days and fed on only bread and water and a bit of mouldy meat on a tin plate.

And he could have said how messages would be sent on a code machine, like they did in Biggles, with little dots and dashes turned into real words to be used by Hitler and his henchmen to bring us down. He could have said all this too. And saved himself the agony.

I'm going to do something about it, and I'm going to do it now. Not a moment to lose. I'm not even waiting for Ingie to come home and ask what she thinks. Whether she approves or not.

It's not easy though, waiting for Mum and Dad to come up to bed, it seems ages, then giving them another half hour at least, hoping they are sound asleep.

Now it's time to act, to put on my slippers and dressing gown, take a deep breath, no turning back now, a true Holdsworth. What on earth would Ingie say if I let Dad down just as I stumbled on the real reason behind his misery?

Tip-toeing along the landing to the creaky little door, gathering the candle and box of matches (put there in case one of Mr Hitler's bombs comes along and blows out our lights), opening the door, just like Ingie did, careful not to let it creak, then taking a few steps inside, the candle and its little pool of light my only company…

A narrow passageway opens up before me, a flat bit, then steps, stretching ahead in the blackness. One, two, three, perhaps more just outside my pool of light. Wooden panelling enclosing me on either side, and over my head, my flickering candle showing me the way. Then the passage doubling back and more steps, four, five, six, bringing me to another pokey little door… Just the other side must be our loft and the answer to those strange noises. The answer to all our problems.

I open it carefully and step into blackness – very frightening for a little boy who hates the dark – wishing Ingie was with me, or Bobby, even Podgy; I'm sure he would bluster in like a big roly-poly, full of laughter like it was all a big joke.

Slowly the door opens and I'm into a different world, like a big empty cavern, not that my little pool of light shows the ends or tops or sides, just the rough wooden floor, with dust and old bits of paper scattered about, and a musty smell like a church, even my soft padded slippers seeming to echo around this blackness.

But it's not crumbly and rotten like Mr Alfie said and Dad agreed. Not what I expected at all, where you could fall through into the room below, bashing your head on the fireplace and lying there, nearly dead, in a pool of blood.

In the middle, a table, and a machine like a typewriter, and papers ready to be typed... It's not a typewriter though, I've seen pictures of things like this, it's for transmitting the dots and dashes. I know it is – I recognize it. Evidence, real evidence; wait till I tell Dad and Dad tells the sinister man with the collar turned up and hat turned down, and the sergeant, and PC Trendle – they'll be up here like a flash, arresting the spy, the real spy, on the spiral stairs or nabbing him in the act of sending those deadly dots and dashes.

Then patting Dad on the back and enjoying one of Mum's cups of tea, sitting comfortably on Dad's sofa, making me a hero at school, impressing Bobby and making him my friend again and all because of what I'm doing now.

A quick look round for some piercing eyes peering at me from the blackness, ready to pounce, just outside my little pool of light. Spooks is what Smith Junior said they are – spooks in black places just like this and in our overgrown back garden at night and the churchyard of course. "Everyone knows about them... making you jump out of your skin...if you're lucky enough... " he said. "Most people just drop dead."

There're some papers under a clip: **MESSAGES TO BE SENT**, it says. Vital Information, right here before my eyes. I move closer still, careful not to let the wax drip and give the game away. **Secret Radio Transmitter. Group H. Station 19. On roof of building. Centre of Reading. Strategic bombing target.**

Then the discovery that stops me in my tracks: these notes, typed neatly, but with some words in pen, real ink like Dad's writing: **Send ASAP.** And then details of this target. **LOOK OUT**

FOR LANDMARKS. THE RIVER. THEN TOWN HALL AND CHURCH. TALL SPIRE. Is it Dad's writing? It looks just like it, neatly done, as he does at his bank, in things called ledgers. "No point in writing something down if you can't read it," he always says. Is Dad the spy after all? And his code, Mr Asap? Is that Dad's name, his spy name? Mr Percy Asap?

It's too terrible to think about...

What now? What on earth does a little boy do when he discovers his dad might be an enemy spy?

Hanged at dawn.

* * * * *

"Can I go, Mum?"

It's a sunny Saturday afternoon and I'm looking up at Mum. The Hoovering's been done and the polishing nearly finished. I'm thinking to myself this could be a good time to ask.

"Can I go and watch Cowman Dance milk his cows, Mum? He said I could. I won't get into any trouble, I promise."

Mum doesn't like the idea one bit but she can't think of a really good reason why I shouldn't go although she's trying hard. "It's very unfriendly in the village at the moment," Mum says. "And with things as they are it would be better to stay at home, it really would." Mum says I could do some of my scrapbook or invite the girls round to play.

I used to like the girls coming round to play, but not so much since Lydia has discovered kissing and wants to try it out on me, behind the garden shed, or in the broom cupboard, where no one could see. I didn't like it one bit. Biggles didn't go round kissing girls in the broom cupboard. He went to the pub with Algy and Ginger, then went home with his dog, like a proper person.

"I'll walk down the little lane at the back of the village hall, Mum. Then cut across Farmer Collins's field. No one will see... I'll be very safe."

Mum doesn't know the little lane, but she's still prepared to bet it's not safe, even on a sunny Saturday afternoon. "Who's going to come to your rescue if you're attacked?"

"Who's going to attack me, Mum?"

Mum thinks hard again. "There's the people in the village... What with your father still under suspicion... anything could happen. These nasty village people." And not just grown ups either.

Does Mum know about Smith Junior, I wonder. He can be a bit funny. Bobby calls him weird. Pushing little kids in the river makes you a bit weird, I suppose.

"Smith Junior, Mum?"

"What about him?"

"Nothing, Mum. But not Cowman Dance... he's a nice man... I know he won't mind."

I wish I could say how Cowman Dance had told me I can come down and watch the cows being milked in Dad's pub. "Any time," he said, leaning forwards with his stoop and flat cap. "You just come on down, boy," he said. "And you can 'elp if you likes." But I can't tell Mum where I've been when I was supposed to be safe at home, tucked up in bed with my mug of Horlicks and Dad on the corner of the bed reading Biggles, doing the *ratta-tatta-tats* and the roaring engines. Or asleep already, dreaming of Biggles bagging a few.

"Well, if your father says Cowman Dance is on our side, then Cowman Dance is on our side. Your father is rarely wrong about these things."

"Yippee! I can go then?"

"Just this once."

So here I am, trotting along the footpath across Farmer Collins's field, quickly, and humming *Run Rabbit, Run* to keep my spirits up and looking out for some nasty village people jumping out shouting "Your dad's an enemy spy!" Then a bit more *Run Rabbit, Run* till my breath's all gone and there's not much left for singing, or running, or anything.

There is a huge animal in the distance, I can see. Perhaps it's Farmer Collins's bull. With a swishing tail and horns all ready for some goring. But it's miles away and I've got my brightest red pullie on, so I'm safe.

We've seen it, Bobby and me, with the others, the farmer's huge bull with its stumpy little legs and a thick neck and angry red eyes. Bobby said it was only a mad person who would go near Farmer Collins's bull and only a mad person who couldn't run fast enough to escape and tell the tale. Minnow said it tossed you in the air and gave you a jolly good goring when you came back down again.

Smith Junior told me that bulls like red things. "Put on something red," he said, telling me as if he was giving me a special message. "I'm telling you just in case you don't know... you being a Townie."

So I'm wearing my red pullover especially, so I know I'll be okay. And the bull is a long way off although I think he's doing some stamping and it looks like a bit of snorting too.

"Coming out of his nose, that snorting," Minnow had said, looking a bit frightened.

"Nostrils," Smith Junior said, "nostrils," knowing lots about bulls as well as everything else.

"Don't worry about a bit of stamping and snorting," he told me. "As long as you're wearing something red, like I told you."

A bit more running and bit more singing and I'm across the field, over the wobbly old stile, skipping across the cloggy farm track and there's Farmer Collins's farm, just as Cowman Dance said, round the next corner, hiding behind a little clump of trees.

"Goodbye, Mr Bull," I call out. "See you on my way back."

Cowman Dance is getting his cows in from the fields, calling "Coo-ie, coo-ie...!" and then a longer "Cooo-ieeee....!" as I come through the gate into the farmyard full of tractors, and ploughs and piles of smelly stuff with a cloud of buzzy flies flying round on top. And he's leaning on his stick, from time to time, seeming to encourage them along: "Come on, me beauties..." He's talking to them like they are his children, scolding the last one. "You always be straggling along, Buttercup. Always be the slowest." Then catching sight of me and saying, "Well, if it isn't the bank manager's lad," calling me "Boy" in a friendly sort of way and saying, "'ow be you then, Boy?"

And me replying, "I've come to watch you milk your cows, Mr Dance. If you don't mind." But I don't say anything about my dad, and if I did say anything about my dad it wouldn't be about the night the policemen came to take him away.

Cowman Dance doesn't mind one bit. "You join in, Boy. What 'appened to your dad 'aven't got nothing to do with milking cows." And the village gossip, he says, "I don't 'ave no truck with that neither."

I walk along with him, giving some cooo-ieeees of my own, like he said, and wishing I had a stick like him. Even a little one would be nice.

I have only seen cows in picture books and in the fields at the back of our house and they seem small then, from a long way off, like toy cows. Now they're next to me, plodding along with their great big feet and their breath, like puffs of steam in the cold air, and their eyes are big and sad and their tails swishing. Shorthorns, he calls them, Cowman Dance, and these Shorthorns follow him into his cowshed and up onto a raised bit where they are milked with rubber pipes coming from the walls, high up, and fluffy bits of hay in the troughs in front of them to keep them happy.

He's explaining it to me because I'm only a Young Shaver, and how Young Shavers don't know about cows. "You being a Townie especially."

"That be the udder," he says, pointing to a thing like a hot water bottle hanging between the cows' legs, and the milk bursting to get out of things he calls teats. He seems to like telling me about these udders and these teats, calling me Boy, Young Shaver, and how he had wanted his own lad to follow in his footsteps and be a cowman, where satisfaction was guaranteed. But his lad had gone into a factory, on a production line, screwing things together, one after another… after another. "Where's the satisfaction in that, Boy?"

I say I don't like factories and watch him start working on his cows.

"And that be where the milk comes from, the teats."

He's sitting on his three-legged stool, his cap pressed into the cow's side, Buttercup, he calls her, washing the teats with his cloth and his soapy water from a bucket. "They gets the muck on 'em, you see, Boy, out in the fields. I 'as to wash 'em off so it don't get in the milk."

And I say "Ohh," with a lot to learn, a Young Shaver and a Townie that doesn't know you get muck on your teats.

And then he takes the pipes with four little rubber things, just like ice cream cones, and puts them on these teats, one by one. Then he's switching the machine on and standing back watching, satisfied, as it makes a funny pumping noise. *Hisss, phutt. Hisss, phut. Hisss, phut…*

And the cow, Buttercup, doesn't seem to mind, standing there, with her sad old eyes, eating some hay in time to the machine. *Hisss, phut. Hisss, phut. Hisss, phut…*

And then the milk goes in the tubes and up to a glass bowl where the pipes go into the wall. "See there, Boy, that's where it goes."

I can see the milk in little spurts, in this bowl, all white and frothy.

"Then into the chiller to get chilled ready for the churns that gets picked up for the London people to 'ave some milk on their breakfast tables next morning."

"Mr Jones used to bring our milk in London," I say. "In bottles with cream on top that Mum saved for my porridge, before I went off to school."

"Ahh, that too no doubt," he says. And then tells me I can help doing the milking if I like.

"You can 'elp washing off Betsy," he says. And I am thinking I might get trodden on by Betsy with her big feet and have to go home and tell Mum how I'd broken my promise not to get into any trouble, when he's saying Betsy wouldn't stand on anyone, not a young lad like me.

"She wouldn't 'urt a fly," he tells me, and how she is the gentlest cow he's ever known. And I bend down, and wash those funny things, these teats as he calls them, and then dry them off, carefully, like he did, and put the ice cream cones on just as I was told.

And then I stand back happy, like Mr Dance, the cowman. "Did I do right, Mr Dance?"

"You be a natural, Boy, I can tell," and says how I am a cowman in the making. "That is if you're not going to follow in your dad's footsteps and be another overdraft man… handing out the money."

166

"I was going to be an engine driver, Mr Dance. But I think I might have changed my mind now."

"Cowman is it?" Farmer Collins is standing in the doorway with his stubbly old face and battered old hat. "You'd like to be a cowman would you, lad?"

I say I would.

"I were just telling the boy 'e's a natural with the cows… Betsy anyway…"

Farmer Collins is on his way to the village in his farm truck with Max, his dog, and I can have a lift if I like. "Picking up the wife, Max and me. She's getting some things at the village shop, you see."

"Thank you," I say. "Mum will be waiting, I expect."

Farmer Collins always seemed nice but Dad said how he didn't even say hello in the Red Lion the last time he was in there, after Dad came back from being questioned by the policemen. But I climb up, next to Max in the cluttered old cab, filled with farm things, straw on the floor, and old bags and some of Mr Alfie's baler twine holding the seats together.

"There be space in 'ere, lad, if you can find it." And he pushes on the pedals with his big old feet and pulls on the gears with his rough old hands and says 'bugger' as we bump along like there's no air in his tyres.

"There were an 'ole in the fence over there," he says, pointing to a patch of land with piggies darting about. "The little blighters found it too." Then he says, "Pity about your dad", after he's told Max you shouldn't say 'bugger' in front of a young lad.

I'd like to tell him Dad is innocent, but don't think it would come out right after what was in our loft, so I just pat Max on the head trying to miss the wet bit on the end of his nose.

"Anyway," he says, "I'll be the first to bet the locals 'ave got it all wrong… I always knew 'e were a good man from the start."

Max looks up at me with his kind face and wet nose and agrees the people have got it all wrong.

"I think he's the best dad in the world," I say as we turn the corner, past the trees where we gather chestnuts with Auntie for Christmas, down the lane and onto the road and home where Mum's waiting.

"Soon be there," he says and toots his horn as a squirrel scampers across the road in front of us and vanishes in the woods. "Vermin," he tells the dog, and Max agrees about that too.

"German Shepherd dog until we went to war, now 'e's just a sheep dog," says Farmer Collins, "don't make sense, do it?" And we pull up with a crunch outside our front gate. "You're welcome any time, Master 'oldsworth, cowman in the making." And he smiles a big, warm smile with his stubbly old face and battered old hat and Max the dog on his way to the shops.

And I duck indoors so I'm not seen by the kids... and not by those who want to shout, "Your dad's an enemy spy..."

Mum's busy preparing one of our favourite pies, a treat for Saturday night, the recipe that Auntie gave her, with some meaty bits (if we are lucky) and lots of Dad's vegetables. There's white dusty stuff called flour everywhere and Auntie's recipe page pinned to the wall. "Now, let me see, cover and simmer for two and a half hours. Must get it in the oven soon." Mum's finished with her recipe then wants to know all about my adventures. 'Farmer's Boy,' she calls me, and asks what Farmer's Boy's been up to since he went off a few hours before.

"I milked Betsy, the cow, Mum, and she's very nice, and Farmer Collins brought me home in his truck with Max, his dog, and he's very nice too."

Mum's pie is on its way to the oven, not a minute to be wasted, cooked in time for Ingie coming home and our dinner tonight as a complete family gathered round the dinner table. And then I tell how I set off down the lane, across the field, and helped Cowman Dance bring his cows in with a cooo-ieee then tried a cooo-ieee of my own before I milked Betsy, the gentlest cow he's ever known. "She didn't stand on my toes once, Mum."

"Well, it wasn't too bad, then." Mum's thinking I was certain to be crushed under the wheels of a tractor or trampled underfoot by a herd of cows. Even having a haystack land on my head. Now she's saying how farming might not be such a bad thing because farm workers are exempted from the war so they can milk cows and drive tractors all day without being shot at once.

Daily Express
COOK'S CORNER

Recipe for Berkshire hotpot

These old country recipes are often fine ration-savers

This recipe for an unusual hotpot is often eaten in the country districts of Berkshire. You need: 1lb calves' sheep's liver, 1/2lb butter beans, 2 tablespoonfuls flour, 2 onions, 1 clove of garlic, 1 oz. dripping or margarine, 1 pint vegetable stock.

The day before you want this dish, put the beans to soak in warm water, to which you have added half a teaspoonful of bicarbonate of soda. Drain the water off the beans and put them in an earthenware casserole. Cover them with cold water and boil them till they are nearly, but not quite, tender.

Cut the liver into pieces measuring about two inches by half an inch thick, and wash and dry them. Melt the fat in the frying pan; roll the pieces of liver in flour and fry them till they are light brown. Remove the liver and put it in the casserole with the beans. Chop the onions and garlic finely and fry them in the fat, then put them in the casserole too.

Drop the remaining flour into the frying pan and add half a teacup of stock, stirring briskly. Pour the sauce over the contents of the casserole, add the rest of the stock, season with salt and pepper and bring to the boil. Cover the casserole and leave to simmer for two and a half hours.

What's yours?
5s. for readers' recipes.

Every district has its food specialties – recipes often have been handed down through families for years. Many of these are economical, using meats that are not rationed – liver, chitterlings, and kidneys and so on. If you know of a good recipe peculiar to your district, send it to us. FIVE SHILLINGS will be paid for each recipe published.

And when Dad walks in, he thinks it isn't a bad idea either.

"So you don't want to be an engine driver after all, Son?"

"Engine driver first, Dad. But if they've got enough, I'll be a farmer."

Then I tell Dad how Farmer Collins said I could go down to his farm any time I wanted. "He's very grateful for the overdraft you gave him... even if he didn't say hello when you walked in the pub last time." And I tell Dad how Farmer Collins might have been upset because his piggies had just got out. "There was a hole in his fence, you know, Dad."

And Dad says, "Hmmm…" And has a puff on his pipe.

I'm thinking how nice it will be to go to Farmer Collins's farm from time to time and escape the villagers and the kids, the nasty ones anyway, and how I'll do as I did before and take the path behind the recreation ground, keeping out of sight of everyone. Then across Farmer Collins's field. It only takes a few minutes, I think to myself. With my red pullie I know I'll be safe.

"You can count on it," was the last thing Smith Junior had said. And smiling when he said it.

Dad always looked forward to his Saturday and Sunday morning lie-ins. The days he didn't have to climb out of bed at six o'clock and trudge off to work. "To that blessed old bank of yours," Mum called it.

"My treat for the week," Dad said. "A nice lie in."

We'd giggle, Ingie and me, when we heard him say it. We couldn't believe dads had treats just like us kids.

With Mr Snitchwell, the manager, off with his sickness there's not so many of these treats, not Saturdays anyway. Even a thing called a rota doesn't help Dad, even though the bank people are supposed to take turns like at school when it comes to cleaning the blackboard for Miss Peabody.

"You're not going in next Saturday as well?" Mum says. "You'll end up with some of Mr Snitchwell's nerves if you don't look out... the hours you're working."

Mum's little moan won't make much difference, Dad says. We're all helping clear away the dishes for our cosy family evening together when Dad says it. After Mum's scrumptious pie. "You might as well throw that rota of yours out the window for all the good it does you."

"Wish I could," Dad says. "But there's important customers to be seen and I can't leave them to Mr Foggarty or Mr Fothergil. Mr Foggarty is a doddery old soul at the best of times and Mr Fothergil isn't senior enough to make decisions."

"No wonder they call you Overdraft Man," Ingie says.

Then there's the balancing to do, down to the last farthing. Dad says it is something that has to be done before they can go home. Dad explained this balancing to me one day, when it rained and he couldn't get into his garden.

"It's like this, Son. You have to count all the money going out of the bank..." Dad was using real pennies as examples, and some shiny sixpences.

"Like Farmer Collins's overdraft?" I asked.

"Yes, that's right, Son." It made me pleased I had thought of that.

"Then the money coming in. Some people put in their savings and others their wages." Dad said you have to take one from the other and what's left must balance out.

I replied "Oh" but didn't understand and Dad went back to waiting for the rain to stop and I went back to my scrapbook. Mum had found something to stick in my pages from the government on how you could make a fresh new jacket from an old coat. *Make Do and Mend,* they called it, with pictures and instructions and it looked good when I stuck it in.

"Well, our son's never going to be a bank manager," Dad told Mum. "And what a relief... I wouldn't wish that on my worst enemy." Dad called it a pestilence, his bank. "Trying to get Head Office to pass the overdraft applications for the farmers and Old Joe and the others." And then there were those who didn't trust Dad because of the questioning at the police station...

"It's time to put all that behind you, Father," Mum says. "It's Saturday evening and our family get-together. Try to find some nice music on your wireless... we'll all enjoy that."

"Or a play," says Dad. "You can't beat a good play on the BBC." The man reading the news is saying how the war is starting to turn our way... starting to get a bit better, in his posh voice, but Dad still wants to twiddle the knobs looking for some nice music... or a play, his favourite.

"Well, if it's going so well," Mum says, "why are we still having to make new coats from old?"

Timmy is on his warm spot by the fireplace, chasing mice in his dreams. Ingie says you can always tell because his whiskers twitch. Mum's taken up some knitting. Ingie is onto her latest book and Dad's still twiddling when, all of a sudden, there's a banging and crashing outside in our garden, a real rumpus Mum called it afterwards when we'd all got over the shock.

Now there's even more banging and some shouting too and whistles being blown and Dad's leaping out of his leather chair, scattering the Radio Times as he goes.

Mum's leaping to her feet too. The ball of wool bounces across the carpet and hits Timmy on the nose. "Goodness, gracious!" Mum's saying, in real amazement. "What on earth can that be?"

And there's shouting: "Stop, police!" And even louder, "STOP, POLICE!"

Now there're some other voices and one is saying, "IN THE

NAME OF THE LAW," and Dad, almost as amazed as Mum, says, "That's PC Trendle, if I'm not mistaken…"

It's all part of this rumpus from outside in the blackness. Lots more bangs and crashes and Ingie's sure our dustbin lid's been sent flying.

Then someone cries "Grab him!"

And PC Trendle's voice replying, "He's grabbed, Sir."

Dad's at the back door now. He can't wait to get it open.

We're all at his side. Ingie and me, who have got to stand back, and Mum who's got to stand back, but not as much.

And as Dad swings the door open, in floods lots of blackness and in the middle of this blackness is a pool of light and a little bunch of men with PC Trendle in the middle holding a man in a grip with one hand and a truncheon in a grip with the other.

"It's the artist!" I cry out. I recognise him straight away from what Mr Alfie said when we first arrived in the taxi. The man with the little white beard and letters after his name.

Ingie recognizes him too. She remembers what Mr Alfie said that first day, when we arrived. "Little Brother is right," Ingie is saying. "It's definitely him. There can be no question about it."

The sergeant with the moustache who did the ups and downs is there too, and the sinister man with the collar turned up and hat pulled down. An undercover man, it turns out, and in charge of the torch and the pool of light.

Now the grabbing has been done it's much quieter and PC Trendle wants to know if he can come in. "Excuse me, Perce… err… Mr 'oldsworth… I have some explaining to do… and it's best done indoors." He's very polite now, not like the last time we saw him in our lounge with Dad's map in his hand. "If you don't mind," he adds, still being polite.

"Yes," says the undercover man. "Constable Trendle, you can stay back and explain to the gentleman what's been going on," and then to the sergeant he says, "Take him away, Sergeant." Meaning the artist.

And the sergeant's saying, "Come with me, my man."

And off they go, the little group, taking the torch with them and there's a cry from the darkness: "Snuff out that light!"

It's Mr Pickering, our ARP officer, doing his duty by King and Country.

"It's all right, Mr Pickering," calls out the sergeant. "I'm arresting a miscreant and I need a pool of light to do it in."

PC Trendle is in our living-room now with the door shut behind him and Dad demanding an explanation. "What on earth has been going on in my back garden?" he asks and PC Trendle says how the artist has been alive all along, and sneaking back at night to transmit his messages on his transmitter in our attic. That's the theory, anyway.

"A deadly deed," he says to Dad, "up the spiral stairway."

"Well, that answers some questions. The strange noises, for a start," Dad says, seeming to be very relieved.

And Mum agrees, it all makes sense, and puts the kettle on, kettles seeming to be the thing you put on after some deadly deeds have been done up your spiral stairway. "You'll stay for a cup, PC Trendle?"

PC Trendle has his helmet off already, it's under his arm, saying how they have been suspicious about the artist all along, but how he could not let Dad in on the secret. "Much as I would have liked," he says, looking guilty about not telling Dad about the suspicions, all along.

"Well I never!" says Mum. But it doesn't make her happy. All this under Dad's nose and Dad being taken off to the station while Mum was getting sideways glances in the village and me getting messages on my desk at school. Mum's not happy about any of this.

Nor Dad. "A face like thunder," Mum says to Auntie the very next day, over a cup of tea and a chin-wag, telling Auntie all about the rumpus. "Father is not holding PC Trendle responsible: he has nothing against him: just those in authority."

Auntie's jaw is set. "This war," she says, showing how she does not approve of wars and how they make your jaw set. "See what it's done to an innocent family... putting you all under a cloud."

Then, after a long silence, in which nothing is said, Mum tells Auntie, "Well, if nothing else, we must look on the bright side, I suppose."

Auntie agrees. "It's the best possible Christmas present anyone could wish for," she says. This cloud being lifted.

And Mum agrees. The best possible Christmas present.

I lay awake in bed after all the excitement had died down. Ingie said her head was buzzing too.

The artist was accused… and Dad's name cleared. You couldn't ask for more. Now Dad can hold his head high again in his pub. And me, when I get in the classroom, or in the playground, I'll have something to tell Smith Junior if he starts saying things behind my back.

But I think to myself, in my head, is this the end of it? There's still the writing in the attic. Dad's writing, it looks just like it.

PC Trendle thinks Dad is clear, and so does the sergeant from Reading… even the sinister man with the collar turned up and hat turned down. And Farmer Collins and his dog, Max. They're sure the villagers got it all wrong too.

What's the truth? What I saw up there in our attic… Is there something I know that the others don't? Is Dad really a Nazi spy, Percy Asap?

It's still too terrible to think about.

Mum says I'm to be prepared for anything at school today, good or bad, she's not certain. "Chin up time again, Son. Just in case…" And the fresh white hanky in my top pocket.

Treasure Island is finished and Ben Gunn has popped out of the undergrowth for one last time and the buried treasure has been found too, and they've even sailed back home to a hero's welcome… "Happy Ever After," says Miss Peabody, looking round the class, and her looking stops when it gets to me. "And another Happy Ever After in our very midst," she's saying. "Young Master Holdsworth has some good news to tell, I do believe…"

And I'm going red, like I do, but not so red today because Miss Peabody says she is "sparing my blushes" and telling how my Dad isn't a German spy after all but an innocent victim in this "awful war" and how he was "caught up by events…"

And some of the other kids are saying they've heard already.

Hands are going up all round the class, and cries of "Miss, Miss, I knew that, didn't I." Especially those who were on my side, Bobby and Colin and pretty Lydia, and even Fatty, who sent me the message "Your dad's an enermie spy" all those weeks ago.

"There, children," says Miss Peabody, looking satisfied with herself, "what did I tell you?"

And I can't help looking satisfied myself. No need for Mum's chin up now. Not even the fresh white hanky tucked into my top pocket.

And when it gets to morning break I'm a bit like Ben Gunn, a hero, but without the whiskers, of course, and everyone's crowding round in the playground wanting to know what happened, especially some gory details, like did PC Trendle bash the artist over the head with his truncheon? And was there blood everywhere?

Everyone wants to be my friend now, not only Bobby and Colin, the postman's son, and Minnow the little lad, and pretty Lydia, but also the ones that didn't want to before. Even Smith Junior who says his dad could have been an undercover policeman and would have pounced long before last night.

But being like Ben Gunn can't last long with Headmaster Williams's bell calling us back to class and Miss Peabody soon onto our new book to take us up to Christmas. "*A Christmas Carol*," she announces with pride. "And does anyone know who wrote this famous story, children?" Smith Junior the Smartie does, and he also knows about the mean old man called Scrooge who thinks Christmas is a rotten old time until some ghosts come along and tell him it's not. Then it ends up with another Happy Ever After.

"What a nice way to bring our school year to an end," says Miss Peabody and sets off at a gallop: '*Marley was dead... there is no doubt whatever about that...*' And then how this dead man, Mr Marley, liked Christmas and had decided to give mean old Mr Scrooge a fright with his ghosts....

Now Mum's welcoming me home with warm slippers and buttered toast and wanting to know what happened at school and how did I get on. "What did teacher say... and the children? Was it good or bad? Did you need the fresh white hanky?"

And I'm saying how I have become a hero like Ben Gunn and how everyone crowded round in the playground and wondered if

I'd helped PC Trendle wrestle the artist to the ground, and did the sergeant put the cuffs on like they do in the pictures?

Then Dad's home from the bank with a good day behind him too, telling us how Miss Perriwinkle in accounts made cups of tea without him even having to ask, and a few biscuits appeared in front of him on a nice little saucer. "I fear I'm running a little low in sugar though, Mr Holdsworth. Just one spoonful, that's all I can afford."

And Dad's not minding one bit, Miss Perriwinkle running a little low. Dad thought it was nice to have them all talking to him again... Although he declined the biscuits, telling Miss Peabody how she deserved them herself after the sterling job she'd done helping with the balancing – "to the last farthing."

Now Dad says it's time to see what the mood is like in the Red Lion, time for the cap through the door business again, dipping his toe in the water. "You never know, it could be just the same as before and only my pint to talk to and nothing to lean against, let alone a comfy seat to rest on."

But Dad gets a bit of the hero's treatment, just like me. "Come and sit 'ere on this seat, Perce, I saved it special," says Old Joe. "The padded one." And he's even kept Dad's favourite beer mug – on the top shelf where none of the others can get it.

Cowman Dance is saying "I knew it wasn't you the moment I see that ghostly apparition in your back garden that misty old night."

And Farmer Collins and Mr Alfie are chummy again, and even Mr Blenkinsop and Mr Right-T-Ho (who made it seem that Dad had a bad smell before) have now changed, as if Dad has a nice smell again.

"Can't be too careful," says Mr Right-T-Ho to Dad. "In my position... behind the counter."

And Mr Blenkinsop has a position, too, making an excuse about not wanting enemy agents in his midst, the Home Guard, that might pass on the Platoon's secret plans to the German High Command.

"Well, you know who your friends are," Dad says on his return. "Fair weather friends," Dad calls them. "Some of them, anyway."

Mum is in agreement. "Thank goodness you won't have to go through all that again," she says. "It's been a real nightmare."

I just wish I could be as certain.

"Here is the 6 o'clock News from the BBC for December 7, 1941

Japan has launched a surprise attack on the American naval base at Pearl Harbor in Hawaii and has declared war on Britain and the United States.

The US president, Franklin D Roosevelt, has mobilized all his forces and is poised to declare war on Japan.

At 07.55 local time the first wave of between 50 and 150 planes struck the naval base causing fires and "untold damage" to the Pacific Fleet. Also attacked were the Wheeler and Hickman airfields. It is estimated that more than 180 aircraft have been destroyed and total casualties are more than 3,300. Three battleships were sunk, one more capsized and four more were damaged. While damage has been inflicted on three cruisers and three destroyers.

Of major significance, three aircraft carriers were at sea at the time of the attack and escaped undamaged.

Although the attack has shocked the American people, there is little doubt that it had been brewing for some years. Relations with the United States have deteriorated over a period of time but particularly since July, 1941, when America saw Japanese policies as a threat to stability in the region... this being especially so as a result of Japan persuading the French government that they could occupy Indo-China including air bases that were within flying distance of British interests in Malaya this action being met by the American and British governments freezing Japanese assets."

Chapter 12

In the Wrong Place at the Wrong Time

Mum said "What on earth have you been doing to your shoes?"

"A bit of walking, Mum."

"It looks more like a bit of climbing trees, and a bit of kicking footballs if you ask me."

"I might have done a bit of that too..."

Mum said the way I treated my shoes, I'd be better off in hob-nailed boots – like a miner. "Then you can kick as many footballs and climb as many trees as you like."

I didn't know miners climbed trees. I thought they went down holes in the ground. "I'd rather be an engine driver, Mum. Dad says I can. Or a farmer like Farmer Collins."

Mum was only joking. A silly joke, like Dad's silly jokes, she said. Being a miner with a black face and a light on the top of your head and these boots you can kick footballs in all day without getting told off.

"It's not just the cost of the shoes," Mum was saying, looking down unhappily at my school bests... "It's the clothes coupons as well. There's so few in our allowance. And what with your father and your sister needing smart clothes for work... I just don't know how I'm going to make ends meet."

Not to mention that awful shopping trip to Reading. Mum's face was set against that too. "The rush and the crowds. And the risk from the bombs."

"Oh, I think we're safe now," says the plump lady on the bus on the way in. The one with the racy red coat and little black dog with bright eyes like buttons. "It's safe now," she's telling Mum. "Hitler's bombers have given up... most of them anyway." And how it's worth the risk just to go to a place called the People's Pantry where you can get a dinner for next to nothing. A square meal, she calls it. "The government has set them up, these restaurants, you know. Sometimes there's even a few scraps left over for Dandy."

Dandy wags his tail at the sound of scraps.

Mum says "I hope you're right." About the bombing. "I wouldn't go by choice... it's just we've got this shopping to do." And Mum tells the lady how the coupons are nowhere near enough for a hard-working family like the Holdsworths. "I've been saving up since last summer for what we need today."

"Tell me about it," says the lady. "My Arthur's elbows 'ave come right through. I've patched 'im so many times the kids call 'im Mr Patchwork."

The bus is filling up. "Pangbourne next stop," says the ticket man. "Move right down please... and let them on that wants to get on." And then tells them to 'old very tightly when they are on.

"Perhaps you'd like to give up your seat for the lady with the little girl," Mum says.

The little girl smiles shyly. Her mum says, "You're very kind."

And I stand, in the crush, in the gangway, and the lady sits next to Mum on my warm patch and puts her empty shopping basket on her lap. "Haven't been in for ages," she says. "Not looking forward to it, not one bit... Reading... in the war..."

"It's value for money at the People's Panty," says the plump lady again. This square meal at a fair price. She tells everyone around her and seems very happy about it. "You can't do better," she says.

The bus is passing from villages to town, the fresh green fields giving way to dull grey houses. "Tilehurst," says the plump lady.

"Not that you'd know it with the signs taken down. To confuse Hitler, of course." And Tilehurst Station, that went long ago, she tells us.

"I didn't know Mr Hitler was coming by train," I whisper to Mum.

Mum says, "Anything's possible in this war."

Reading is very busy. Just like London when we lived there. Buses and cars and lorries and people rushing about. Mum thinks we'll get off in Broad Street. Nearest to the shops that count, she says.

The little girl with her Mum and empty shopping basket get off in Broad Street too. And the plump lady with Dandy the dog.

"'ave a good day," says the driver. And tells us not to be late for the return journey.

"Them that misses it, misses it," says the ticket man. Mum says he doesn't want to be caught in the Blackout.

"It could be size sevens, he's growing so fast," Mum tells the young girl in the shop and the young girl reaches for a thing called a shoe-horn and prises my feet into shiny new shoes on a little padded stool and sits on the padded bit and says, "Your little piggies 'aven't got no room to breathe, 'ave they? Shall we try the 'alf size up? I've just got one pair left."

And Mum tells her how Clarks are the best shoes in the world. "If the housekeeping stretches to them... and the coupons, of course."

The young girl tries the half size up and then says "They can breathe now, your little piggies, I can tell." And they can. Black lace-ups with patent leather uppers that are not for kicking footballs and if I come across a tree asking to be climbed, I'm to ignore it.

I stand up and plod about in my new shoes and look at them in a long, thin mirror. "I won't climb trees in these, Mum."

Mum says we'll take them and fishes in her purse for her three and sixpence and her coupons and says "Thank you very much," and we set off down Broad Street in the crush, with my new shoes in Mum's shopping bag, looking for a baking tin. "If the war hasn't taken them all."

The war hasn't taken them all, just the customers, in Woolworths, where Mum tries first. "Sorry, sold out," says the lady from behind the baking tin counter with no baking tins on it. "Try the ironmongers in the shopping arcade."

And we do, into the crowds again, and Mum's in luck, the last one... although there's a dent in the side. "Take it or leave it," says the man in a brown coat with a thing called indifference on his face and a pencil behind his ear, and Mum parts with more money and tells him that a smile costs nothing. And he says, "Don't you know there's a war on?"

And in this war where a smile costs nothing we're searching for Wellsteeds and Dad's new shirt. "Stay close, I don't want you lost in the crowd."

I've never been in a lift before but I am now and it zooms up and up until the man working the levers says "Third floor, Menswear."

And Mum asks, "Shirts?" then goes down the end to see Mr Brown and Mr Brown has just what Dad needs, size 16, with little holes for cuff-links that no proper dad would be seen dead without.

"You won't do better, not in wartime," says Mr Brown and shows Mum how the collar comes off when it wears out.

Mum says "Nothing but the best for my husband and the Midland Bank."

And smiling Mr Brown agrees. "In an official position, is he?" Then asks, "You run to a spare?"

And Mum can run to a spare. "The man who invented detachable collars deserves to be knighted."

It's time for tea and a snack. Not the People's Pantry though, Mum's taking a leaf out of Dad's book. "A bit of space and a touch of class in Lyons Tea Shop. That's where your father would go."

Down Friar Street and past the church with a statue of a lady Mum calls Old Queen Vic and a big grey building with a clock that turns out to be the town hall where the mayor lives.

"Mum, there's the lady with the little girl we saw on the bus this morning – they're going into the place where you get one of those square meals. And the plump lady with the little dog. He's nice, isn't he?"

There's a dull thud, miles away. And another closer. And a siren starts to wail... Mum clutches my hand and we're starting to run...

There's a whoosh and a roar.

I can recognize aeroplanes quicker than anyone I know. Just hearing the engines is enough. Smith Junior reckons he's better than me, but he's not. This is a German, I know it is. It's a Dornier, a Dornier bomber, you can't miss it. *Ratta-tatta-tat... ratta-tatta-tat.* And they're the machine guns. I know them too.

The whoosh and roar is over our heads now and it's a screaming noise. Mum's tugging my hand, the bag with my new shoes and Dad's shirt and the baking tin with a dent in the side. I catch a glimpse over my shoulder, just the one. There's two long cylinders tumbling from the screaming, roaring aeroplane. I can see the pilot too, his grim face and leather helmet. He's pulling the plane upwards, and the long cylinders keep on tumbling down...

B O O M! I am blown over. I can hardly breathe... like someone's sucked all the air out of my lungs. I can hardly see... like someone's thrown sand in my eyes. And I can hardly hear... like someone's ringing a million tiny bells in my ears...

And I can scarcely call out... "Mum, where's my mum...?"

I wake up in a big room with a smell you get at the doctor's and there are nurses wearing little white hats and starched aprons, some scurrying around, others leaning over the people in beds. And the people in the beds are making groaning noises. They are all children like me.

"Welcome to Royal Berkshire Hospital," a nurse is saying, close to my face, with a sponge and towel. She's wiping the dust from my eyes and tidying my hair. I am one of the lucky ones, she tells me, and how I escaped the bombing. "Lucky you" she says in her whisper. "Now I must clean you up for doctor." But she needs my name first. "So we know who we've got and who we haven't." Then she can finish the cleaning up.

My head is aching. I can't think. "Where's my mum?"

"I must have your name first – then we can find your mum."

I'm trying to think. My ears are still ringing. I can still hear those tiny bells. Millions of them. And I feel sick too.

"Take your time… you've had a shock… a big shock…"

I say my name like I do at school when teacher asks. Parrot fashion, teacher calls it. "Richard Michael Holdsworth. Seventh of the eleventh nineteen thirty two – " Parrot fashion – it's the only way I can remember it.

The nurse is writing it down and smiling. "Well, you haven't lost your memory then. Even with a bash on the head."

I want to know where Mum is. I remember we were shopping, we were going for our tea. "Then the bomber came," I say. "Mum had just bought my new shoes and Dad's shirt and a cake tin with a dent in it."

"No wonder, with what you've been through."

There's a doctor standing next to the nurse now. He's much younger than Dr McGilligan. But I know he is a proper doctor because he's got a white coat and one of those things hanging round his neck that doctors use to hear if your insides are working properly. With rubber tubes and a cold bit that goes on your chest. "How is this young lad then, nurse?"

"He seems fine, Doctor. Apart from concussion and a few cuts… that's what the ambulance men said when they brought him in. He was one of the lucky ones, apparently. He wasn't in the People's Pantry like the other poor souls."

"Can you help find my mum, Sir? We were running away from the bomber but I don't know what happened next."

The doctor has a worried look. He says he's sure she's somewhere safe… nurse will find her. "After she's finished here. We have lots of other patients and lots to do, you know…" First he wants to check me over. "To make sure the ambulance men didn't miss anything."

He puts the cold thing next to my chest, just like Dr McGilligan, and I say 'nointy-noin' and he smiles and shines a torch into my eyes and asks me if I can move my legs and my arms… then feels my neck and things. "That seems fine. No broken bones… just the cuts… and the concussion…" Then he takes my temperature, like Mum does, with the little glass tube under my tongue that you mustn't bite on because the stuff inside makes you die instantly, then says, "Only a bit above normal… just as I expected." And tells the nice nurse, "It's over to you now nurse…"

The nurse is wiping my arm now, my right arm, where I've got my cuts. Then the left one. It stings. "Just a few cuts and scratches and a bit of a bonk over your eye," she says and is going to get me dressed. Not putting on my clothes, it's patching me up, that's what getting dressed means in hospital. There's sticking plasters and the bandage round my head and some funny-smelling stuff. "Iodine," she calls it, and says how it will stop the infection getting in... where the bomber got me.

She's going off now, the nice nurse. "I'll just pop into the other wards to have a quick look for your mum." Then she's lost amongst all the others scurrying around.

"Copped it, they did. All of 'em." It's a boy from the next bed. He seems pleased about people copping it. "A German bomber – I saw it. And I saw the pilot too... he had an evil face... All Germans have evil faces... my dad says so."

I was there," I say. "With my mum. I saw him."

"Copped it with the bombs, I expect. They all copped it... I expect your mum did." He seems pleased about the bombs too.

I don't know what to say. He seems to know it all.

"And the machine guns," he says. "You should have heard the machine guns... there were millions of them. *Ratta-tat-tat... ratta-tat-tat...* I expect your mum copped the machine guns as well. And there was a little girl, with her mum. She's dead and so is a fat lady with a dog. She got it too... they all did."

I say perhaps they are safe and in the hospital somewhere. "Getting better."

"Nah, they're all dead. I heard the ambulance man say. I just got blown over. I'm only in 'ere for them to look at me. They calls it observation. Then I'm goin' 'ome to 'ave my tea."

The nurse is at my bedside again and she's smiling and saying she has good news. "Your mum is in the next ward, in Benyon Ward. I went down to see her. She's a bit bruised and she can't put any weight on her foot yet... she was trapped under a piece of masonry. But she'll be all right. And she sends her love."

"But Mum's all right?" I say. I can't believe it.

The kid in the next bed says, "I bet he's going to blub now... I can tell..."

The nice nurse is searching in her pocket. "Here, have my hanky?"

I think to myself everyone has to cry sometimes, even boys when their mums get bombed. Ingie would say it's alright... she'd make an excuse for me. She'd say she's read it in her story books somewhere.

I want to see Mum, but I can't.

"I'll take you down in the morning. Your mum's sleeping now and you should get some sleep too... you've had a big shock." And she's tucking me in like Mum does. "I'll puff up your pillows... make you comfy for the night."

I don't get much sleep even with puffed up pillows. People are making noises all night, like they are dying and nurses and doctors are scurrying about everywhere. They are having emergencies. The doctor that tried my bones and listened to my inside says it every now and again. "Emergency, nurse! Here... quickly... quickly! Another emergency," he says. I can hear him all through the night. And then the kids are taken off to be fixed, I see that too. They're lifted out of their beds, very gently, and wheeled away on trolleys.

"They are going to have bits cut off them, I bet," the nasty kid tells me. He says he's seen it at the pictures. "They always cut bits off you to keep you alive. On the operating table," he says. "The doctors have masks on their faces and coats made of rubber so they don't get blood all over them."

And then he turns over and goes to sleep and snores ever-so loud.

In the morning, when he wakes up, he says "I bet I was snoring."

And I say he was and he says his mum reckons he snores so loud he'd wake the dead.

I wish he'd have an emergency, I think to myself, and then they'd wheel him away.

Then, suddenly, Dad's standing next to me and Ingie too. Dad's saying things about "Brave soldier" and Ingie says she's counted the bandages.

"I can see three," she says. "On your arms and one big one across your head. Have you got any more, Little Brother... on your legs and other parts?"

And I say I haven't.

Dad says three is enough. "Brave soldier," he says again, and tells me how they have come in to take me home in Mr Alfie's taxi but Mum's staying because she can't walk properly from where the piece of masonry got her.

"It must have been dreadful," Ingie says. "For you two. With the sirens going and the bomber coming. Were you frightened?"

"I was a bit when I saw the bombs dropping," I say. "And, Dad, the bomber was so close I could see the pilot... even his face. And it was a Dornier, Dad. I know it was a Dornier, I'd seen them in my books."

Ingie says it wasn't on the wireless and it wasn't in the papers either. "The government doesn't like the people knowing or they might think the Germans are winning the war – then they would all panic."

Ingie says the first she heard about it was in her office. "They talked about nothing else... the bombing raid over Reading. "You'll have more than enough to fill your scrapbook, Little Brother."

"Not if they haven't written anything," I say. "I can't fill my scrapbook with something that's not there."

Dad says he got a call from the hospital, in his bank, right at the end of the day. Just before they balanced. Next of kin, they called Dad. That's when he knew about it. "Are you next of kin?" the man said. "My heart was in my mouth," Dad tells us when the man said he was from the hospital. "I have to tell you..." the man went on...

Dad thought the worst... then the man perked up a bit and said how Mum was only bruised and I had some concussion and cuts and how he could come in and take me home but Mum had to stay in for a bit longer. "A day or two at most."

"Mum can't stand up," I say. "Some masonry got her foot. The nice nurse said. But she didn't say which one."

Dad's going off to see Mum now. And Ingie's got to get me ready to come home. She's got to get my things from the nurse, the stuff

I had in my pockets, which are called personal possessions: my hanky, my penknife and the mint with a hole in the middle saved for a rainy day.

Ingie helps me into my clothes, pulling my pullover carefully over my head so it doesn't knock my bandages off, then she says I can have a suck of my sweetie with the hole in the middle because it's always a rainy day when you've been bombed. "Everyone knows that," she says.

We wave goodbye to the nice nurse and the horrid boy and go down to see Mum, and Mum is sitting up in bed with puffed up pillows, just like mine, and Mr Alfie is saying how lucky we are, Mum and me, escaping from the bomber. "Not many peoples get bombed and lives to tell the tale," says Mr Alfie from the end of the bed, with his weddings and funerals cap to show how important it is.

Mum gives me a big cuddle and says how the cut on my head nearly got my precious eye and how lucky I was and how God was smiling down on me and keeping me safe. But I might get a black eye from the cut… He wasn't smiling on that bit, my precious eye, because it would be going black in a few days just like being whacked in a boxing ring by a boxing man.

"Two treats, Mum," I say. And I tell how Ingie has let me have a suck of the sweetie, saved for a rainy day, and now I was going to get a black eye to show the kids at school.

Mum says "I thought I'd lost you when I woke up and no-one seemed to know where you were until the nurse came along."

"I lost you, too, Mum," I say. "And then the nurse said she'd found you and how you'd got a bad foot in Bunion Ward."

Mum says Benyon Ward.

And I say, "Oh." And Mum tells me we were in the same boat, which means you lose your loved one and don't know where they are. Except they're somewhere in the same boat you're in.

We are going home now, leaving Mum with her poorly foot to be looked after by the doctor and nice nurse. For a couple of days, when Mum should be able to walk again. Auntie is coming in to the Artist's House to look after us, Dad has made arrangements.

"What on earth would we do without her?" Mum says. And none of us know... Auntie's being a diamond again.

And Auntie says, "Goodness, gracious me!" when we come through the door, back from the hospital. Dad, Ingie and me. And Mr Alfie still wearing the weddings and funerals cap.

Auntie's "Goodness, gracious me" is for me, Brave Soldier, injured in the line of duty and not complaining one bit, Dad says. "A nasty cut on his right arm and another on his left, but not as much, and a bonk on the head."

"Don't forget my black eye, Dad. Mum says it'll come soon. Something to show the kids at school."

And Dad says the black eye as well. "Although I don't know it's something you should be showing off." Then Dad tells Auntie about Mum's foot and how she can't walk properly.

"Some masonry got her, Auntie," I say. "A bit from the town hall where the Mayor lives."

"You two were so lucky," says Auntie. "Some poor souls lost their lives... if you believe what they're saying in the village."

"That's what they said in the Red Lion last night," Mr Alfie says.

Auntie doesn't usually believe what they say in the Red Lion. But she doesn't mind this time. "If that's what they say... nearly 50 dead... you were so lucky, you and your mother."

"And more injured," Mr Alfie chips in. He's heard that too. "That's what they reckon," he says, "although they don't put it in the papers and on the wireless in case the people gets in a panic."

"I'm very happy to look after you while Mother's recovering," Auntie is saying. "The least I can do... those terrible bombs... "

And Dad says how he'll be going into the hospital each evening with Mr Alfie to make sure Mum's coming along all right. "For a day or two, perhaps," Dad says.

And Mr Alfie is happy to oblige. "I'll say tat-ta, then," he says, on his way out. "Until tomorrow when we goes in."

Headmaster Williams, in assembly, tells us he has an announcement to make, after he's ticked our names off in his book, then played *All Things Bright and Beautiful* on the piano. "There is one of us here that might not have been here at all..."

He is talking about me, I think, with my bandages and black eye that's on its way, if you believe Mum. "A very lucky boy indeed."

And Reverend Curd is there too, in assembly, to tell us how God saved Mum and me from the bomber and how this is proof – "if proof be needed" – that He looks after his flock, and that young Master Holdsworth is part of this flock and watched over by Him in moments of need, like when a German bomber comes your way.

And all the others are looking at me with my face going red (as it does) and not that worried about being in this flock but thinking to myself how I'd rather be in the playground showing the kids my bandages and telling them all about the bomber and how Mum and me were knocked over and ending up in hospital with nurses and puffed up pillows.

But the best bit is the black eye. "Mum says it will be here tomorrow," I say, in morning break, after sums.

Lydia says how her dad came home with a black eye once and her mum said, "What 'ave you been doin'? Not getting yourself in a fight, I 'ope."

"And Dad says he walked into a lamppost... in the dark... just round the corner."

Bobby says he expects black eyes take a bit longer to come if you get them when you've been bombed. "Stands to reason," he says.

Next morning when I look in the mirror, there it is, my black eye just like Mum promised and I race to school to show everyone. "It's here... it's here!"

Dad has written something for my scrapbook. He says he heard it on his wireless the night before, when I was in bed, and thought it would be useful. "It tells what the Americans are doing, Son. Tanks, and guns and aeroplanes, lots of them for the war effort, lots for us." He says it was from their President, who is the same as Mr Churchill only he is President Roosevelt. Dad wrote it down, what their President said, and I stick it in my scrapbook.

I hear Dad say to himself, "It's going to take years to pay off this war, pay back the Americans." I don't know what he means but he looks very gloomy.

"I am announcing to Congress tonight our policy for achieving overwhelming superiority in munitions, aircraft and ships for the Allies - a superiority so overwhelming that the Axis can never hope to catch up with it.

"Production for 1942 and 1943 will be as follows: Aircraft 60,000 this year and 125,000 next year. Tanks, 45,000 this year, 75,000 next year. Anti-aircraft guns, 20,000 this year, 35,000 next. Merchant ship building, 8,000,000 tons this year, 10,000,000 next.

"I hope these details will become common knowledge in Germany and Japan and give them a little idea of just what they accomplished in the attack on Pearl Harbor. It is our policy to convert every available plant and tool to war production, from the greatest plants to the smallest, from the huge automobile industry to the village machine-shop. The workers are standing ready to keep the wheels turning and the fires burning twenty-four hours a day and seven days a week. Civilian use of valuable materials would be cut and cut, and in many cases completely eliminated. More than one-half of the national income will be devoted to national defence in the coming year.

"In a word, the new policy I am announcing tonight meant an all-out war by individual and family effort in a united country..."

At the bottom, I write: January 6, 1942. In my best writing.

Chapter 13

The Americans Cometh

Colin Lamplin, the postman's son, tells us he's never seen so many tanks and trucks and guns in all his life and he's eleven and grown up. "Never, ever," he tells us. Nor Bobby, my friend, and he's grown up too. Nor Minnow, the little boy, nor Fatty. Not even Smith Junior, who's seen everything.

Bobby tells us they are Americans, all of them, he says. He went to the pictures in Reading a while ago on the back of his brother's motorbike, that's where he saw them. "They were on the news," he says, "the Pathe News. Just before the big picture."

We're all listening, really impressed.

"Lots of people cheered when they came on," he says. And he tells us they stamped their feet... most of them, anyway. "The Yanks are coming... the Yanks are coming!" And the girl who took the tickets said, "'andsome lot, aren't they?"

Colin knows the little trucks are Jeeps, even though he wasn't at the pictures. His dad told him. "Dad doesn't have to go to the pictures to know about Jeeps," he says.

They're here to win the war, Bobby reckons. "That's what the man said on the Pathe News, anyway." And Bobby knows the

Daily Express

Tuesday, January 27, 1942

U.S. ARMY LANDS IN ULSTER

SECRET JOURNEY: NOT TOLD WHERE THEY WERE GOING

American troops stand at the alert tonight on the battlefield of the British Isles. Within seven weeks of the U.S.A. declaring war on Germany they have taken their stations by the side of our soldiers and Allies as they did a quarter of a century ago.

They crossed the Atlantic without losing a single man, U.S. warships participating in the convoy. Well trained, well armed, and with the most modern weapons, they are, in the words of an officer, "all pepped up and roaring to go."

America, true to the word of President Roosevelt, has rushed to this country several thousand of her finest soldiers. Their proper title is "The United States Forces in the British Isles", but this has already been contracted to U.S.A.F.B.E.

It was dawn this morning when the ship that brought the Americans tied up by the quayside at a Northern Irish port. A few hoots on the sirens, the blowing of whistles and the shouts of the gay-hearted soldiers made it seem like the arrival of the great Trans-atlantic liners in the days of peace.

Raiders over

But it was war alright as the troops were landing German planes came over. Fighters went up and ground forces went into action, but no bombs were dropped.

Yet the arrival of the Americans had been kept so secret that at first only a few people were in the street as they marched along.

As the gangway of the troop ship was lowered the band of the Royal Ulster Rifles struck up "The Star Spangled Banner". The Americans sprang to attention and the flags of the two nations fluttered side by side. The British on the quayside saluted. Then came a burst of song from the troop-lined deck as they sang out "God Bless America" and "Home on the Range" followed by "There'll always be an England".

Major-General Russell Hartle, in Command, came down the gangway beaming with outstretched hand to greet the British representatives. He wore his steel helmet and the calf-high laced gaiters worn by all ranks. After him came Major-General James E Chaney, U.S. Commander-in-Chief, British Isles.

They were greeted by the Duke of Abercorn, Governor of Northern Ireland, Sir Archibald Sinclair, Air Minister, and Mr Andrews, Prime Minister of Northern Ireland.

194

> On behalf of Britain and the Government, Sir Archibald welcomed the troops. He said: – "From here, assuredly, you will sally forth with us to carry the war into the enemy's territory and free the oppressed people of Europe. Your safe arrival here is not an isolated manoeuvre but a part of the general disposition of our resources which is being made under the responsibility of your President and our Prime Minister."
>
> "It is a gloomy portent for Mr Hitler, and nor will its significance be lost on General Tojo. Your arrival reveals a part of one great plan to smash the Dictator Powers wherever they may be found."

tanks and trucks and guns are American because they have stars painted on the sides and the letters USA, which means America. "The man said that too."

We're on our way to school with satchels over our shoulders. I've got my school books in mine, the homework I did last night, and the dinner money Mum gives me every morning. Fatty Tucker is dragging his along behind him. "I 'avent got nuffink in mine," he tells us. "Didn't do no 'omework. Don't like jography..."

We're more interested in the American tanks and trucks and guns roaring through the village, past the post office and the butcher's, as we stand and stare, our mouths wide open, not quite believing what we are seeing. We all agree we haven't seen anything like this in our whole lives (even Smith Junior, which must be a world record, according to Bobby) and there's so much noise it makes our ears hurt.

Lydia, the evacuee girl, tells Lizzie not to be frightened. She cups her hands and puts her mouth close to Lizzie's ear and shouts, "You won't come to no 'arm if you keeps close to me!"

Then we wave to the Americans. Lizzie waves and Lydia waves (when she's not cupping her hands over Lizzie's ear) and one of the Americans riding in a tank waves back. "See, I told you they won't do you no 'arm!" she shouts cupping her hands over Lizzie's ear again.

They're going up the hill towards the Manor House and it's a bit quieter for a minute with some of Colin's little Jeeps coming past. "That was the tank commander," Colin shouts. "The one waving."

Colin knows about tank commanders too. His dad told him about them after he'd said about the Jeeps. Then more trucks and tanks roar past and it's getting really noisy again. We're waving and the Americans are waving and one throws a packet covered in waxy stuff and we dash into the road and fight to get it.

"Have some gum!" shouts the American with a big smile and white teeth and more packets come tumbling through the air and we rush and scramble and stuff our pockets with American gum. Mine's got 'Spearmint' on it.

Mr Blenkinsop, the butcher, comes rushing out of his shop. He's standing and staring just like us, and wiping his hands on his apron. "Keep back, you kids," he tells us. And Mr Right-T-Ho, he's come rushing out of the post office. He tells us to stand back too. "Get crushed under them wheels and you'll know it."

PC Trendle, the policeman, cycles up. "Noisy so-and-so's," he says over the roar and leans his bike against the big oak tree outside the post office, and birds scatter from the branches and fly around our heads. Smith Junior tells us they've been scared by the tanks.

"You don't say," says Bobby.

PC Trendle's taken the notebook from his top pocket and his new pencil. Smith Junior reckons he'll be writing it down. *8.30 in the morning... the Americans have arrived...* "He's got to make out a report," Smith Junior says. "All policemen have to make out reports when something like this happens."

A tank careers across the village green, scattering Farmer Collins's geese and sending them running and squawking, web feet flying, into the pond. The tank cuts up the ground leaving great track marks next to Mr Jiggins's sign, KEEP OFF THE GRASS.

"PC Trendle will put that in his report too," Smith Junior reckons.

Colin says "I bet they're going up to the mansion to make their camp."

His dad went up there the other day but there was a guard on the gate and he wouldn't let him in. He was an American and Colin's dad had to give him the letters and came back saying something was up. "My Dad always knows when something's up," he says. "As well as Jeeps... and tank commanders."

All us kids think it's the best thing that ever happened, having an American camp in our village, none of us can believe our luck. Except Smith Junior, the Smartie, who wants to get to school. "Come on, you lot," he says. "If we don't we'll be told off by Headmaster Williams. And get lines."

"Blinking school," says Fatty, kicking a stone. "Sums today. And jography." The stone bounces up the road, hits the dustbin outside Mrs Fuller's house and goes *ping*.

Bobby says we'd better. "We can see them on the way home. After school's finished."

Then another tank roars past. Followed by another. We're all waving and the tank commanders wave back. "Nice, aren't they?" says Lydia.

Fatty says they will have gone off to war by then. "After they've had their tea. I bet we miss them."

"Don't be daft," Bobby tells him. "Americans don't have tea."
"Everyone has tea," says Fatty.

"Well, they don't have tea in the pictures I saw in Reading. They have coffee and candy and played a game like rounders with gloves."

"Baseball," says Smith Junior, from miles in front of us, over his shoulder. "You lot coming or not?"

And we drag ourselves away, slowly, leaving the Americans to roar through the village as we traipse up the road to school, through the school gates into the playground where the sissy girls are skipping and the little kids playing on the swings.

Mr Williams the headmaster stands on the steps to the porch. He's ringing his bell and calling out "Come on, children... Late ones get a hundred lines... Persistent offenders get a clip round the ear."

"Told you," says Smith Junior. "About the lines."

"We've been watching the American soldiers, Sir," says Bobby, who doesn't mind talking to teachers, even Headmaster Williams, and even without putting his hand up first. "There's thousands of them, Sir, and they're going to help us win the war. My brother says they're the best in the world."

The bell stops ringing. Mr Williams looks down from the top step. "Is that so, Robert. But what about our brave men? Mr Potter

197

who went off to France and young Tom Ledbetter in the desert with Montgomery. Aren't they the best, then?"

"My brother said the Americans are the best, Sir. We saw them at the pictures in Reading, on the newsreel. He's got a motorbike now, you know."

We climb the red brick steps and push through the front door and line up for assembly and morning prayers, not concentrating one bit. Mr Williams plays *Onward Christian Soldiers* on the piano, and we sing the words, except Bobby and Colin, who have their own words, and Fatty who just la-la's. Then we're saying our prayers, with our eyes closed, and thanking God for looking after our mums and dads and sending us the Americans. Then going into class and doing Miss Peabody's sums.

"What's persistent?" says Fatty, in a whisper, as Miss Peabody turns her back, writing on the blackboard in big letters L O N G D I V I S I O N.

Bobby says they are the ones that get clipped round the ear most.

"They're the persistent ones," he says.

"Bobby's right," I tell him. "And offenders are people who steal things." I heard Dad say the people who stole money from the bank were offenders and how they went to prison.

Minnow says some get hung, in his whisper so only Bobby and me and Fatty can hear. The worst ones, he says. "Especially if they murder someone nice."

The sums aren't going very well today, Miss Peabody's Long Division. Even Smith Junior gets some wrong. "You lot keep putting me off," he says. Bobby tells us he can still hear the American tanks and Colin is sure there are lots of Jeeps. A paper dart flies round the room and Minnow (who is best at making darts) has to stand in the corner. "I don't know what's got into you today, children," says Miss Peabody.

Just when we are getting really fed up with long division, Mr Williams is standing in our doorway and saying to Miss Peabody, "I want all the children in assembly... straight away." A man is going to talk to us. "An address," says Mr Williams.

And the man is one of the Americans and we all get excited and go into the assembly room and some nudge the kid next to them, saying he is an important soldier, and others saying he's an important American soldier. Now Mr Williams is coming out of his study with the man looking very smart in his uniform, with stripes on his arm and some medals and carrying his hat, and Colin says he is a general. And each boy's looking at the one next to him and whispering excitedly, trying not to let Mr Williams hear, saying, "Yes, he *must* be a general."

And our general telling us he is Captain Swartz from the American base and how he and his men are guests in our country and how they want to be our friends and not be any trouble although, sometimes, there might be some disruption when they do things called manoeuvres. And Mr Williams tells us how we are to treat our American guests with respect and not to get in their way, especially when they are manoeuvring. "You wouldn't want to be accused of hindering the Americans in the war effort, now would you children?"

And we all nod and agree and lots of boys start saying how they wouldn't do any of this hindering, or get in their way, and heads are nodding all round assembly, and then we go back to our classroom where Miss Peabody gives us more long division, saying, "Now, where did we get to, children?" And us all groaning...

But at least the Americans have arrived. And Miss has forgotten about Minnow having to stand in the corner.

* * * * *

School can't end soon enough. Bobby says we're to run home as quickly as we can, have our tea, then meet on the village green so we can go straight up to see the Americans. And he says it's best if we don't tell our mums in case they say we can't. Colin and Minnow and Fatty and me and Bobby, of course. Smith Junior says he'll be busy with his homework. "Anyway, I've seen soldiers before," he says. But can't remember where.

Pretty Lydia with the pigtails wants to come too. And her little sister.

"You two won't keep up," says Colin, "we'll be running very fast." But Lydia says they will run as fast as Fatty, and Bobby lets them come as long as they don't get in the way of the Americans.

And we run across the field, through the long grass, with butterflies and bees all around us, to the mansion grounds, hanging onto the fence and our faces pressed against the wire so it leaves criss-cross marks on our cheeks and the Americans are everywhere, covering their tanks and guns with stuff that looks like Auntie's lace curtains. Only their lace stuff is painted with green and brown patches.

"Camouflage," said Bobby, who saw some of their lace stuff when they went to the pictures. "It's very good for hiding tanks and guns so the enemy doesn't know where to find them."

And there are lots of huts and each one is like a big 'C' upside down and they're putting all their stuff inside so the enemy can't find that either. Their helmets and the bags that go on their backs. "Their kit," says Colin, who knows what you call a bag you put on your back.

We are all very excited, even pretty Lydia and Lizzie, who is too little to understand, seeing the Americans everywhere with their tanks and trucks and loads of Jeeps tearing about their camp.

Some of the tanks are being lined up in rows. Lots of tanks and lots of rows.

"Look at that," says Fatty. Then says, "Wow!"

"There's our tank commander!" cries Bobby. "The one we saw this morning."

"We saw more than one," says Colin. "We saw lots."

"But he was the first one to wave."

Our tank commander sees us hanging onto the fence and comes over.

Some others do the same. Big American soldiers with heavy boots and their trousers tucked into their socks and tin helmets and some with stripes on their jackets.

"It's because I waved," says Colin.

"Don't you be frightened," Lydia tells Lizzie.

"Hey, you kids, haven't you seen an American soldier before?"

"Only at the pictures in Reading, Sir," says Bobby. "When my brother took me... you were very good."

"And we saw you this morning," says Colin. "I remember you looking out of your tank. I waved."

"Say, you're right, I remember, we were going up to our new base, through your little village. Pretty, isn't it?"

And they squat down and look straight into our faces, the tank commander who is tall and one that is not so tall with a nice smile and some others, and they are all very friendly. Me, Bobby, Colin, Minnow, Fatty and pretty Lydia, we think they look great. And Lizzie too, but she's too frightened to say anything to American soldiers.

"I'm Hank," says the tall one, "and I'm mighty pleased to meet you all."

And one with dark curly hair is Jimmy. "Jimmy Delaney," he says. "From Detroit and I'm pleased to meet you kids too."

And we tell them our names, including Fatty, who says he isn't really Fatty, but Martin. And Minnow says he isn't Minnow either – he's Arthur. And I say I am Richard and that's my real name but I don't tell them I got it from a German man who wrote music. I just say my dad's in the bank.

"We have kids like you back in the States. Good-looking kids," says Hank, our tank commander. "And who are these pretty little girls, then?"

"I'm Lydia, Sir," says Lydia, still with criss-cross marks on her cheeks. "I'm from London and this is my little sister who is shy and won't tell you her name but it's Lizzie, short for Elizabeth."

And another one is called John T and he has a sister like Lydia but a bit older. He's from West Virginia in a place called Charleston and she's called Charlene. "I just hated leaving her behind…"

Bobby says, "Your general came to see us at school. He said how you're going to win the war. As long as we don't get in your way when you're having a manoeuvre."

And they all laugh like Bobby's said something really funny.

Then they dig into their pockets and bring out sweets and other nice things that we can't get because Mr Hitler has sunk all our boats. And chewing gum, which he can't sink because we don't have chewing gum.

"That's Captain Swartz," says the tank commander. "Swartzie, to us. He's not a bad guy. Here, have some more candy and gum… Uncle Sam gives us plenty…"

"Wish I had an uncle like yours," says Lydia. "My uncle's a miserable old man and doesn't give us anything. He's Uncle Peter and we don't like him very much."

And the Americans all laugh again, with their white teeth and wide smiles. Then the Tank Commander says they had better get and do some work. "If Swatzie says we've got to do manoeuvres, we'd better get and do them, eh guys."

And they go off to do some. And we run home, all the way, through the long grass with butterflies and bees and warm sunshine then down the lane with the birds singing and our pockets packed with candy and gum from Uncle Sam.

It's easily the best day of my life.

"Mum, look what the American soldiers just gave me…"

Chapter 14

We're All on the Same Side

John T Millard is from Charleston, West Virginia. And Jimmy Delaney is from Detroit, an altogether different ball game, a big city where they make the automobiles, Dodge, Buick and his favourite, the Cadillac.

Neither has ventured more than a few miles from where they were born. Home-spun lads, they both say, although John and his family, Mom and Pop and sister Charlene, went on a vacation once, to New York City, in the summer of 1933, it was. They got back on the train after a couple of days, not liking it one bit.

No, both the Millards and the Delaneys have barely scratched the surface of the US of A, let alone the rest of the world in all their years, just nineteen birthdays in the case of John T, and one more for Jimmy.

Until now. Now they have signed up to fight this war, in the 101st Paratroop Division, the Screaming Eagles, to be precise, and find themselves walking down a leafy country lane in Bumblethorpe, in deepest Berkshire, and they have no idea what awaits them.

And the regulars in the Red Lion, PC Trendle, the roly-poly policeman, Mr Right-T-Ho from the village stores and my dad, deputy manager at the bank, with Old Joe, behind the bar, amongst the others, have no idea what awaits them either. One thing is certain: when John and Jimmy pass through the door, pushing past the blackout drape and ducking under the low beams, it will be the start of a totally new world for them. And never to be the same again.

Dad tells all this with relish, which means he is pleased with it, at breakfast next morning, with Mum and me listening just before Dad rushes off for his bus and the bank.

"I watched them come into the village, Dad," I say, "the Americans, in their tanks and Jeeps and trucks. There were hundreds of them. My best friend Bobby White says he has never seen such a big army, not even at the pictures."

"Those Americans," says Mum, rearranging the knives and forks and pulling the tea cosy tightly down over the tea pot.

Mum doesn't seem to approve. Not as much as Bobby and me, and all the other kids; when we watched them tearing into the village the day before, we thought they looked great. And not as much as Dad, who says we should give them the "benefit of the doubt", he'll wait and see. For the time being, anyway. Judging by John and Jimmy, anyway, and the others who came into the Red Lion the evening before. "They seem to be a nice bunch of lads," he tells Mum.

There was at least a dozen of them, apparently. "And I've never seen so many locals in there either," Dad said. "I got the impression they were giving the Americans the once over. It was the busiest I've ever known it, by far."

"Are they here to win the war, Dad?"

"Well, I think they could make a real difference, Son. A real difference."

Mum says, "They've made a real difference to Mr Jiggins already."

"Goddammit," Hank had said. If the Americans had been told once they had been told a hundred times, the English drive on the opposite side of the road, the left-hand side. It was the first and last thing his commanding officer instructed him. "Drive left, soldier, drive left."

And that's what he was doing. Best he could, it was such a narrow strip of road, the Little Piddlington road, Hank had seen nothing like it, not in the wide open spaces of Texas, anyway, as he led the 101st through the village and up to the mansion and their new base on the hill behind the village.

But it didn't allow for Mr Jiggins, who recognised no such distinction between left and right. "Left and right, they be all the same to me," said Mr Jiggins, as he free-wheeled down the hill with his broom handle balanced over his handlebars, only to meet Hank, his tank, and what seemed like a hundred-million invaders coming the other way.

It was an accident, Hank explained. And John T and Jimmy saying the same; it was the last thing they wanted... it really was... and the villagers listening in silence, PC Trendle, especially, pencil and notebook at the ready. And young Polly Bishop, too, behind the bar, brought in by Old Joe to help cope with the rush.

"These Americans be good for business," he had heard. "You'll need help if you're not to miss out, Joe."

"We're sure sorry for what happened... all of us guys," Hank said. And asked about Mr Jiggins in Battle Hospital in Reading, with his leg held high, on some sort of pulley contraption, and they even began filling a pint mug with loose change from their pockets to offset the damage done.

"We're guests in your country and to start by knocking one of your elder statesmen off his bike, first day, that's no way to win friends. We're all on the same side in this goddamn war, you know." But it was an accident, pure and simple. "How is the old guy, anyway?"

PC Trendle said: "I don't know about him being an elder statesman, he's the road sweeper, not the Lord Mayor," and laughed in a jolly sort of way and thought it safe to put the pencil away, in his top pocket, next to his whistle. "'ave no fear," he tells the Americans, "I'll bet our Mr Jiggins will be making a full recovery – 'e's as tough as old boots, you know."

"One boot, now," Mum said over breakfast, seeming not so convinced about the Americans invading our village.

And next evening John and Jimmy and all the others from the 101st – Hank especially – were cramming into the Red Lion to hear about Mr Jiggins and how he had been sitting up in bed taking his medicine and giving as good as he got.

"Now don't you fret," Polly was telling Hank, who she'd taken to calling Handsome Hank. "It weren't your fault." With her fulsome figure and high heels that had clickety-clacked all the way down Love Lane and past the post office and village green. And her mum and her younger brothers and sisters (all seven of them) waving her goodbye. "Now, don't you go making a spectacle of yourself," Mrs Bishop had said as Polly trotted off. "And keep yourself for young Tom when he gets back from the front and that fighting of 'is."

Soon Old Joe was emptying the pint mug and emptying it time and time again, the Americans turning out their pockets most evenings they walked in the door. And that was every evening.

"'ere," said Old Joe, holding up a shiny coin with an eagle on one side, and words he didn't recognise on the other. "What's this, then?"

"That's a quarter dollar," said John T proudly. "You see, some of us from over there are having a little trouble with your money over here... Your pound notes, for a start, and your shillings and your pence, they don't make sense. And what about this cute little thing with 12 sides to it..." John T's voice seemed to trail off...

"That be a thruppenny piece," Old Joe told him, with all the Americans crowding round listening and eager to learn. "And four of them thruppenny pieces make a shilling and 20 of them shillings make a pound. They be the King's legal tender," said Old Joe, as if he had a love for it.

Hank had a pocketful of the money Old Joe loved so much and he spread it out on the bar, shillings and pence, the lot. "Well, what's this shiny little fella here?" he said, holding up a sixpenny piece. "What does your King call this?"

And Old Joe told him. The penny next, 12 making a shilling, then the farthing, four in a penny. And the half-crown, which is two and a half shillings and the ten bob note which is ten shillings and also half a pound, Old Joe knew his money, he'd been counting it for years, just like my dad. Only in his case, he said, "never enough".

"He's got one hell of a memory, this King of yours," said Jimmy. "We just make do with dollars and cents."

Dad didn't mention the guinea, which is 21 shillings, one more than a pound, how racehorses and expensive cattle were valued. He thought it was complicated enough.

Hank took back his silver quarter dollar, saying it was good where he came from, in the States. And made as if to bite it with his pearly white teeth just to show it was not just shiny on the outside and soft on the inside.

"You're a card," Polly decided, perched on her heels, giving Handsome Hank her best smile.

And Old Joe told him how you don't have to eat our money. "We 'ave crisps when you gets peckish. And they comes with their own salt, in a little bag." Old Joe seemed as proud of a packet of Smiths crisps as if it was his own. "Tuppence," he said, "to you." And how they went down best with a pint of bitter. "I'll pull you another, Yank, if you wants," he said.

"It's Hank," said Hank.

"Hank, Yank. All the same to me," said Old Joe, and asked if he wanted this pint, or not.

And Hank did and more than that, he was going to treat everyone. "Drinks all round," he said with his wide smile and pearly white teeth. "And be quick about it, Landlord, we're all dying of thirst out here." And Old Joe obliged, helped by Polly, of course, lining them up. The last time he'd done that was when our King first sat on the throne. "Crowned," he said.

The Americans were making friends and they were not slow at doing it, Dad was the first to agree. "Yes, line 'em up," said Hank again. Dad had a pint. And Mr Right-T-Ho had a pint, and our police constable one, too.

"And what about pretty Polly?" said Hank. Polly had a shandy. "Anything stronger and I gets all tiddly," she told him. "And I'm not myself at all."

And Hank said, "Who are you, then, Polly?" in his Texan drawl and tilted his Paratrooper's cap and gave a wink in her direction.

And Polly giggled and said "That's for you to find out," and poured his before the others.

"You seem to be going to that pub a lot these nights," Mum said to Dad when he got back. "Since the Americans arrived..."

"They're here to help us win the war, Mother," Dad said. "To launch an attack on Fortress Europe..."

"From the Red Lion?" Mum enquired.

"From the Red Lion," Dad said. "I think I'll go up there again tomorrow night too... just to find out what they're up to..."

"Well, as you've asked, I'll have a ginger beer, thank you very much," I hear Reverend Curd say politely to Dad's landlord behind the bar at Dad's pub.

And I hear Old Joe say to the reverend, "You best 'ave something. I don't 'ave people in my pub that don't buy nothing. Even if they say they're come in 'ere with good news."

It is a Thursday and Dad and me are at his pub, and I am sitting quietly in my corner writing up my scrapbook while Dad has his medicine and Reverend Curd has his good news: an idea, a dance for the American soldiers, he tells them, and how it's going to be in the village hall just as soon as he can get some people to help organise it.

"The poor boys are miles from home," says the reverend with his wobbly head and skinny old bones balanced on the edge of Old Joe's padded stool. Everyone is listening to what he has to say about his dances, all the regulars, before the Americans walk in for their nightly drink. "It's intended to be a surprise," he says.

There's Mr Trendle, Mr Lamplin, and Mr Right-T-Ho from the village stores. And Mr Alfie has popped in. He says he's on his way to the Cat and Fiddle in Tufton Hardwick for the darts match. "I can give a lift to anyone who wants," he says. "A needle match," he calls it. " Anyone coming?"

And the reverend is saying to them all, "A dance seems such a nice way of showing how much we appreciate them coming over here and helping us in our hour of need." And he has another sip of his fizzy ginger beer. "I trust I can count on your support..." He's looking round and not seeming to know what sort of replies he's going to get. Then, seeing me in my little corner, saying how it can't be right. "Surely not," he says: "a young lad in a place of alcohol. Looks to me like we might be breaking the law somewhere round here."

"'e don't do no 'arm," says Old Joe sharply. "The bank manager's lad... now do 'e want 'elp with this dance, or not?"

Dad says, "Don't worry, I'll make sure he's in bed soon..."

"Well, I need help selling the tickets, that's the first thing to do," says the reverend, leaving me in peace. "And I really don't know where to get a band. One for the hot numbers... I believe that's what you call them these days, hot numbers..." And he tells them how the ladies from the Women's Institute have already offered to make the sandwiches while Miss Peabody has promised to take care of the bunting. "My assistant, you see... I don't know where I'd be without her."

Only Mr Scrimper doesn't seem happy. From my little cubby hole I watch as all the regulars start nodding their heads, saying what a good idea the dances are and how they would have thought of them if the reverend hadn't got there first. And PC Trendle says, "I can't see no problems.... long as there's no problems."

And my dad tells the reverend what a nice touch it is. "I'm sure the American soldiers will be very grateful."

But not Mr Scrimper. He's still shaking his head about the sandwiches. "The fillings, especially," he tells the reverend. "What with the Rationing, me and the missus 'aven't got enough for our needs – show me someone who 'ave – and now you're thinking of giving some to the Americans. Can't agree with that."

But Reverend Curd tells them he has the answer. "Me and Miss Peabody are going to cycle up to see the commander at the American base and ask for help." The reverend says how we all know the Americans have more than enough and how they're sure to be able to spare something for such a good cause. "It's fingers crossed time," he says. "I'll ask very nicely, of course."

Then he wonders about Bing Crosby. "For the music, that is," and everyone round the bar starts to get excited and chatter among themselves and Polly says, "You've got Bing Crosby coming – why didn't you say?" Then tells them how she loves his crooning. "I've got all his records, you know."

"Not Mr Crosby himself, silly. But someone like him... that's who we want... doing the songs of the day, The Wiffenpoof Song and the like. Not that I've ever met a Wiffenpoof you understand, but I'm sure he's very nice."

Everyone goes quiet thinking how they would have liked to hear Bing Crosby in our village hall until PC Trendle pipes up. "Well, if you're really stuck for a band, I can recommend Georgie Plowright and the Melody Four from over Yattendon way." PC Trendle's puffing up his chest and making himself a helpful policeman, then saying how he's got his telephone number in his back pocket. "If needs be," he says. "Young Georgie is no Bing Crosby, but what he lacks in style he more than makes up for in effort."

And Mr Lamplin tells them the same. "On a good day you can hear his vocals ringing out across the fields... if the wind's in the right direction, that is. On 'is tractor. A Fordson, I do believe."

"He'll need a lift home afterwards, of course," says PC Trendle. "Can't expect him to walk all the way back to Yattenden. Especially if you want the encores... I'm told he'll be rattling the rafters by the time God Save comes round."

"Seems just what we need, Constable. It's volume that counts in today's world. Wait 'till I tell Miss Peabody."

"Pleased to help," says PC Trendle, doing some scribbling in his notebook – "*MELODY FOUR, YATTENDON 205*" – and handing it to the reverend. "Give Georgie a call", and to himself he says "This new pencil's coming in handy these days."

Old Joe's promising to sell tickets from behind the bar and Mr Right-T-Ho will make up a little sign saying GET THEM HERE. "It'll go in the post office window first thing Monday morning, I promise." And Mr Alfie says he'll play his part too. "I'll run 'im home after... no charge, of course... if the encores be as good as you say."

"It's all coming together nicely," says the reverend. "I'm so glad I popped in. Your support has been invaluable..."

And at that moment the door swings open and a group of Americans push in, laughing and joking, ducking beneath the blackout drape and making straight for the bar. Polly's greeting them with a smile – the tall one especially, the one who led them into the village in his tank, Handsome Hank – and has their drinks lined up ready. "Poison," they're calling what my dad says is medicine. They're the soldiers that Bobby and me saw, with the other kids, on our way to school and afterwards when we went up to their camp. The soldier who said his name was John T is there, he's the little one, and Jimmy from the place where they make the cars. Then the tank driver, Hank, he's first in. And Walt, who they call Cowboy because he rides a horse on a ranch which is like a farm only bigger.

Hank is the one I remember especially. He gave us lots of sweets and gum from his Uncle Sam.

"Good news, men," says the reverend excitedly. "We're putting on a dance for you... with a real live band... and the singing tractor driver... lots of hot numbers. I'm told that's what you Americans like."

"A dance..." says Hank. "Well, that's a mighty fine gesture, Reverend. A live band too. And a real singer... what do you call him... the singing tractor driver? I don't believe we have them back home."

The little one with the smiley face, John T, is saying. "You've got it in one, Reverend: the hot numbers: that's what us guys want."

"This calls for drinks all round," says one of the others at the bar. One I haven't seen before. He's a bit older and he must be in charge because he has some stripes on his uniform. They're calling him Sarge.

"Wait 'till we tell the others back at base camp, Sarge." And they are all laughing together. "The hot numbers. Wild horses won't keep us away."

Now they're going to buy Reverend Curd something to drink... as a reward, they say. "What's your poison, Reverend?" says Hank. "A Bourbon on the rocks?"

Our reverend isn't having anything on the rocks. "I'm very happy on my padded stool, thank you... with my ginger beer."

And that makes them laugh even more.

Mr Right-T-Ho thinks they're the happiest bunch of soldiers he's seen in a long time. "Even with the threat of battle hanging over your heads."

And the sarge is saying how they'll worry about that when the time comes. "It's got to be done. There's no ducking our responsibilities."

"All of us together," John T reckons.

And Jimmy says how they're going to give Hitler a bloody nose. "Nothing less than he deserves."

Old Joe tells them that some of the men from the village have been fighting since it began. "Not 'alf way through," he says. Mr Potter and now young Tom in the desert. "Young Tom is Polly's intended... since school days... Some says wedding bells will be a-ringing the minute 'e gets back from fighting that Rommel."

And then they see me, in my corner. "Say, if it isn't one of the kids from the village... Didn't we see you yesterday... at the camp?"

And I'm nodding.

"Cat got your tongue?" says Hank.

"He hasn't, Sir," I say. "He's at home in front of the fire. But I'll have a squash, Mr Hank, please... if my dad says so."

And Dad does say so.

Then I show him my scrapbook. "I put all the war news in here, Sir. From my dad's wireless and his papers... And my dad gave me a list of how many tanks and guns you're going to make... from your President." And I say I'd like something about them, the soldiers, if possible...

Mr Hank promises he'll get a few words written down for me. "I bet one of our clever guys can knock something up for your scrapbook... if your dad says we're going to help win the war."

"Nice kids you got here," says the one with the smiley face, the one they call John T. "They're very polite," he says.

I think he's talking about me and Bobby and the others.

Dad looks pleased but now he thinks it's time to go home. "Mum will be back soon."

"The cat will be waiting," says Hank. And the Americans are all laughing again.

Mum and Dad are going to the dance. "It will be just like old times, Father," Mum says. "When we were courting... I hope you remember your steps."

And Ingie is going too, it's her first ever. "Lucky me going to the dance. Unlucky Little Brother, staying at home..."

"Soppy dance," I say.

"The Americans will be there..."

"I bet they're only going so Reverend Curd won't get upset. They'd rather be driving their tanks and Jeeps. And Hank's going to get something for my scrapbook. He's great."

Mum's lending Ingie one of her old dresses. Taken in and with extra bows to make it look pretty, she says. And the bottom bit raised. The hemline, Ingie says showing off with words you use when you are old enough to go to the dance.

"Anyway, I'd much rather stay at home reading Biggles. And doing my scrapbook. I bet Hank gets something great for it... he says he will."

Ingie is trying on lipstick.

"Ingie," I say, "do you know they're going to parachute onto the Germans? They're called Screaming Eagles. I think they're really brave, don't you?"

Ingie doesn't have much time for people parachuting onto the Germans. "You're daft," I say.

Mum says to Dad, "Our daughter should have a new dress, a proper one, that's what she deserves. All this Make Do and Mend, it's fine for Mr Churchill, he doesn't have to go to the dance."

"Well," says Dad, "when the war's over you can have all the clothes you want. Even if the Germans win."

"Heaven forbid," says Auntie, getting upset about the Germans winning. And Make Do and Mend. "Hadn't you better be off? I came over early so you wouldn't miss anything."

I bet they won't win, I say to myself. With the Screaming Eagles landing on the German soldiers, they won't stand a chance. "Will they, Dad?"

Dad thinks the Germans could be waiting ready.

"That wouldn't be fair."

"This dreadful war... it just goes on and on," Auntie says, still worried about the Americans coming and Making Do and Mending. "Hitler's got a lot to answer for," she says.

Babysitting is what it's called – Auntie coming over and plonking herself down on our sofa, looking after Timmy and me, while Mum and Dad and Ingie go off to the dance. Even if I'm not a baby, which I'm not. "There's nothing you can do about it, babysitting," Bobby says. "That's what grown-ups call it... and you've got to put up with it until you're out of short pants and can do some babysitting of your own... for another kid."

Fatty says he thought it meant sitting on a baby. Until Smith Junior, the Smartie, told him he was stupid.

Fatty said, "I was only joking. Everyone knows you can't sit on a baby."

Ingie's admiring herself in the mirror and Dad tells her, "You look very pretty."

"I wonder if anyone will want to dance with me. One of the handsome Americans, perhaps..."

Mum's sure they will. "They won't have met many girls as lovely as you."

Auntie says that one of them had been seen around the village with Miss Peabody, our teacher, and they were holding hands, which Auntie doesn't think is right. With Americans, anyway. "Apparently she went up to the American camp with Reverend Curd and that's where they met." It's the smiley one, Auntie says.

He's called John T, I say.

"Well, at least he's well-mannered and very cheerful."

Mum does one of her Hmmms... "Those Americans. Going out with our girls while our men are away fighting."

"Walking out." Auntie says that's what it's called and how it should be stopped along with holding hands. "And rumour has it that the tall one is seeing that Polly Bishop, the hussy, from Love Lane. And her promised to poor Tom the young village lad who's away fighting in the desert with that nice Mr Montgomery."

Auntie's dipping into her bag and coming out with a ball of wool and knitting needles. "Mittens..." she says. "For our soldiers on the front..." Then saying how we shouldn't really complain about the Americans coming over to help win the war. "You can't ever have enough... not Americans... mittens I mean."

Dad tells Mum to hurry up or they will miss the first dance. And Ingie's got to hurry up too.

I get a kiss on the cheek and Mum says, "You can stay up until we get back as long as you don't give Auntie any trouble. We'll tell you all about it when we come home."

"As if he would," says Auntie, her knitting needles going nineteen to the dozen. That's what Ingie calls it, like a chin-wag, only with knitting needles. "As if he would," Auntie says again. "Giving trouble."

Auntie's calls out for them to have a good time. But the door's closed already. "And don't be too late."

"When I'm older, Auntie, do you think I'll be able to go to the dance?"

Auntie thinks I will. "And give those Americans a run for their money..."

Auntie's in two minds. "It's way past your bedtime." That's Mind Number One. "On the other hand, your Mother did say you can stay up until they come home."

"Is that your Mind Number Two, Auntie?"

And Auntie says it is.

"I like that best."

"Well, you would, dear. But it's late and I'll be getting a telling off if you're not safely tucked up in bed."

We've been having a little chat and Auntie's enjoyed every minute of it. "You on your scrapbook and me doing my mittens. What a busy pair we've been."

Timmy stretches and yawns. He's asleep and missed everything.

"There's no-one to talk to in Rose Tree Cottage since you moved out. It's a bit lonely at times," Auntie says. "Just me and Fluff... and he doesn't say much."

"We've only been talking about school lessons, Auntie, and you showed me how to cast off."

"Well, it's nice..."

It's gone eleven and I've never been up this late and everything's exciting, even Auntie's casting off. I wouldn't like to be outside in the dark though, by myself, with the hootie old owl and some of Smith Junior's spooks... "These spooks," he said, "a known fact – all the villagers will tell you." And he said how they might be in our garden but the best ones were in the churchyard and how he'd show me one night when nobody was around... and the skeletons in the tombs. "There's lots of them... where they have broken open. It's terrific. Just don't fall in or you'll never get out again."

I didn't want to fall in.

"Don't tell your mum and dad though... it'll be our secret, you see."

I haven't decided yet. I'm not that keen on skeletons... and I can give spooks a big miss. But he did ask me specially and we're sort of friends now. Not best friends... that's Bobby. But we're friends.

Auntie says she's going to get my warm milk... then it's off to bed with me so I'll be missing Mum and Dad and Ingie coming home and saying all about the dance.

Then suddenly I'm saved and the latch on the door clicks open and in walks Mum and Dad and Ingie.

Auntie tells Mum, "No scolding necessary. He's just off to bed."

But Mum's not scolding. "It's been such a lovely evening, I'm sure we won't mind a little lateness."

Dad thinks it was too. "Very successful." And Ingie's head is still spinning, she has had such a good time.

I'm having my warm milk snug in my dressing gown, listening to what happened. Auntie and Mum and Ingie have treated themselves to tea and a biscuit while Dad's having a splash of Bells. "Well, it is a special occasion, isn't it?" Reverend Curd's dance. Then we hear all about it. Even Timmy's woken up.

"It was so successful," Mum says again, flopped down on the sofa and telling us she hasn't danced like that for years.

Auntie says how it sounds as if everyone enjoyed themselves. Mum and Ingie especially. "Quite flushed," Auntie says. "It must be the swirling around on the dance floor." Dad's not flushed. It seems dads don't swirl around dance floors.

"You did spend a lot of the time at the bar," Mum tells him.

Dad says he did *some* dancing. "The gentle ones... Remember my lumbago." Dad was chatting to the Americans about the war. "They said they would be going off soon..."

"I'm glad the Americans had a good time," Mum says. "It can't be easy being miles from home and their loved ones."

Ingie danced lots and lots, and all with the Americans, the village boys looking on and getting more jealous by the minute. "Ben taught me the new dance – the jitterbug. He's from New York, you know. That's where it came from, the jitterbug. He told me so."

Dad chatted to Hank and Jimmy and the one they call Sarge. "And then there was that nice young man from the barracks in Reading, Robert Bowen." Dad says how he got married just before sailing to England and into the war.

"New York, Little Brother, did you hear that?" Ingie seems very pleased with the place where the jitterbug comes from. "The Big Apple," she says, "that's what they call it." But doesn't know why. "It's the biggest city in the world and he's invited me to come and stay. When the war's over... meet his ma and pa..."

217

"What's a ma and pa, Ingie?"

"That's American for mum and dad," Ingie says. But has no idea why they don't call them mums and dads like we do. "Everything's different over there... it's very exciting, Ben said."

I say, "Ben this, and Ben that", and am about to get my ears boxed.

Mum says, "Guess who danced with the smiley one?

And Auntie can't. Then she can. "Not prim Miss Peabody...?"

"Nearly every dance... Including that silly jitterbug thing, throwing herself into it." Mum thinks she must be quite taken with him.

Dad says it won't be long before the Americans go off to war. "Robert said they were packing up lots of their equipment, but none of them knew where or when. The announcement would be made soon, he thought."

Dad asked lots of questions.

"It's top secret," they said.

"Did you see any spooks, Ingie? On the way home, I mean. Or in our garden?"

Ingie didn't. "Spooks? What are you talking about, Little Brother?"

"I just wondered," I say. "Jumping out on you..."

Chapter 15

Day of Reckoning

"I'm not frit of you… I've fought Rommel in the desert and it will take more than a Yank to frighten me here in my village."

It is young Tom returned home from the war and come straight round to the Red Lion with a score to settle and his fists raised like pictures I have seen of boxing men in olden days, with bare knuckles and the words underneath, 'The Noble Art of the Pugilist'. Tom is like one of these pugilists and all the men in the bar are keeping their distance, in a little circle, so these fists cannot reach them, and facing him is Hank the American who doesn't seem to want to be part of it.

"Come on," Tom is saying to Hank, "put 'em up…" And how he wants this score settled right now. "Big brave American that you are… "

Dad and me are keeping back too. "What's happening, Dad?" I ask. And Dad says how it is a bit of a disagreement between two men and how we should leave before anything nasty happens. But we don't because Dad hasn't finished his pint yet.

"Come on, Yank… Put 'em up!" some of the men in the bar are saying. "Or else we'll think you're frit, like young Tom says. You and your fine places you keep on about… them deep canyons and wide open spaces that can't be beat…"

But others seem to be siding with Hank and saying how they should stop all this silliness. Mr Blenkinsop, the butcher, is one and he says, "Forthwith" because he likes big words. And he says if there is going to be any fighting done it should be against Hitler and not amongst ourselves.

But old Mr Timms wants to see this score settled like young Tom says, here and now, not a minute longer. "Let 'em go at it," Mr Timms tells Mr Blenkinsop, the butcher. "Let's see some blood spilt."

And Old Joe says, "Not on my floor."

Polly says she is thinking of going weak at the knees, from behind the bar, the thought of blood, she says. And does a bit of screaming when Tom throws a practice punch in the direction of Hank, who she's been seeing while Tom was away and who's the cause of this disagreement.

According to Auntie, who seems to know these things.

But Hank still won't put his fists up. "No way," he's saying. And tells them, "It's just damned silly," in a pleading sort of voice. And all the other Americans gathered round him, his friends, John T and Jimmy, agreeing. "Can't we sort this like gentlemen – with a handshake? That's how you do it in these parts, isn't it?"

But the men in the bar are starting to make hissing sounds, saying how Hank must be frit, as young Tom says, a brave young lad who has fought Rommel in the desert while Hank has been walking out with his girl, childhood sweetheart, Polly Bishop from Love Lane.

Dad says how it could turn nasty, the way things are going. A brawl, Dad calls it, in Old Joe's pub with people getting injured, pint glasses knocked over and even the domino board sent flying. "Just as I was about to win," says Mr Alfie, who hasn't won in ages.

Old Mr Scrimper from the council houses doesn't want to see pints getting knocked over. "There's not enough to go round as it is," he says. "From what I can tell it's no better than the sandwich fillings."

"We'd best send a deputation to fetch the constable," says Mr Blenkinsop, still using long words. "Before this goes any further."

There is some pushing and shoving from those who want to see it go further, and those who don't, when suddenly Constable Trendle appears in the doorway with his truncheon and tells them, "Now then, now then… what's going on 'ere?" and declares how he won't stand for any nonsense on his patch.

Everyone is talking at once, a real hubbub is what Dad said to Mum when he described the scene afterwards, and PC Trendle calls for names and addresses and a hush while he writes them down. "I can't hear myself think," he says, keeping his helmet on even though he's indoors. And his truncheon at the ready.

This hush falls on the crowd, and everyone looks a bit guilty, especially young Tom and Hank, who have lots of explaining to do.

"I've a mind to make out a report to the chief constable," says PC Trendle, telling them how they should know better. "Whatever next?" he tells them and says again about his patch.

"Quite right too," says Old Joe. "Fighting in my front bar with paying customers likely to get themselves incapacitated."

Now PC Trendle wants handshakes all round and tells young Tom how he's a mind to tell his dad, who would surely give him a thick ear… "Punishment enough." And Hank too, "If you 'ave such things as thick ears in Texas."

Young Tom goes off, hang-dog Dad says, and there are mutterings all round the bar that the matter hasn't been resolved and still no handshakes exchanged from what Dad can tell.

"Learnt their lessons," says PC Trendle hopefully. "For the moment anyway." Then he's loosening the strap on his helmet, where it goes under his chin. "I think I'll 'ave my regular now, Joe, if you don't mind."

Hank and Jimmy and John T and the others have gone. Dad says how quiet the pub has become and we go home, down the lane, hoping Mum hasn't got there first.

Yes, it's very quiet in the village.

> ### "Here is the 9 o'clock News from the BBC for June 6, 1944
>
> *"D" Day has come. Allied troops were landed under strong naval and air cover on the coast of Normandy early this morning.*
>
> *The Prime Minister has told the Commons that the Commanding Officers have reported everything going to plan so far, with beach landings throughout the day and mass airborne landings successfully made behind enemy lines. More than four-thousand ships, with several thousand smaller craft, have crossed the Channel; and some eleven-thousand first-line aircraft can be drawn upon for the battle.*
>
> *The news was broken by General Eisenhower, Supreme Commander of the Allied Expeditionary Force, early this morning, saying that the goal was the liberation of Europe as part of a concerted united nations plan in conjunction with 'our great Russian allies.'*
>
> *BBC correspondents accompanied troops and reports have been coming in throughout the day.*
>
> *His Majesty the King will broadcast this evening."*

"Well, that's it," says Dad, standing tall, by our fireside. It looks like he might give his pipe a filling. "The beginning of the end, perhaps." Dad doesn't seem to know what else to say or do.

He has listened with Mum in silence while the man on the wireless said all about D-Day. It seemed very important.

Dad says eventually, "Well, it appears they've established a foothold. From what you can tell, anyway."

Mum says, "I wonder if it will mean the war will end any quicker."

"Unless our forces are driven back into the sea..."

"Is that where the American soldiers have gone, Dad? D-Day?"

Dad says, "That's where they've gone, Son. That's where they will be now… Fighting along with our men. No wonder the village is quiet."

"I hope they're safe," Mum says. "They seemed a nice bunch once you got to know them. The one that danced with our daughter, anyway. Ben someone…"

The man on Dad's wireless is saying how they had received the first report. From their correspondent… Dad says, "Shush… We must listen…"

"It's a first-hand story from a man who flew over to France in one of the planes towing the gliders. John Macadam, on his return, has just recorded this description of events.

'The big test came on the run-in. We had skirted the belt of flack to bring the glider exactly over the landing zone. It was a trying time for any aircraft, but for a tug and a glider linked by a strand of rope it looked like suicide. But I was glad to be there if only to see the pitch of mutual trust and regard those R.A.F. air crews and their glider boys of the Army have reached. There was no question of casting off and getting out of it. The skipper said: 'Glider pilot, are you all right? Okay? Great! Well, hold on, son, there's a lot of stuff flying around here but we'll get through it…'

Then the tough little glider sergeant pilot's voice: 'We're all right, carry on…' We entered cloud… We could see nothing. The skipper kept on talking to him and always the gruff little voice came back: 'Okay skipper.'

Then the rear-gunner yelled, 'The glider's hit.' The skipper said: 'Glider pilot, glider pilot, are you all right?' There was a short pause and then the voice came back again: 'All right, we're with you.'

> *The navigator all this time had been working with his maps and his rulers. He was shouting to the skipper and when we came out of the cloud and away from the flak, why there was the landing zone just as we had been studying on the maps for days and days beforehand.*
>
> *'Casting off,' said the little gruff voice and we could just hear a faint "Thanks skipper, and good luck…" And the tug lunged forward, free of the glider's weight. I looked down as we turned for home. There was nothing but blankness now… the glider swooshing down onto the target landing zone… occupied France…'*
>
> *That's the end of the report."*

"Come on, Son, let's get up to the Red Lion."

It is a Thursday and Mum has gone off to her game of bridge. "I'm sure I won't be able to concentrate this evening," Mum had said when she went out, half an hour earlier. "With everything else that's going on."

Dad says he can concentrate. "Come on, Son… Let's get up to the Red Lion. Let's not waste another minute."

"Some winding down, Dad?"

"That and the Americans arriving back from France, Son. They might be in the pub tonight. You never know. It would be nice to see them again, wouldn't it?"

Even the kids at school were excited when they heard the news. "The Yanks are back!" Colin, the postman's son, yelled to me and Bobby rushing across the playground, just before Mr Williams called us into assembly. "Dad saw them on his rounds this morning. He came home specially to tell Mum." Colin was very excited about it.

Bobby too. "It'll be great. Just like we had it before – gum and candy and everything."

It's a bright, sunny evening and Dad's striding along with me beside him, through our side gate and up the path to Dad's pub, me trying to keep up.

"They probably had a terrible time over in France," Dad says. "Some of them may have been injured. Some may still be in hospital." Dad takes a long time to say it, from our gate to the top of the lane. Then says, "Some might have been killed. Some of our friends, perhaps. You must be prepared, Son."

It's not a bit like it used to be when we climb the steps and through the door. A sombre mood, Dad calls it. Not like it used to be, not one little bit.

Dad's saying his "Good Evenings" as he always does, politely to Old Joe, and all those gathered round, and I go to my little corner and wait to hear what's being said about the Americans and what happened since they went off.

Then the Americans arrive. But not laughing and joking like before. They seem serious and sad. They seem to have become old men overnight.

And as the villagers see them the questions start: from Mr Blenkinsop, the butcher, and Mr Pickering our ARP officer, as well as Old Joe. And Mr Lamplin, the postman, Mr Right-T-Ho, from the post office, and Mr Alfie, not asking much. Farmer Collins by the fireplace with Cowman Dance calling me the bank manager's boy. "A cowman in the making," he always says when he sees me. All of them want to hear what happened when the Americans went off on D-Day.

And the Americans: some of our friends, just as Dad said. John T and Jimmy, and Hank, of course, and the man they call Cowboy (I think I heard them say his real name is Walt) and Joe from a place they call the East Coast. But I don't see the Sarge. And Ben's not there either, the one that showed Ingie the jitter-bug dance thing. And Hank's got his arm in a sling... just like Jeremy Ramsbottom when he fell out of a tree last year.

"Now, Polly," Old Joe's saying, "just because he's got himself an injury don't mean you've got to cluck round him like an old hen."

And Polly's saying, "'e's got an injury that needs treating and I know just the treatment… some of Mum's special injury ointment. Kills the germs deep down, you know."

Mr Alfie says how they can turn nasty. "Them wounds… Sceptic before you knows it."

Hank says, "Copped some shrapnel, Polly. That's all. It'll be on the mend before long. Just gotta bide my time."

"Well, I 'ope they bandaged you proper, that's all."

Hank is grateful for all the kind words. "It's great to be back with you guys." And the villagers all gather round hearing what happened, after they went off to fight on D-Day. And Jimmy and John T and the others saying the same. "It's just great to be back." They can't believe what they came through.

"It's been real tough," they say. "The flight over in those slow old C47's… the parachuting… the blackness…"

And the villagers want to hear how tough and aren't going to mention young Tom… the night he came in looking for a fight. They just want to know about the Americans and D-Day. The flight over… the parachuting… the blackness… everything… They want to hear *everything*.

"Don't forget those slow old C47's," says Jimmy. "I reckon I could run faster. Picked us off one-by-one, the Jerry anti-aircraft guns."

Dad tells the Americans we listened to the man on the wireless, a BBC war correspondent, safe in our living room. "He was in an aeroplane towing one of the gliders… Painted a graphic picture."

"Sure was bad," says Hank. "We parachuted into a hell hole, this graphic picture of yours. All of us, the 101st, the Screaming Eagles."

The men round the bar nod their heads. They heard it on the wireless too. "I wouldn't want that," says Old Mr Scrimper. He's never parachuted into a hell hole in his life…

John T says, "Then the flack, thick as stair rods. They didn't warn us about that at training camp."

Mr Scrimper hasn't come across any flack either. Thick as stair rods or not.

Hank says, "Some of our guys copped it before they even hit the ground."

"And some found themselves landing in water," John T says. "Up to their necks... the landing zone flooded and the kit dragging them down... No-one warned us about that either. "

"Weighs more than 150 lb, our kit," says Jimmy. "That sure takes some humping for a little guy like me."

"Then there was the fire fight, " John T tells us. "The Jerries gave us hell... Threw everything at us. The fire fight. That's what we call it."

"And that's when I caught it," says Hank. "Shell came over our heads... exploded right amongst our bunch. My fight was over."

"That's where the Sarge copped it too," John T tells us. "And Ben... it was right on them... they stood no chance..."

Men round the bar stare into their pints. There's nothing to say, no questions to ask now. They didn't know about flack... stair rods... darkness... men dragged down... And then to cop it all, in the fire fight...

"Ben and the Sarge caught the full force," says Hank. "I was lucky, a couple of feet either way and I'd be history... The shrapnel just got me in the shoulder..."

There is silence now. Old Joe is polishing a glass. I watch him put it back on the shelf then take it down again and polish it once more. "Perhaps you don't want to talk about it," he says eventually. "Only if it 'elps."

"Perhaps it does... perhaps it doesn't..." says Hank.

"It's war," says Mr Blenkinsop. He's the only one who wants to talk about war – to talk about what happens when men fight men. The Somme, that's where he fought and he's proud of it. "You'll have nightmares... You can be sure of that... for months after. Years perhaps..."

"Gee..." says Jimmy, "... years."

I'm sitting quietly in my corner. I've got my scrapbook open on my lap. I think it best not to say anything. My pictures from Dad's paper, Mum's Make Do and Mend instructions, Dad's news reports from his wireless...

Hank seems to cheer up, he catches sight of me in my corner. "Hey, the bank manager's kid... I promised I'd get something for your scrapbook... And I didn't let you down." He takes a piece of crumpled paper from his pocket.

I think it's okay to smile.

He tells me I look like the cat that's gotten all the cream. "One of the guys wrote it out... he went in on Omaha Beach. Robert Bowen from Brock Barracks in Reading." Mr Hank says he's documenting the war as he sees it. "And happy to do a copy for the bank manager's kid." But Mr Hank says it's no fairytale. "I wouldn't read that before you hit the sack or you'll get nightmares just like us."

And I get my piece of paper on the Americans for my scrapbook. "Thank you, Mr Hank. Wait till I show my friends at school."

"Don't thank me – thank Robert. He's the guy who wrote it out in hospital with me... he'd done his leg in... but he'll be okay. They say he'll be back long before I am."

"This is it men, let's go!" Lieutenant Aspinwall's voice rang out as he pushed along the crowded aisle. He had led the platoon with fervour since the day he had joined the company, a fair and compassionate man and a credit to the officer corps. We had just learned of the birth of his daughter and knew he was very happy about it. I thought he should have been company commander because he outclassed all the other officers in the company.

We filed up the companionway to the pitching deck, carrying our heavy loads like acrobats on a high wire. The Channel was covered by a mass of ships, fighting the choppy water, which made them bob like corks. Destroyers darted through the mass, firing shells at the shoreline whole LSTs and LCIs disgorged troops into smaller craft. They steamed shoreward towards a string of vehicles lying disabled in a line short of the beach. Some were afire spewing black smoke skyward. Airplanes shuttled back and forth with loads of bombs that they dropped somewhere inland. Warships farther out in the Channel hurled salvos of shells at the beaches. The noise was deafening, the spectacle inspiring...

As we waited on a side ramp for a smaller landing craft to pick us up, one of the Navy crewmen said, "If I was in your shoes I'd be shitting my pants." Grethel shot back, "What do you think's in mine?"

John Meadows, also expressed his feelings. "You got to be joking" he said to the crewman, "anything's better than this goddamn tub." He was one of the seasick ones.

An LCVP manned by two black coxswains eventually pulled alongside and we clumsily went down a scramble net to the deck below. I could see the other boats like ours, some with silver coloured barrage balloons tied to the superstructures by cables. As we pulled away Navy crewmen shouted words of encouragement and we joked about them missing all the fun. Our fears were disguised well. We were too proud to show them.

I was huddled in the front of the boat with Lt. Aspinwall, Tech. Sergeant O'Guin, Fred Grethal, Pappy Bates and John Meadows. Behind us were Bruno Primas and Jimmy Gilstrap, rifleman from my squad. Once we hit shore our lives would change in ways none of us could ever have imagined. Although we were not thinking it at the time, we were about to embark on an experience that would affect us forever. The gruesome nauseating signs of battlefields would haunt me for the rest of my life, shake my confidence and alter my personality.

The others in the bow of that boat with me would fare much worse. Aspinwall, Grethel and Meadows would be shot to death before it was over, Bates would die of injuries following a glider crack-up, and O'Guin would lose most of one leg when he was struck by a .50-caliber bullet from one of our own planes. Primus and Gilstrap would lose legs too, after stepping on Schumines. No wonder someone would tell me later, "You must have had an angel on your shoulder to have survived."

I looked at the shoreline. The beach seemed like a Chinese fire drill, disorganized squads of men straggling from the water and dashing for the openings in the seawall, stalled and burning vehicles abandoned in the surf, German shells shooting up geysers of sand and water as they landed with gigantic explosions, and dozens of small LCVP's just like ours landing more men on the beach. Dozens of large LSI's rolled with the waves, their landing nets crowded with struggling men.

We were still several hundred yards from the beach when a German shell came screaming our way, everyone involuntarily drawing his head into his shoulders and clutching at the sides of the boat. It dropped between our boat and the next with a crash, shrapnel shards whining over our heads. Suddenly, one of the Navy coxswains pitched forward on the boat, his brain pierced.

We passed a half-sunken LCVP, one of those that had unloaded the 4th Infantry Division earlier that morning. As we went by we noticed bodies trapped under the water or floating nearby, their faces white and staring. I looked away. Soon the boat turned off its engine and shuddered to a stop on the beach, lurching forward. The ramp then dropped with a great splash. Aspinwall looked sternly into my eyes, and said softly. "Let's kill some Germans, Sergeant." He then turned to the rest of the men in the boat and yelled, "Let's go, men. Keep together. No straggling."

The water seemed ice cold when I landed in it, right behind the platoon leader's heels. It was chest-deep and turbulent and the weight of my gear and the soaked uniform threatened to pull me down. I stumbled in shell holes. It was like trying to wade through a vat of glue. It seemed to take forever to reach the beach but I finally made it.

A shell screamed in, exploding close by in a great geyser of sand and shrieking shrapnel shards. Involuntarily I hit the sand, much too late to do any good. A loud voice from the base of the seawall shouted, "Get moving, goddammit! Get off the beach!" It was from one of the beachmasters.

I needed no urging, surging to my feet and taking off to where others seemed to be going, a 10ft-wide hole in the seawall. The sand was like sticky goo. A string of bodies lay in my path, one man with nothing but a bloody blob for a face, another looking as he were asleep. Along the base of the wall a deep ditch had been dug. It was filled with wounded and Navy men shouted for us to come through the broken seawall.

But the gap was partially blocked by a stalled tank with bodies around it. One lay in the depression in the sand as if it were of some protection. Company C streamed through, leading the battalion over the causeway that led inland. On either side of the causeway were flat stretches of salt marsh grass, wire obstacles and what looked like bayberry bushes. Tanks and trucks were stalled along the road, their occupants huddled in ditches because of the incoming shellfire. I could see high poles with teller mines attached to the top, anti-glider defenses, and signs saying "Achtung! Minen!" An American lay prone in ankle-deep wire, both hands missing, the middle of his body a bloody hole and a string of entrails strung out behind him...

Chapter 16

Will the Real Winner Please Stand Up...

Hank is standing there and young Tom is standing there and Polly from Love Lane. She is standing there, facing them, a hanky clutched in her hand. It looks like there have been some tears.

Young Tom has said his bit and Hank has too. They are waiting for Polly to make a decision, say her bit. So Dad says.

There is silence around the bar. From the men, the locals, and the Americans.

Old Joe behind the bar and Mr Alfie at the dartboard, saying nothing. No darts being darted. And Mr Blenkinsop and Mr Right-T-Ho at the shove halfpenny board. Nothing being shoved.

"You could cut the atmosphere with a knife," Dad says.

There is some shuffling of feet and polite coughing.

Cowman Dance finds a reason to go out and see his cows. "'aven't seen them for all of fifteen minutes," he says, "on the way up 'ere." Farmer Collins says the same. "Got to check 'em regular," he says, and they stumble out of the pub in a hurry. It seems they don't like Dad's atmosphere.

"Well, Polly," says Old Joe eventually, "You best say your bit, make your decision. Then we can move on, there's beer to be served."

And Dad whispers, "Polly has got to choose between Hank the American and young Tom from the village. She can't make up her mind."

Miss Peabody has.

Mr Lamplin, the postman, told them the evening before. "I heard her say how she has chosen to stay in the village. Not to go with the Yank after all." It was when he came in for his evening pint that he overheard them. "She seemed very upset," he said. "And the Yank were consoling her with fine words… " In the porch. "I thought you were my gal," he told her in his American drawl.

Mr Lamplin looked satisfied. Being first to bring the news to the locals.

"And she wouldn't come in," he said. "She was saying how she'd never been in a pub in her life and wasn't going to start now."

"I've made up my mind, John T," she told him. "I'm very sorry but the village needs me… and the children."

"Well, life goes on," said John T, resigned. "I was hoping to take my English rose back to my home town… Charleston in deepest West Virginia."

The men round the bar were nodding their heads. Bumblethorpe might not be as glamorous as deepest West Virginia. But it's where her heart lay.

And Miss told us in school too, when Bobby asked. English composition, first lesson after break. "Are you going to leave us, Miss?" She seemed to take a deep breath as if making a really big decision. "We'll miss you, Miss."

"It's easy, English Composition," Smith Junior whispered to me. "I can do that standing on my head… I'll write about village history, the church and the churchyard, who's buried there, the tomb stones… it'll be great."

Miss Peabody took another deep breath. "Well, I expect you'll find out sooner or later, children, so I might as well tell you now," she told us all. "I've decided to stay here in Bumblethorpe. To stay with you, I feel you're my own, my family."

Old Joe says again. "Well, Polly, the teacher 'ave decided. What about you? Is it to be young Tom… standing there all sad and forlorn, your childhood sweetheart, or 'andsome Hank from Texas and 'is Wide Open Spaces? We wants to know."

Polly looks down... then up again, seeming to be determined to say her bit. That's what they want.

"I'm sorry, Tom, she says. "You've been my love for as long as I can remember... since the time you carved my name on the wall in the playground, two hearts and an arrow joining us together."

Everyone in the village knows that. Common knowledge, Mr Alfie called it. "Tom loves Polly" etched with the pen knife, the one he got on his thirteenth birthday.

"A girl couldn't ask for more," she admits.

Polly is staring at the floor again. The men round the bar shuffling their feet... some polite coughing. It must be Dad's atmosphere again. There's no darts being darted nor halfpennies being shoved... Even though Mr Alfie and old Mr Timms are locked in combat on the darts and Mr Blenkinsop and Mr Right-T-Ho on the shove halfpennies.

"It's Handsome Hank I love now..." she says, swayed by his injury, the one that could have made him history, a couple of feet either way, not the Wide Open Spaces nor the Grand Canyon that's so deep you can't see the bottom. "He needs my love," she says. "And Mum's injury ointment... It was 'anded down from Great Grand-ma, you know. Rose petals, clover seed and touch of elderberry... all mashed together. It cures all ills."

"It's going sceptic that's done it," Mr Alfie tells them, from the dart board, in a knowing sort of way. "Them injuries turn nasty before you knows it." He says he only needs a double top for victory. "One dart, Mr Timms, and you owes me a pint."

Young Tom can't believe it. He's etched Polly's name, two hearts and the arrow by the swings... "I done my best," he tells them.

There would be tears, but he's a man now... The soldiering has given him that. Mr Blenkinsop is an authority, he insists. "Soldiers don't burst into tears... except when you drop a cannon ball on their toes."

Old Joe's agreeing. "Makes a man of you, the Army", and how there's sympathy for him, young Tom, around the bar. "I'm sure I'm speaking for everyone 'ere."

And he is, Hank included. "Gee, I'm sorry, Tom. Taking your girl. But you must come and visit us... I'll show you the Wide Open Spaces and the Grand Canyon. That's worth the trip alone... "

Young Tom is standing there. There's nothing to say, he says. He doesn't want to see the Wide Open Spaces and he couldn't care two hoots for the Grand Canyon no matter how deep it is. Bumblethorpe is good enough for him, in his soldier's uniform, freshly ironed by Mum and his Army boots... a size too big... "I've nothing to say," he says again. "Except I'll never forget you, Polly... That I won't."

Handsome Hank is silenced too. Just a few words. The shoulder is bad... worse than first thought. He's returning home for treatment. "They say I could lose the arm if it's not caught in time." He's not fit for fighting, that's for sure. While his comrades mop up the last of Hitler's resistance, he's being shipped back to the States, the next available plane.

"I'll send for you, Polly... We'll be wed as soon as arrangements can be made."

Young Tom's dad, the squire's foreman, is standing in the doorway. Dan Ledbetter, he's heard it all. "Come on, Son, let's get home, there's things to do, there's work on the estate, alongside me."

They all nod their heads, all of them round the bar. "The squire's a good man," they say, "a good governor... you can't do better."

Young Tom's dad is sure as sure can be. Tom has a future once all this is over... "Come on, Son. Your mother's got your tea on the table... Don't keep her waiting."

"The war's as good as over, Mother. Do you hear me, the war's as good as over..."

Dad has swept into the kitchen... his coat thrown across the kitchen table, his hat sent skimming towards the hat peg.

Mum says, "Have you been drinking, Father?"

Mum gets a kiss instead of an answer, and a great big hug... "Time for a bit of gay abandon, Mother. The war in Europe is virtually over. It's on the news." And another kiss.

"Two in one day," Mum says.

"Yes, there's little resistance from the Germans now. Even Hitler's reported to be dead." Dad's saying how everyone out in the streets is elated.

Mum is on one of her steak and kidney pies, dicing the vegetables. She's in the kitchen and not quite as elated. "Who won then?" Mum asks, flattening the pastry.

Dad looks surprised. "I take it that's a rhetorical question, Mother?"

"I don't call that much of a victory. Fifty-two million dead. And I still can't get a single kidney for my pie."

The American Fifth Army and the British under General Montgomery have swept all before them since D-Day... through France and into Germany. They've reached the Rhine. Dad says they can relax now. The hard work's been done... "Our allies, the

Russians, are rolling into Berlin as I speak. The powers to be in London and Washington seem to think it's the right policy."

Dad thinks this doesn't bode well for the future... but it's a fact of life... nothing he can do about it now. "Hitler warned about the Russians... the Communists. Only history will tell whether he was right or wrong."

Dad gives Mum another big hug. "But the war's over, Mother. That's the main thing. It's over..."

Mum says, "Now look what you've done. You've got flour all over your best suit."

* * * * *

"I'm going to tell my friends," I say.

"Don't be long."

I slip out of the back door and across the field. Smith Junior said he wanted to show me something in the churchyard, it's my chance while Mum and Dad are celebrating. Perhaps those spooks. Or skeletons. Not that I'm much keen on either. But he did ask specially, and we're friends these days. Sort of, anyway. He lets me call him Smithy.

You can't come to any harm with friends...

"Glad you came" he says. "I've got things to show you." He's heading towards the back of the cemetery, amongst the really old tombstones. What looks like slabs of stone, made years ago, and crosses with mossy stuff and writing about old people who died before any of us were born. "Look, down there," he says. "Can you see?" He's putting his hand on my shoulder and wants me to lean forward and look down into the gap where the slabs have come apart.

I don't think I will. Another day, perhaps. It's very dark and spooky down there and I wouldn't want to fall in.

"Smithy," I say. "The time you told me about wearing something red for Farmer Collins's bull... Cowman Dance says bulls hate red."

He's looking at me with that smile again.

The End

List of Illustrations

	Ref. No.	Page
Come into the Factories © Imperial War Museum	PP 00289	Front cover
Dig for Victory © Imperial War Museum	PP 00287	Front cover
101st Airborne Screaming Eagles © Terrance Collins		Front cover
Supermarine Spitfire © The Daily Telegraph		Front cover
Bumblethorpe village © Richard Holdsworth		x
Peace in our time © Imperial War Museum	D 2239	12
Hitler's Storm Troopers © Imperial War Museum		21
Gas masks – be prepared © Imperial War Museum	HU 36137	27
Your Britain © Imperial War Museum	MH 13415	36
War is Declared © Imperial War Museum	HU 36171	47

	Ref. No.	Page
Look before you Sleep © Imperial War Museum	PST 0753	51
The Artist's House © Richard Holdsworth		98
Phoney War © The Daily Mail		102
Use One Not Two © National Archives	INF 2/70	113
Dig for Victory © Imperial War Museum	PP 00287	116
Eggs, Bacon, Fat © National Archives	INF 2/70	120
Scrap steel © Imperial War Museum	CP 5529	129
Winston Churchill © Imperial War Museum	HU 55521	135
The Blitz © Imperial War Museum	AP 725 OD	146
New from old © National Archives	INF 2/98	170
GI's on manoeuvres © Imperial War Museum	NUT 20820	202
GI's at play © Imperial War Museum	EA 9010	213
Omaha Beach – June 6, 1944		231

About the Author

Richard Holdsworth has enjoyed several lives!

Hardly an exemplary scholar, Richard scraped through his 11 plus but came top at milking cows and driving tractors for the Squire in Bumblethorpe - the village at the centre of Six Spoons of Sugar. At 20, with Agricultural College behind him, Richard worked his passage on a cargo ship taking stud cattle to Australia. In the Outback he worked on Keynton Station, brought out the Supreme Champion bull at the Royal Adelaide Show, became a journalist with the *Stock and Station Journal*, and later joined the Melbourne *Herald and Weekly Times* where he met Heather, his Australian wife to be.

What happened next?

Back in Britain they built their own Volkswagen camper, explored every nook and cranny around Europe, borrowed £150 from the Midland Bank, and set up a fledgling business building campers that eventually took top honours and sold worldwide. After selling the business in 1995, Richard went on to design and consult for major UK motorhome manufacturers and he established a leading

German manufacturer on the UK market. In between times he preserved one of the last locomotives built in the GWR Swindon works.

World War II and Six Spoons of Sugar.

Richard wanted to tell the story of the war through the eyes of a little boy snatched from the leafy suburbs of South London to a country village in the depths of Berkshire. Named after his Father's hero, German composer Richard Wagner, he was always going to be treated with suspicion by the village kids and there were more bad days than good. But by the time the 101st Airborne "Screaming Eagles" arrived in the village, life was on the up and Richard made many friends. Now some 60 years on, he has tracked down some of the survivors - the men he once looked up to and asked "Got any gum, chum?" Harold Heffner from Ohio tells it like this, "I remember your Pa... and I remember you kids... You all made us very welcome."

The Future

Richard writes for various magazines as well as having penned Six Spoons of Sugar – while two more autobiographical books are planned plus a book of humorous short stories.

"There's never a dull moment," says Richard

APPENDIX

1939

Sept	1	Germany invades Poland.
Sept	3	Britain and France declare war on Germany.
Sept	17	Russia invades Poland.
Sept	21	American President Roosevelt addresses Congress on the need to lift the embargo on the supply of military hardware to Britain (and others). From this comes Cash & Carry.
Sept	29	Russo–German agreement to divide Poland.
Nov	11	W.S. Morrison, Minister for Food, introduces food rationing.

1940

April	9	Germany invades Denmark and Norway.
April	15	British forces land in Norway.
May	10	Germany invades Holland, Belgium and Luxembourg. Prime Minister Chamberlain resigns – Churchill takes over.
May	14	Germany invades France. Anthony Eden announces formation of Local Defense Volunteers (Home Guard).
June	4	British and French forces evacuated from Dunkirk.
June	8	British forces leave Norway.
June	10	Italy declares war on Allies.
June	25	France surrenders.
July	10	Luftwaffe launches Battle of Britain.
Sept	2	United States provides Britain with 50 destroyers in exchange for land rights to seven British foreign bases.
Sept	7	London blitzed by German bombers.
Sept	13	Italy invades Egypt.
Nov	15	Coventry bombed.

1941

Jan	5	British forces attack Italian troops in North Africa.
Jan	22	Australian forces capture Tobruk.
March	9	Italy invades Greece.
April	6	Germany attacks Yugoslavia and Greece.
April	17	Yugoslavia falls.
May	2	Rudolf Hess parachutes into Scotland with peace plan.
May	25	Battle for Crete.
June	22	Germany invades Russia.
Oct	6	German forces reach Moscow. Leningrad besieged.
Dec	6	Russian counter-attack. Germans retreat.
Dec	7	Japan attacks American fleet at Pearl Harbor. American President, Roosevelt, declares war on Japan, Germany and Italy.
Dec	8	Japanese forces land in Malaya.
Dec	11	Germany and Italy declare was on US.
Dec	26	Hongkong surrenders.

1942

Jan	15	Japan invades Burma.
Jan	23	Japanese forces land in New Guinea and threaten Australia.
Jan	26	First American troops arrive on British soil.
Feb	15	Singapore falls.
March	11	America's Cash & Carry Act replaced with Lend Lease in which Britain purchases military goods to be paid for at a later date.
May	8	US Fleet engages Japanese in Battle of Coral Sea.
June	7	Battle of Midway.
Aug	13	General Montgomery given command of British Forces in North Africa.
Oct	23	Montgomery leads the defeat of German forces at Alamein.
Nov	8	Anglo-American forces land in North Africa.

1943

Feb	2	German forces surrender at Stalingrad.
May	13	German forces surrender in North Africa.
July	10	Allies invade Sicily.
Sept	3	Allies invade Italy.

1944

March	4	First daylight raid by American bombers over Berlin.
June	6	D-Day invasion.
June	13	First German V1 bombs fall on London.
Oct	5	British forces land in Greece

1945

Jan	17	Russian forces capture Warsaw.
March	23	Allied forces under Montgomery cross the River Rhine.
April	6	American forces land on Okinawa.
April	12	American President Roosevelt dies.
May	1	Berlin surrounded. Hitler commits suicide.
May	2	German forces surrender in Italy.
May	7	Germans agree to unconditional surrender.
Aug	6	America drops atomic bomb on Hiroshima.
Aug	9	America drops atomic bomb on Nagasaki.
Sept	2	Japan signs unconditional surrender.